ACCLAIM FOR

MURDER OF INNOCENCE

"Three Chicago pros tell the archetypal story of our time: violence and madness within the realm of respectability. A powerhouse!"

— **Studs Terkel**

▼

"The challenge of true-crime writing is to penetrate the killer's cortex and discover where and how evil first took root. Here, the authors prove more than equal to the task...a powerful indictment."

— **Vincent Bugliosi**
author of *Helter Skelter*

▼

"Joel Kaplan, George Papajohn, and Eric Zorn give journalism a good name with a thorough investigation of Dann's tragic life."

— ***Boston Herald***

▼

"A modern horror story that surely will be numbered among the best true-crime stories of the year."

— ***Flint Journal***

▼

more...

MURDER OF INNOCENCE

The Tragic Life and Final Rampage of Laurie Dann, "The Schoolhouse Killer"

Joel Kaplan, George Papajohn, and Eric Zorn

WARNER BOOKS

A Time Warner Company

"BROWN-EYED GIRL" written by Van Morrison.
Copyright © 1967 Songs of PolyGram International, Inc.
International Copyright Secured. All Rights Reserved. Used By Permission.

WARNER BOOKS EDITION

Copyright © 1990 by Joel Kaplan, George Papajohn and Eric Zorn
All rights reserved.

Book design by H. Roberts
Cover design by Anne Twomey

Warner Books, Inc.
666 Fifth Avenue
New York, N.Y. 10103

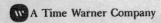 A Time Warner Company

Printed in the United States of America

This book was originally published in hardcover by Warner Books.
First printed in paperback: October, 1991

10 9 8 7 6 5 4 3 2 1

*For Isadore and Rose; Gus and Ethel; Jens and Frances,
and,
especially, for Johanna*

ACKNOWLEDGMENTS

This book grew out of a *Chicago Tribune Magazine* article titled "What Was the Matter with Laurie Dann?" We wish to thank metropolitan editor Ellen Soeteber for rearranging our schedules to give us the time to do that original piece, and magazine editor Denis Gosselin, former editor James D. Squires and managing editor F. Richard Ciccone for their advice and encouragement.

Several other *Tribune* editors supported us as we tried to juggle our responsibilities while continuing to research and write this book. They include Dean Baquet, Bill Garrett, Gene Quinn and Owen Youngman.

The three of us have covered various aspects of the Laurie Dann story since May 20, 1988, yet this book could not have been as thorough without the help of several *Chicago Tribune* reporters who also reported the story. Those reporters who shared with us their notes and records as well as their insights include Ray Gibson, John O'Brien, William Recktenwald, Jessica Seigel and Kate Seigenthaler. Other current and former *Tribune* staffers who covered parts of the story were Bob Blau, Tom Burton, Jean Davidson, Bob Davis, Dan Egler, Bob Enstad, Mike Hirsley, Dave Ibata, Steve Johnson, John Kass, Peter Kendall, John Lucadamo, Barbara Mahany, Linnet Myers, Pat Reardon, Dave Silverman, Wes Smith, Steve Swanson, Karen Thomas and Terry Wilson.

We particularly appreciate the assistance of two of our colleagues, Ann Marie Lipinski and Mike Tackett, as well as that of Frances Zorn at the University of Michigan. Their comments and suggestions on early drafts were enormously helpful.

Winnetka Police Chief Herbert Timm, Lieutenant Joseph Sumner and Sergeant Patricia McConnell were generous with their time and gave us access to important records compiled by the Laurie Dann task force.

Others who've helped include Gerald T. Rogers, Jack Corn, Mary Ellen Hendricks, Andy Martin, Sue Tolpin, Dan Brogan, Chris Hubner, Joe Hajost, Jon Kamerman, James DeBruzzi, Dave Schabes, Steve Libowsky, Dr. Mark Gunther, Dr. Syed Ali and Dr. Patrick Staunton.

We owe a special debt to *Tribune* reference librarian Susan Miller, who tracked down difficult information in her spare time and offered words of encouragement at the appropriate moments.

Finally, we wish to thank our editor at Warner Books, Rick Horgan, and our agent, Dominick Abel, who guided us through this difficult process.

CONTENTS

AUTHORS' NOTE

All material in this book is based on interviews with the scores of people who had contact with Laurie Dann, or is taken from police records and other documents. In many cases, people agreed to relive very painful and emotional memories so that this account could be as complete as possible.

Some minor characters in the book spoke only on the condition that their names not be used. Agreeing to use pseudonyms is always a difficult bargain for a journalist to make, but we decided to sacrifice smaller truths in the interest of getting to certain larger truths in the story of Laurie Dann. The only major characters for whom we used pseudonyms were the Glenview boy who dated Laurie in high school; her friend from Northbrook who also attended the University of Arizona; and the University of Arizona student who dated Laurie and later became a doctor.

We spent many hours with Russell Dann, his family and his friends in order to detail his marriage and Laurie's deterioration. A few people with important insights into Laurie Dann, however, declined to be interviewed for this book. They include Laurie's parents, Norman and Edith Wasserman, and her brother, Mark. Highland Park police officer John McCafferty, now retired, said he did not want to discuss any aspect of the Dann case. His colleague, John Burns, also retired, said he would not make any comment beyond the public record of the police reports.

We have, therefore, relied on police reports, interviews with acquaintances, adversaries and law enforcement personnel, news articles, videotapes and public documents to reconstruct scenes and dialogue.

In many instances, we present Laurie Dann's perceptions and memories of people and events. In evaluating such passages, the reader should be mindful that Laurie's unstable mental and emotional state raises questions about her reliability as a witness, and that her observations may reveal more about her than about those she is discussing. Laurie Dann voiced many serious accusations against the people in her life, particularly Russell Dann. In all instances involving accusations of criminal conduct, such accusations have proved unfounded.

Children live in a small world. Their homes and families, their schools, playgrounds and athletic fields; this is their world. And it was precisely that world that was invaded and ripped apart on May 20. And all that can be assumed, all that can be taken for granted, all that can be counted on, all that is the right of every child—life, peace, security, spontaneity, innocence—was taken away that day by firearms. And in the weeks after that event we could not be comforted, for our children were not.

—Rev. Andrew Dietsche, Christ Church of Winnetka

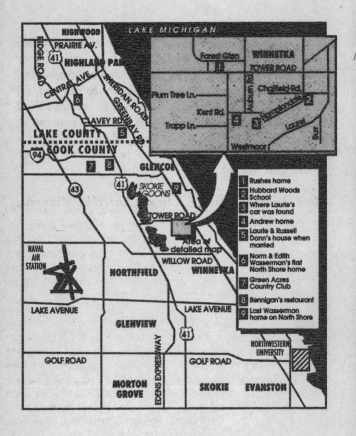

LAKE MICHIGAN

HIGHWOOD

PRAIRIE AV.

RIDGE ROAD

41

HIGHLAND PARK

Forest Glen 1

WINNETKA

TOWER ROAD

CENTRAL AVE.

6

SHERIDAN ROAD

GREENBAY RD.

Plum Tree Ln.

Auburn Rd.

Chatfield Rd.

2

Hamptondale

CLAVEY RD.

Kent Rd.

4 3

Locust

LAKE COUNTY

5

Trapp Ln.

Burr

COOK COUNTY

94

Westmoor

7 8

GLENCOE

SKOKIE LAGOONS

41

9

43

TOWER ROAD

Area of detailed map

NAVAL AIR STATION

NORTHFIELD

WILLOW ROAD

WINNETKA

LAKE AVENUE

LAKE AVENUE

GLENVIEW

41

GOLF ROAD

GOLF ROAD

NORTHWESTERN UNIVERSITY

MORTON GROVE

SKOKIE

EVANSTON

EDENS EXPRESSWAY

1 Rushes home
2 Hubbard Woods School
3 Where Laurie's car was found
4 Andrew home
5 Laurie & Russell Dann's house when married
6 Norm & Edith Wasserman's first North Shore home
7 Green Acres Country Club
8 Bennigan's restaurant
9 Last Wasserman home on North Shore

1

A Beautiful Day
for a
Carnival

Laurie the baby-sitter had let herself go to hell.

Her body, which only five months earlier had been trim and shapely, was swollen with fat—her eyes looked tired and her hair was clumsily cut above the shoulder in a way that lent unflattering emphasis to her drooping jaw. Her admirers had once compared her to a Barbie doll and remarked on how young and fresh she always looked, but now every trouble in her life seemed to have caught up with her at once.

Yet Marian Rushe, one of Laurie's best clients, was not inclined to judge her harshly. Marian was an accepting person, open to everyone, and she already had plenty to concern herself with that morning anyway. She'd just hustled her daughters, Mary Rose, nine, and Jennifer, thirteen, and son, Robert, eleven, off to school and at the moment Laurie showed up at the door she was simultaneously trying to clean up the breakfast mess and find windbreakers and shoes for her two youngest sons, Patrick, six, and Carl, four. The boys were giddy and chattering with excitement. Laurie, their favorite sitter, was taking them to a kiddie carnival.

It was a brilliant spring morning in Winnetka, Illinois, an older, exclusive suburb of thirteen thousand on the shores of Lake Michigan seventeen miles north of downtown Chicago. Skies were clear and the temperature was on its way up to the mid-seventies. Laurie was wearing white Bermuda shorts and a tan T-shirt from the University of Arizona College of Medicine with a skeleton in the logo. She was carrying a plastic Mickey Mouse mug—the kind with feet on the bottom and ears on the lid—and a paper plate filled with baked Rice Krispies treats.

She'd been a regular sitter for the Rushes for more than a year, then mysteriously vanished after the previous Christmas. Her disappearance more or less coincided with the arrival of Marian's sister from Ireland, who came on an extended visit and took over most of the baby-sitting chores. The few times Marian had called Laurie to fill in, no one answered the phone at her house or else an older man picked up and said simply, "Laurie is out of town."

It had been a surprise, then, two days before this bright morning, when Laurie showed up unannounced at the door. She'd looked haggard and at least forty pounds heavier than when Marian had last seen her. She'd dyed her brown hair auburn and thickened it with an unhandsome perm.

Marian had invited her in for a visit. "How have you been?" she asked in a voice still light with a brogue she hadn't lost in the four years her family had lived in the Chicago suburbs.

"So-so," Laurie said. There'd been a death in her family, she said, and her allergies were kicking up. But otherwise she was okay—working as a nurse at Evanston Hospital and living at home. "I missed you and the kids," she said. "I thought I'd stop by and catch up."

"Well, it's great to see you," Marian said enthusiastically. Next to Laurie she was a big woman, five feet eight inches tall and sturdy, with pale Irish skin and dark brown hair. "Are you still planning to get married in June?"

Laurie nodded. "I'm having my engagement ring reset again," she said, apologetically fluttering her bare left hand. "The first time didn't work out. It wasn't right."

"That was his mother's ring," Marian said, recalling their conversations from many months earlier.

"Yeah, it's like an heirloom."

"And he's...in the restaurant business?"

"Right," Laurie said. "A chef."

The women sat and talked for about an hour. Laurie spoke happily about her upcoming honeymoon in the Virgin Islands and said work was going well. She reacted calmly when Marian told her the family was going to move soon to Long Island because the Bank of Ireland, where Marian's husband worked, was closing its Chicago branch. "The house will be going on the market Friday," she said.

"Are you already packing?" Laurie wanted to know. "Do you have a moving date? Are the kids upset? Have you found a new place in New York?"

Marian answered her questions and they moved naturally on to other topics. Toward the end of the desultory conversation Laurie said that the real reason she had come over was to ask if she could take Patrick and Carl to a carnival at her hospital Friday morning. "It's especially for younger kids," she said. "I'm sure they'd enjoy it."

"I don't know," said Marian. "Patrick goes to kindergarten in the afternoon, and—"

"Oh, we'll be back by eleven," Laurie assured her. "We'll leave around nine, and I'll have them back in plenty of time for school. They'll love it, I promise."

Marian went along with the plan. Laurie had always been somewhat quiet and awkward, especially around adults, but the kids loved her. She could play as if she were one of them, transforming herself down on the floor from a thirty-year-old woman into a child again. She'd taken them to the park, out for ice cream and even on excursions to her parents' house in the nearby suburb of Glencoe. Things had gone so well that Marian had enthusiastically recommended Laurie to several friends and neighbors who were engaged in the always difficult search for mature, reliable baby-sitters in the North Shore suburbs.

So on the morning of May 20, 1988, just before nine o'clock and a little ahead of schedule, Laurie rang the front doorbell. Marian let her in, watched her carry the Rice Krispies treats and the Mickey Mouse cup to the kitchen and set them down. When Marian left the room to continue helping Patrick and Carl get ready to leave, Laurie picked up a gallon jug of

2 percent milk on the counter and filled the Mickey Mouse cup, sealing it again with the no-spill lid.

"I'm taking along some milk, in case the boys get thirsty," she called out.

Marian thought this was a peculiar choice of beverage— milk would spoil on a hot day and she had juice in the fridge that would be a better choice—but she said nothing. It was Laurie's little outing, a reunion. Why make an issue of it?

Laurie waited a few minutes in the kitchen, consulted the clock and said, "Okay, I guess we can leave now."

Marian shepherded the children out to Laurie's car—not the old blue Honda Accord hatchback she usually drove, but a white, spanking clean 1986 Toyota Cressida. Four doors. Vanity license plates—her father's initials followed by three zeros. The sunroof open to enjoy this beautiful day. Marian belted Patrick and Carl into the back seat, told them to behave themselves, and waved as Laurie pulled out of the driveway.

She walked back into the house and went to the kitchen to continue cleaning up. Dishes. Bowls. Silverware. And the milk was still out! It looked weird, a little orangy, as though one of the kids spilled his juice into it for a joke or just to be annoying.

She smelled the milk. Nothing. She took a small taste. Normal. Hmm. When you have a houseful of children, you can't be fussy about every little thing. She put the milk away and went about the rest of her chores.

And Laurie, who was supposed to be heading south with the kids toward Evanston, was instead, at that moment, racing north.

2

The Good Life

Norm Wasserman, a lean and meticulous young account-ant who had lived in Chicago apartments all his life, took out a $14,000 mortgage in 1955 and built a house on a vacant plot of land given to him by his wife's relatives. It was a long, sturdy bungalow with an uninterrupted expanse of windows across the front room opening on a street lined with drooping shade trees. The day that Norm, his wife and young son moved into their own home on their own land marked the realization of his parents' immigrant dream.

His father, Morris, and mother, Betty, had come over by boat from Russia when they were young and childless. Morris found work as a truck driver, and the Wassermans ended up in North Lawndale, a middle-income West Side neighborhood where nearly half of Chicago's Jewish population lived after World War I. It was a quiet, mostly residential area graced by elaborately landscaped parks and parkways and dotted with more than a dozen synagogues, most of them Orthodox. Idele Wasserman, the couple's first child, was born in 1926, followed three years later by Norm.

In the 1940's the neighborhood began to turn rapidly as the upwardly mobile Jews dispersed into the higher-status neighborhoods that had opened up to them. When Idele was starting her second year of high school, the Wassermans rode one of the migratory waves to the prestigious, white-collar South Shore neighborhood where they took the top floor of a three-story on South Phillips Avenue. The North Lawndale they left behind is now the city's most blighted neighborhood, and the site of Norm's boyhood home has become a vacant lot filled with abandoned cars.

The greater South Shore area in those days was close-knit—like a small town or suburb in many respects—and heavily populated by families that had fled Nazi Germany. When the Jewish population was at its peak, some two dozen synagogues dotted South Shore and the adjacent Hyde Park–Kenwood neighborhoods. So many of the residents were prosperous that the area became known informally as the Golden Ghetto.

Norm had just started attending South Shore High ("The School of Our Dreams," the slogan went) when Morris Wasserman died of a heart attack. Suddenly Norm, a studious, soft-spoken kid who was overshadowed in many ways by his vivacious older sister, was the man of the house.

He won awards for scholastic achievement and a varsity letter for playing on the school tennis team. His yearbook photographs show him with his hair fashionably slicked back above dark, ruminative eyebrows.

He graduated from South Shore High and lived at home while going to the University of Illinois at Navy Pier in Chicago, which has since closed. The school offered only a two-year program of study, and Norm completed sixty-seven credit hours in a liberal arts curriculum between January of 1947 and December of 1948. He transferred to Roosevelt University in downtown Chicago where he studied business for a year before leaving school in 1950 without a degree.

That same year he left school he married Edith Joy Lewis, a quiet, curly-haired redhead who'd been a year behind him at South Shore High and grown up in an apartment building the next block over. They had both been in the Student Services League at school.

She was the third child of Mae Lewis and her husband, Dan, an attorney who'd started practice at the age of twenty after becoming the youngest person ever to have passed the Illinois bar exam. The newlyweds moved into an apartment over a row of stores on the busy South Shore intersection of Colfax Avenue and 79th Street just a few blocks from where they'd grown up, and Norm studied to take the certification exam to become a public accountant.

He passed the exam in July of 1952 when Edith was pregnant with their first child. Mark Ira Wasserman was born in October in Michael Reese Hospital, the same hospital where his father had been born twenty-three years earlier.

The Colfax Avenue apartment was neither big enough nor in a suitable location for a growing family, especially once Mark started walking. So Norm and Edith eagerly took the opportunity to put up a house on Lewis family land on the 8700 block of East End Avenue nearby in the Stony Island Heights neighborhood.

In the 1950's, Stony Island Heights was an enclave of upper-middle-income Jewish professional families. Because so many doctors lived in the western third of the neighborhood the area was called Pill Hill, and to live there had a definite cachet.

Norm's accountancy practice thrived, and he and Edith decided to have one more child. On October 18, 1957, Laurie Ann Wasserman was born.

The Wassermans became an archetypal 1950's nuclear family—the hardworking dad, the stay-at-home mom and the pair of well-behaved children. Norm was the provider, the steadying force, the wearer of the pants. Edith was the caregiver, disciplinarian and professional's wife. Slowly, however, the dream life in Chicago began to erode. Industrial growth and a comparatively favorable civil rights climate brought a large number of southern blacks to Chicago and greater South Shore in the postwar era, and by the late 1950's many Jews were beginning to feel a pressure to relocate.

This time, the Jewish migration was almost exclusively northward along Lake Michigan—particularly to the Rogers Park neighborhood in the city and to the suburbs of Evanston, Lincolnwood, Niles, Wilmette and Skokie, where entire neighborhoods were being built for and marketed to Jewish families. The more successful families went still farther north to the old-money North Shore communities of Winnetka, Glencoe and Highland Park, where large mansions and homes of vintage elegance lined the distinctive ravines.

Chicago's North Shore suburbs were settled in the early nineteenth century by pioneers who enjoyed the dense woods, the bluffs overlooking the lake and a hilly terrain unusual in northern Illinois. The villages and towns were organized and incorporated in the latter half of the century, some with an eye toward becoming utopian communities. It was a vision that few of the suburbs ever really relinquished.

Frank Lloyd Wright and his students built prairie-style homes in among the Queen Anne, the Colonial and the Victorian. The town centers retained an understated and intimate air while rapidly growing suburbs elsewhere—some equally wealthy—were overrun by the sordid combination of franchised businesses and tract subdivisions. The North Shore was more than a place and more than just an impressive array of per capita statistics and restrictive zoning laws. It was an attitude.

Norm and Edith Wasserman naturally looked to the best of these suburbs in 1963 when they decided it was time to leave South Shore. They were not yet able to afford one of the grand homes near the lake in Highland Park, so they settled for a brick tri-level on Sumac Road on the less prestigious southwest side of the city.

They occupied the last house on the block, and other families noticed that they didn't seem inclined to have much to do with them. They often drove out the long way—the way that would not put them in the position of having to pass any of their neighbors or wave to them. When Edith did drive by, she usually stared straight up the road or turned her head away. The bitter rumor circulated that she believed Laurie and Mark were too good for the other kids on the block.

Mark, who was nearly a teenager and had his father's compact, wiry build and his mother's red hair, was older than most of the neighborhood children anyway and already in-volved with his classmates and other activities. He had friends over occasionally to play Monopoly or other board games, but was known on the block as that shy, quiet boy who was doing very well in junior high.

Laurie, on the other hand, was often outside with the kids. They were mostly boys and they played lineball, kickball, hopscotch, army, four-square and a game of hide-and-seek tag called Queen Bee in which one of the girls would sit at the top of a slide and her protector, a boy, would try to find the others before they got to the girl on the slide. They also gathered in an elaborate tree fort one block south where they made up games and formed clubs that disbanded and reorganized every couple of weeks under new names. As they got older they went pool-hopping, sneaking into backyards on warm summer nights and splashing around and laughing until homeowners shooed them away.

Laurie was a reticent, funny-looking little girl with an oversized nose and sailboat ears. She was always a follower in the group, never suggesting anything and never arguing. The kids accepted her, for the most part, but it sometimes bothered them that she almost never smiled and every so often would fix them with a blank stare that seemed to come from a million miles away.

"Laurie!" they would tease her. "Are you still there? Laurie!"

Once in a while her mother allowed her to invite a few of the younger girls into the pristine interior of the Wasserman home to play with Laurie's huge collection of fashion dolls and plastic, long-haired trolls. Entering the house was always a little intimidating, though—Edith's nickname among some of the kids on the street was "The Bitch" for the way she would peremptorily call Laurie inside. "You forgot to clean your room!" she'd say. "Come set the table!" "Dinnertime!" Sometimes she'd whack her on the butt when she came through the door. Laurie then wouldn't emerge for hours or even days except to get in the car to go out to eat. The Wassermans went out to dinner more than anybody. Edith hated to cook so much, Laurie used to tell people, that she didn't even own a can opener. Her playmates watched as Laurie would sit in the car in the driveway looking morose while her brother, who always seemed to get most of his parents' attention, bounced in his seat and laughed.

Norm's favorite leisure activity was tennis, which he played on mornings and weekends at the Highland Park Racquet Club. Edith, much less athletic than her husband, was known to go bowling in the afternoons with the sisterhood of B'Nai Torah. The Wassermans weren't particularly religious, but they did help raise money for the temple and showed up reliably for services on the High Holy Days every fall.

Laurie went to West Ridge Elementary School four blocks from home, and there, too, was known for being shy and basically serious, though not the exceptional student her brother was. In the fourth grade she showed up with surgical bandages on both sides of her head for several weeks. After they came off, her ears didn't stick out anymore.

Her parents sent her to Chippewa Ranch Camp in Eagle River, Wisconsin, during summers when she was in elementary school. It was an all-purpose camp, offering eight weeks of lakes, trees, swimming, sailing, riding, crafts and games. When Laurie was nine, the whole family went to Disneyland.

For sixth through eighth grade she went to Red Oak Junior High, where she was too meek to say hello to those who greeted her or to attend the semiscandalous boy-girl parties her peers were throwing. She was a reasonably good student, and most of her schoolmates had no idea that she also attended special classes for troubled and learning-disabled children held at Washburne Junior High in nearby Winnetka. The classes, which were more or less modified group-counseling sessions, attracted a grab bag of kids from the North Shore who, for one reason or another, didn't fit into the mainstream. They were the loners, the low achievers, the behavior problems, the oddballs. Laurie's group had two girls who thought they were witches, a couple of students who were borderline mentally retarded, several with reading disabilities and a handful with drug and alcohol problems.

The North Shore has always been a pressure cooker for adolescents. The high schools there are among the best in the nation, public or private. Nearly all the students come from affluent families where the expectations for social, athletic and particularly academic success are extremely high, and an average kid can easily feel as though he's a disappointment to everyone, including himself. Teens on the North Shore take their own lives at a rate three times higher than the national average, and local therapists call the area the Suicide Belt.

When Laurie got up the nerve to speak to the others in the special education class, she told them she didn't feel she was good at anything, that she couldn't communicate with her parents and that she felt like an outcast in her own family because she didn't feel loved or needed. Whenever anyone suggested a solution to her or offered the least advice that involved changing her behavior, Laurie lashed out to defend herself, suddenly wild and unsprung.

She'd already shown several signs that there might be more to her introversion and sense of worthlessness than just a garden-variety dissatisfaction with family life. When she was five years old she'd adopted peculiar rituals that involved touching the same objects over and over and fixating on good numbers and bad numbers. These rituals disappeared as she got older, but her family history suggested the possibility of future mental problems—both Edith's mother, who died in 1966, and Norm's grandmother suffered from clinical depression, an ailment with a strong genetic component.

In the homeroom portrait taken for the 1969 *Red Oak Leaves* yearbook, Laurie Ann Wasserman knelt at the far right of the front row of her sixth-grade class, her head turned toward the boy next to her. She was the only child of twenty-three not facing the camera.

3

Laurie Wasserman Grows

The 1971 *Red Oak Leaves* junior high yearbook included a prophecy and last will and testament for each graduate. Laurie's last will read: "Laurie Wasserman's spelling quota to lucky Jeff Worth." Her prophecy—"Laurie Wasserman grows"—referred to how short and physically undeveloped she was. It was such a brief prophecy, her classmates later remembered, because Laurie was such an unremarkable girl.

Beginning in September of 1971, she attended Highland Park High School. She struggled, earning grades that were a terrible disappointment to her parents—her brother, Mark, had also been a mild and unmemorable kid in high school, but he had made National Honor Society and earned a 4.5 grade-point average out of a possible 5.0, creamed his SAT's on the second try and gone off to the University of Illinois at Champaign-Urbana, one of the top state schools in the country, where he was studying economics and headed for an honor's degree.

Laurie, on the other hand, had achieved almost nothing except live up to her junior high yearbook prophecy—she'd grown. In the summer before high school, her body, so recently childish, had developed pleasing amplitudes, and the boys were starting to pay attention. Chuck Brotman, a popular sophomore whose family lived in Deerfield, noticed Laurie right off and thought she might be worth making a play for even though she was on the funny-looking side. One day in the cafeteria, shortly after he'd broken up with his girlfriend, he turned to Laurie as he and a group of friends walked past her and said, "You. You're going out with me."

Laurie's eyes widened. "Okay," she said.

Chuck had sort of meant it as a joke, but they started going out anyway. He dated her for two months and introduced her to heavy petting. Still, the whole relationship started to embarrass him. He didn't care much for how bland she was and seeing her did nothing to enhance his image, so he made it a point to keep his distance when they walked together in the hallways at school. He finally called off the romance, and she hated him for it. He was surprised that such a mousy girl was capable of showing such intense contempt with just her eyes.

•

At the start of Christmas vacation her sophomore year of high school, Laurie met Barry Gallup at a departure gate at O'Hare International Airport. Their families were both taking the same ten-day package tour to Hawaii, and Saul, Barry's father, happened to recognize Norm from their high school days together on the South Shore. Such seeming coincidences happened so frequently among the transplanted Chicago-area Jewish population that they weren't even surprising—everyone knew everyone or someone else who did. Sophie Gallup, as it happened, was acquainted with Idele Wasserman, Norm's sister.

The Gallups were then living in Glenview, a middle-income suburb due west of the North Shore, and Barry was a senior at Maine North High School. Laurie was bashful around him at first, but the two had plenty of opportunity to ease into a friendship on the flight to Honolulu and, later, at the Holiday Inn on Waikiki Beach where they all were staying. While their parents went sightseeing and dining, Barry and Laurie walked together by the ocean and stole unsupervised moments alone in the hotel corridors and, when they could manage it, the bedrooms. It felt like love, and on the return trip their parents were amused and surprised to see Laurie sitting on Barry's lap.

The relationship continued back home. They dated every weekend and went to movies, concerts and school dances. In the afternoons they liked to sit in her bedroom in Highland Park and listen to the 45 of "Brown-Eyed Girl," by Van Morrison, brown-eyed Laurie's favorite song:

> *Laughin' and a runnin', hey hey,*
> *Skippin' and a jumpin'*
> *In the misty morning fog*
> *With our hearts a-thumpin'*
> *And you,*
> *My brown-eyed girl.*

Barry graduated in June and she wrote in his yearbook:

…I know you'll have a good time in college and I'll come see you even if you don't want me. I have to see how you do. I would never be able to forget you and I'll always love you.

Love you,
Laurie

They never spoke directly of marriage, but Laurie talked abstractly about having children—she wanted to give them French names, like Armand or Danielle, not horrible names like her father's. She hated that name. She made fun of it when he wasn't around, referring to him disrespectfully as Norman.

Barry's impression was that Norm and Edith were too busy with other things in their lives to pay much attention to their daughter. Norm appeared to be totally wrapped up in work and tennis. Edith seemed concerned only with appearances— if Laurie were dressed right, if she would be able to get into a proper college. Laurie told him that Edith spoke disparagingly of "the shacks of Glenview" in his hometown.

He noticed that when Laurie approached her mother with a problem, no matter what it was, Edith seemed to trivialize it, as though she couldn't be bothered. "Oh, Laurie," she would say.

Edith was focused at the time on the family's impending move one town south to Glencoe, the second wealthiest village on the North Shore behind only waspy Kenilworth, the richest suburb in the nation. She had located a $105,000 single-story house on the west side of Sheridan Road, the tony avenue that follows the contours of Lake Michigan from Chicago up into Wisconsin. The L-shaped 2,600 square foot limestone ranch was on a half-acre lot in the southeast corner of the suburb, just north of a wooded, tortuous stretch of Sheridan known as the Ravines. It had five bedrooms, three bathrooms, a finished basement and a semicircular driveway—a modest home by Glencoe standards and one of the smallest in the immediate area, but a big step up for the Wassermans.

While many teenagers would have found switching high schools midway through a hardship, the move offered new opportunities for Laurie. She'd get a chance to start over with a fresh group of kids and teachers at New Trier East High School in Winnetka and leave behind the unpleasant memories of Highland Park where she'd made few friends. Academically, her sophomore year had been as disastrous as freshman year. Maybe at New Trier she could turn things around.

As part of her new beginning, she had plastic surgery over the summer to reduce the size of her nose. She had been complaining about it for years, and the transformation once she had it sculpted down to size was nearly miraculous. She was suddenly a beautiful young woman. Her big smile became her most noticeable facial feature.

She gave away all her play dolls to a girl at the other end of Sumac Road and she walked with her head high down the street one last time. The neighbors could hardly believe it was the same Laurie Wasserman.

•

Wade Keats, for his part, could hardly believe his good luck. He was attending a hockey camp in Aspen, Colorado, in August 1973, when, one day, lying out by the pool at the condominium complex, he saw a girl to die for. She was about his age, darkly tanned and eye-catching in a yellow bikini. He stared at her longingly, and she noticed him and returned the look. After a few back-and-forth glances he approached her. She was wearing a gold necklace with a charm that spelled out "Laurie," so he said, "Hello, Laurie. How are ya?"

They began talking and discovered they were both from the North Shore and staying with their parents at the complex. Wade was from Winnetka, and was pleased to discover that this quiet but friendly girl was going to be a new student at New Trier, his high school, that fall. "Small world," he said. "I'm going to be a senior there. Maybe I can show you around."

Again a vacation romance blossomed for Laurie, and again it transferred back home where she and Wade went out often—to movies, to dinner, to the Par King miniature golf course and to the lakefront lot at Gillson Park in Wilmette where they made out in the car. Even though she was still technically seeing Barry Gallup, Laurie and Wade were virtually going steady by the time the school year began. Wade would pick her up at home every morning in his gold 1965 Ford Mustang with a black vinyl top, and she would run out to the car wearing his army jacket. She clung to him in the halls, where they kissed passionately at each parting.

She was nervous during her first weeks at New Trier, the most prestigious, academically distinguished and status conscious of the North Shore high schools, and happy to have Wade around to ease the transition for her. Perhaps her need for him was unhealthy, but Wade didn't mind. Laurie had caused something of a stir at school when she showed up, the new girl with the long silky hair and the expensive, tight-fitting clothes. Wade was just as happy to keep her to himself.

The result, though, was that Laurie made a bad impression on the other girls at the school and was unable to ingratiate herself into any of the cliques. She tried out for such group activities as cheerleading and Girls Club—a social organization that sponsored pep rallies and athletic fund-raisers—but didn't make the cut and walked away hurt and angry. She would complain later that the school was very anti-Semitic.

When she wasn't with Wade she took to lurking on the

periphery of groups of girls, and she even picked out one particularly pretty classmate and brought her gifts of candy and earrings so she would be allowed to stand nearby.

During classes she sat slumped indifferently in her chair, usually off to one side of the room. She remained an academic lightweight and her schoolmates noticed with disdain that she sometimes cheated on tests, once even walking up behind the teacher during the confusion at the end of an exam period and copying directly off the answer key.

Barry Gallup was also going through a rough period of adjustment as a freshman at the University of Illinois. He was not happy with the new friends he was making and he missed Laurie.

One weekend she came down to visit Barry and her brother, Mark, then a senior at the university, and Barry rented a room for the night at the student union so they could be alone. When he tried to explain his problems to her, she brushed him off in almost the same way he'd seen Edith brush her off so many times in the past.

"Don't tell me," she said impatiently. "I can't help you with that."

The mood later turned romantic, but just as it looked like they were going to get to spend their first whole night together, Laurie interrupted the intimacies and asked Barry to walk her back to her brother's apartment where she was supposed to be staying. "What would Mark think?" she asked, gathering herself together. "God, what would he tell Norman?"

•

Laurie gave Wade Keats his army jacket back around homecoming in October and told him she wanted to break up and date other boys. But a month later she accepted his spontaneous offer of a ride home after school and they ended up making out in her driveway for old time's sake. Her mother rushed out of the house to break up the action and order her daughter inside.

Laurie was interested in other boys, Barry was still in the picture and her other romances continued to overlap. Those who were drawn to Laurie were attracted in part by her fey helplessness—she was almost like a little bird that needed protection. If you gave her the benefit of the doubt, her frequent silences seemed mysterious and enchanting.

A boy named Scott who sat next to Laurie in U.S. History dieted off fifty pounds before he could work up the nerve to ask her out. She refused him four times, each time inventing a kind excuse. Finally he got the hint—she was too cool for him.

Rob Heidelberger—a strapping athlete who played football and basketball, ran track and drove a hot 1968 LeMans convertible—had better luck. In the spring of 1974 he saw her several times standing alone in the hallways looking heartbreakingly lost and friendless. He introduced himself to her one day when she was standing at her locker and asked what her name was, what grade she was in, where she lived and so on. She bubbled with silly laughter at his subsequent flirtatious wisecracks, and he asked her out.

They went to dinner a couple of times and cruised around after school in the LeMans listening to Beach Boys tapes. Laurie had a job at the Highland Park K Mart and didn't hesitate one time to slide items through for free for her new boyfriend. Later, when she was assigned to restock shelves with refund items, she punched in on the clock and left the store. When she returned at quitting time to punch out, the manager caught her and fired her.

Rob asked her to the junior prom, which was held at the elegant Orrington Hotel in nearby Evanston. He borrowed his father's car for the occasion, but on the way to pick her up he was distracted trying to tune the radio and hit the brakes too late to prevent a minor collision that knocked a small hole in the radiator.

He had to call his father, who came and got him and took him home so he could drive the LeMans instead, all of which made him well over a half hour late to the Wassermans'.

"God, you're late," Laurie seethed when he finally arrived.

"I was in an accident," Rob said.

"Well, let's hurry up," she said. "I can't believe you're so late."

She didn't ask him how he was or if he had been hurt, and she held on to her anger most of the evening. Rob took her home before midnight and went off with friends to a sunrise party on the beach in Wilmette.

Back in school the next week Rob approached Laurie at her locker again. "We should break it off," he said. "This really isn't going anywhere."

She didn't argue.

•

Barry tried to talk up the University of Illinois, but Laurie deflected him by saying she wanted to go farther away for school, maybe to Arizona. The weather was better there. The parties were wilder. But in truth she didn't have the grades for Illinois or Arizona, and she was coming to the end of the road with Barry anyway.

When Barry asked her if she would accompany him and his family to Canada on vacation, she said she would. Then, after thinking about what going on such a trip might mean, she backed out.

Her excuses were vague, but the night before Barry was to leave, he received a phone call that spelled out the real reason.

"You don't know me from Adam," said a boy who identified himself as a New Trier student, "but you should know that I've been going out with Laurie. We've been having a great time together, including sex. She really likes it from me. She thinks I'm great. And those times when you dropped her off for work at K Mart or the country club? Well, she called me up and I came to get her and we went out."

Barry was stunned and hurt, but, in a way, he appreciated the intelligence. The end was merciless, quick, clean, final.

4

Playing House

Despite Laurie's mediocre high school record she was able to get into Drake University, a small, private school in Des Moines known as one of the colleges of last resort for under-achievers among the overachieving scions of the North Shore. Close to 95 percent of New Trier graduates go on to college, so not going or waiting a couple of years isn't really much of an option. You find a school, you pack your trunk, you kiss Mom and Dad goodbye.

She enrolled in the fall of 1975 and took courses in education to prepare her for a career as an elementary school teacher. She carried a full, fifteen-hour load and earned A's, B's and C's, working uncharacteristically hard in an effort to get her grades up so she might transfer to a school like the University of Arizona with a climate and social atmosphere more to her liking.

At Drake she ran across Chuck Brotman, the boy who'd used her and dumped her when she was a freshman at Highland Park High School. He was pleasantly surprised to see her and thought nothing of calling out a friendly greeting.

She said nothing, but fixed him instead with a hard, malevolent stare that recalled their bitter breakup four years earlier. He would feel that same stare nearly ten years later when he looked over and saw her at a nearby table at the wedding reception of a mutual friend.

"Don't you look at me," she snapped at him then. "Don't you ever look at me."

•

The social milieu at Drake was just as drab for Laurie as she had feared, so after freshman year she sent her improved transcript to Arizona.

Arizona accepted her into the college of liberal arts where she again signed up for courses in education. Later in her career at Arizona she switched to the home economics department in the college of agriculture to study the merchandising of clothing and textiles. With such a specialty, a student could expect to land a middle management job in retail clothing sales, a field Laurie already knew a great deal about from the consumer end.

Her father did accounting work for several women's stores in the Chicago area and had long been able to get good deals on the latest fashions and hottest labels for both Laurie and Edith. Laurie had a particular passion in those days for the crisp, understated preppie styles that quietly revealed her family's wealth.

Her wardrobe made a good impression when she went through sorority rush, but she was still an unexciting wallflower in many respects. The sisters at Delta Gamma found her too bland for their tastes and cut her early on. She was infuriated, not so much because she didn't make it as a DG as because Jane Sterling, a gorgeous high school cheerleader who'd been a year behind her at New Trier and was also going through rush, totally snubbed her at the parties. Didn't even say hello. Didn't even appear to recognize her.

Laurie had better luck across the street at Alpha Delta Pi, where she was one of thirty women accepted into the pledge class that fall. Some of the sisters found her tolerably sweet but a little dull; others thought she was just a complainer who was only interested in the sorority because it offered yet another way to meet men, as if she needed it. She was five feet three inches tall by then, weighed a little under a hundred pounds and always had a deep, smooth tan. Her hair was straight and silky, parted down the middle in the style of the day and falling just over her shoulders in back. Her phone rang constantly. She became notorious—even admired in some circles—for making dates with five or six different guys for one evening, then canceling all but one at the last minute.

She didn't earn a C average her first semester and so was on academic probation at the sorority second semester when the pledge class went on "Walkout," a traditional wilderness retreat to build spirit and deepen friendships. When the time came to leave for the trip, Laurie didn't show up and threw everyone into a big worry. It later turned out she was spending the weekend at the apartment of a boy she'd just met.

Her Pledge Mom, an upperclasswoman and the vice president of the sorority, finally confronted her: "You don't seem interested in being part of the group," she said. "Why don't you resign now so we don't have to kick you out?"

Laurie quit.

The summer after her first year in Tucson, she returned to the midwest and took a two-credit home economics course at the University of Wisconsin in Madison. She leased a room in the Towers, a private luxury dorm. A twenty-seven-year-old man who dated her that summer found her downright extroverted, talking to strangers at bars when they were out together and flaunting the effects on others of her extraordinary appearance. But beyond that she was typical, he thought—shallow and spoiled—like a thousand other North Shore girls with more money than brains.

She went back to Arizona in the fall and took a room in a town house at Euclid Terrace—an eighty-eight-unit complex known variously as the Zoo or Animal House because it was occupied by some of the hardest partiers on campus. Three hundred and more people would pack into each of several keggers every weekend, and Monday morning it was not unheard of to find beer bottles, bicycles and even motorcycles at the bottom of the Euclid Terrace swimming pool.

Laurie didn't really take to crazy partying. She drank, but only a glass or two at a time, and marijuana just never interested her that much. She was happy, then, to find a soulmate in Pearl Gelb, a quiet, plain but friendly fashion merchandising major from Northbrook, a suburb near the North Shore. Like Laurie, Pearl had attended Drake before transferring to Arizona.

Pearl and Laurie met while sunning themselves by the pool at Euclid Terrace, and they soon were playing tennis, going out to dinner, seeing movies and hitting the bars together. Laurie made it clear to Pearl that academics weren't particularly important to her—she was looking for a husband. Her search took her through a variety of run-of-the-mill boyfriends, then one day she reported that she'd found a live one, Stephen Witt, a handsome, Jewish premed student with dark hair and an athletic build.

They'd been in the same Normal Personality Psychology class in the spring semester of 1978, but didn't actually meet until they recognized each other at a party one Friday night the next fall. He asked her out to a football game the following afternoon. The more they got to know each other, the more they seemed like an ideal match—they were both attractive but somewhat insecure people who had gone from mate to mate with almost no interruption, and they shared a desire that bordered on need for frequent, overt displays of affection. Pretty soon they were hanging on each other at parties like high school students in love, and Steve's friends were a little nauseated.

The new couple took swing-dance lessons, tried all the new restaurants and went to loud clubs. He always paid even though she was the rich girl and he was the pharmacist's son.

They spoke of the future in general terms, not yet daring to presume that they would spend it together. He shared his dreams with her of a career in medicine, and she told him how she hoped to get into elementary school education someday, though he got the distinct sense that she was much more interested in having children and being a housewife than she was in being a professional.

Pearl took a dim view of the relationship as it became more serious. Laurie was far too clingy and dependent, and she seemed easily manipulated by Steve. If he had time to see her, he would; if he didn't and had to study, too bad. He also reserved the right to date other girls, and this, Laurie said, made her crazy. She was so obsessed by the progress of the relationship that she stopped going to classes and quietly dropped out of school for the balance of the semester. Later, when Steve found out, he was furious. The excuse she gave—that she was getting bad grades—didn't square with her overall grade-point, which was rising to a 2.81, slightly lower than a B.

She reenrolled for winter term, and when she came back from Christmas vacation she told Steve she wanted their relationship to be exclusive from then on. He agreed, but the arrangement seemed to do nothing to calm her insecurities. She raged at Steve or went into extended pouts whenever he spoke to another woman for any length of time. More and more, Steve's friends were finding her aloof, self-centered and stuck-up. She talked about her father's money far too often and she hovered over Steve always, even at big parties. His friendships suffered because she never gave him time to see anyone else.

Before Laurie, Steve had always resented the long tedious hours he spent in the library grinding away with the other premeds, but as her dependence on him grew he found himself actually looking forward to retreating to the study tables and hiding in his books. It was the perfect excuse to get some breathing room, and as a happy consequence he pulled straight A's for several semesters.

He kept the romance going partly out of convenience. Between keeping up with classes and trying to prepare for the Medical College Admission Test, he had neither the time nor inclination to engineer a new social life. Laurie was there, a given, someone who took care of him, loved him, told him how great he was.

He drove her the 1,800 miles from Tucson home to Glencoe at the start of the summer and stayed four days at the Wassermans', long enough for Norm to take him to the Highland Park Racquet Club and thrash him in tennis. Steve came away with the impression that Laurie's father was an extremely strong-willed, controlling figure compared to her subdued mother.

When Steve returned to Tucson to take classes and volunteer in a hospital, he left Laurie behind to work for the

summer as a waitress. She insisted on a protracted and lugu-
brious goodbye scene as though some tragedy had occurred,
and as Steve drove away he felt even more uncertain than
ever.

They remained faithful to each other over the summer
and wrote or called often. In the fall they moved into separate
furnished units in the Colony Apartments, a complex similar
to Euclid Terrace only slightly less frisky. Technically, Laurie
was sharing an apartment with three other girls, acquaintances
she had met through a mutual friend, but she almost never
spent time with the other women either in or out of the
apartment. She never talked to them about school, she never
talked to them about her friends, she never even talked about
herself. She had no pictures up in her room of her family or
anything else in her past. Everything was Steve, Steve, Steve.

She virtually lived with him. She did his laundry, she
folded his clothes, she cooked and she cleaned, all of which
allowed him to keep focused on getting into medical school the
next year. It was great, but he had the horrible feeling she'd
be a millstone in the long run.

Early in the winter semester, Steve sat Laurie down and
told her that because he hadn't been admitted to medical
school yet, he'd decided to go away to the University of
Southern California for dental school the next fall. He didn't
want her coming with him.

"I need to be by myself for a while," he said.

She was crushed. "But why?" she wailed.

"I've lost all my friends here already," he said. "I don't
want to go somewhere and right off the bat not make any
friends because of you wanting to spend so much time with
me."

Laurie tried anger, tears and promises. "I'll try to be less
possessive," she said. "I won't do it anymore."

Steve weakened. Maybe, he said. Maybe once he had some
time alone things would look different.

At his suggestion she sought out a social worker at a
student clinic to help her learn to be less demanding and
possessive. Steve even went along to the first couple of
appointments, but he gave up when it became apparent

that Laurie simply wanted to blame him for their problems and find excuses for her own behavior rather than learn to change it.

He was nervous nearly all spring. It was true that he'd been accepted at Southern Cal, but he was actually holding out for the Arizona College of Medicine, where he was on the waiting list. When he cleared the wait list, he didn't tell Laurie, since she was already making plans to leave town. Instead he took another apartment, this time across campus and with a roommate, in an effort to put more distance between himself and the woman he no longer wanted.

She was shattered by the end of the affair. Steve was her best shot, her only hope at a successful college career. Her fantasies of the two of them setting up house in Tucson, having a lot of money and raising a family had faded away. She called her mother for consolation.

"You'll find another boyfriend," Edith said.

When it was too late for Laurie to change her plans, Steve told her that he had, in fact, been admitted to medical school at Arizona and he would be staying in Tucson after all.

In July of 1980, with only a promise from Steve that they would get together in Boca Raton, Florida, at her parents' new vacation condominium during Christmas vacation to see how things stood, Laurie withdrew from Arizona. She was twenty-two credit hours shy of the 125 hours required for a degree, and she hoped to finish up at Northwestern University on the North Shore while living at home with her parents. She clung to the hope that she and Steve would end up together if only she could get herself straightened out.

Laurie believed she had a social knack that would help her excel in such fields as psychology, teaching or nursing, and when she returned home she made plans to finish her degree at Northwestern University. That fall of 1980, just to try out the school, she signed up to audit a psychology course in an open enrollment program. It bored her and she dropped out.

Her failure to complete her education only compounded the pain Norm had felt in the spring of 1975 when Laurie's brother, Mark, announced that he was quitting law school after less than one year to pursue a master's degree in advertising. The story Laurie told was that Norm had written Mark a letter saying how much the decision had hurt him; Mark had written back saying he realized his father would be disappointed, but that was too bad.

Laurie and Steve continued to talk on the phone from time to time and she continued to tell herself that things would probably work out again during the reunion in Boca Raton. But when the big week finally came, the feelings were gone, nothing was the same. He'd gone on with his life and she was stuck in hers. They drove around, swam, hit tennis balls, sat on the beach, talked and found time to make love even though they slept in separate rooms—but the realization sank in that it was really, really over. When it came time for Steve to leave for the airport, Laurie couldn't bear to accompany him, so Norm drove him to meet his plane.

"Well, you've got a career ahead of you," Norm said, alluding to the obvious rift. "You've got to worry about that. No sense being tied down."

"That's for sure," Steve said.

Norm nodded. "We'll take care of Laurie," he promised.

•

A few weeks later, Steve called Laurie and made it official. "This isn't working out," he said. "It's not going to work. We really have to break up."

In the weeks and months that followed, Laurie hounded him by telephone with weepy pleas to get back together, to give her another chance. She told him it was unfair of him to break up with her over the phone—he ought to have the guts to do it in person.

But Steve felt no temptation, only relief. In his mind they'd broken up when she left Arizona, and he was happy to put the whole thing forever behind him.

Laurie Wasserman was history.

5

Russell

The summer following her breakup with Steve, Laurie signed up for Introduction to Sociology and Social Problems at Northwestern's continuing education program, but then withdrew. In the fall of that year, she shifted directions and signed up for courses in dance, acting and playwriting. She couldn't finish those classes either.

Nevertheless, to her friends she seemed to be thriving. Those who met up with her at restaurants and bars in those days thought she was prettier and more self-confident than ever, moving with a certain authority, glowing.

She continued to crave the college experience and so moved into the Lake Shore Club, a Northwestern dormitory at 850 Lake Shore Drive on Chicago's Gold Coast. The old graystone building was just a few blocks' walk from the Oak Street Beach to the north and the fashionable Michigan Avenue shopping district to the west, and nearly everyone who lived there was studying health sciences at the nearby Northwestern Medical Center.

The men in the Lake Shore Club were so bewitched by Laurie's looks that they chanted "Laurie Wasserman, Laurie Wasserman" at her in playful admiration. The only strange thing about her was that she constantly wore purple, one of Northwestern's school colors. It was such a memorable fixation that when the residents played the Galaxian video game they referred to the purple-colored aliens as Wassermans.

She helped support herself at that time by working as a cocktail waitress at Green Acres, an all-Jewish golf and tennis club in Northbrook. She'd had similar waitressing jobs at Northmoor and other country clubs in high school, but Green Acres, with its heavy complement of well-to-do single men, was ideal for her at that stage of her life. On one particularly crowded night in the spring of 1981, she was flattered by the attentions of one of the members, a bright-eyed, mischievous guy with a round face and slightly lopsided grin who'd been giving her the eye as he ate dinner in the restaurant. He hit her up with a little small talk on his way out.

"What's your name?" he asked.

"Laurie," she said, but so softly he misunderstood.

"Well, Linda," he said. "What do you say sometime I call you and we get together?"

Laurie smiled. "I'd like that," she said.

He touched her lightly on the end of her perfect nose and said, "See you later, cutie."

•

The flirt was Russell Dann, a twenty-five-year-old sales executive at his family's Northbrook-based insurance company. He was cocky, outgoing, ingenuous and, Laurie thought, he looked a lot like Davy Jones, one of the four actor-musicians who performed as the Monkees. Their 1960's TV show, which was still in syndication and being shown every morning at eleven o'clock on Chicago's Channel 32, was one of Laurie's favorite prework diversions, and she had a particular crush on Davy.

Russell and Laurie were similar in some respects. They were both the youngest children of well-to-do Jewish families on Sheridan Road. They were both on the small side. They both had trouble early on in school—Russell's problems were attributed to a mild dyslexia. They had both gone to Highland Park High School at one time, and then on to private, less competitive colleges.

But where Laurie had been a reclusive, insecure child,

Russell had been rambunctious and popular, a ringleader, a scamp. Everyone called him Rusty in school, an impish nickname to go with all his wisecracks, stunts and practical jokes. In elementary school music class he and his friends were the ones who screamed and bumped heads together dancing the cancan. By junior high he was riding his minibike hell-for-leather through the streets. One time he crashed into a wall at a friend's house and put his head through a pane of glass. The cuts all along his neck and under his chin were severe and very bloody. His friend was frantic.

"Don't you get worried," Rusty ordered, cupping his hands and pressing them against his throat to stanch the blood and hold the skin together. "You stay calm. You've got to help me."

He got to a phone and reached his mother. "Mom," he said evenly. "Is Dad home?"

The cuts took 150 stitches to close and left tiny scars that nicked his face into adulthood.

At Highland Park High, Rusty was happy-go-lucky and mostly guileless, a good-time kid who was so lively he could be a teacher's favorite even though he was no better than an average student. As he got to be a junior and a senior, his parents' house on Sheridan Road became a social center where the half-dozen guys he considered his closest friends always knew they could come in the evenings to shoot baskets, order pizza and maybe smoke dope and get drunk down on their private beach. They threw back beer literally by the case. In the winter they'd pile into Rusty's Volkswagen bug, "Albert," and drive across front lawns knocking over snowmen for sport.

Once, when Rusty was speeding down the expressway with three buddies in Howard Norton's car, he decided to blow up the ashtray with a firecracker. It blew, the car filled with smoke, everybody laughed and Howard started speeding. A passing police car gave chase and eventually trapped the boys on a dead-end street. Rusty had the firecrackers in his pocket and decided not to stick around. When the car came to a stop he opened the door and ran. The officers ran after him but he was far too fast for them. He hopped a six-foot fence and got away, and the story was repeated often in his circle as an example of Rusty at his most ballsy.

He was only five feet seven inches tall, but a fierce soccer and tennis player for the Highland Park Giants. He inherited a general athletic aptitude from his father, a former football and baseball standout, and racquet skills from his mother, Elaine, who had lettered in tennis at the University of Illinois. He was also a reckless skier who spent winter vacations in Aspen with his friend Paul Zucker. Rusty made friends with the owners of the Continental Inn in Aspen, and they in turn allowed him and Paul to sleep in basement quarters for $10 a night. In the evenings they would try to pick up girls, but they were so aggressive that only the most desperate ones would have anything to do with them.

Senior year, a private academic counselor directed him to Ithaca College in upstate New York, an expensive private institution that attracted numerous wealthy Long Island kids who didn't have the academic credentials to get into Cornell, the Ivy League school in the same town. He dropped Rusty, a nickname he thought made him sound like a dog or a three-year-old, in favor of the more appropriately adult Russell, and began working toward a liberal arts degree with an eye on one day getting into public relations or business. After his sophomore year he decided to transfer to the University of Denver because the skiing was better out there.

His steady girlfriend at Ithaca, Ann, transferred with him. She was beautiful, thin, sweet and shy, just the way Russell liked his women. He helped bring the quiet ones out of their shells and they helped temper his carefree excesses. He and Ann spent their first semester senior year in a foreign study program in London. He returned to Ithaca to get his degree and Ann indicated she was willing to move to the Chicago area with him when he was through. He talked her out of it. He was too young to settle down. Life was just beginning.

Russell felt a little aimless after graduation, which was good news as far as his father, Armand, was concerned. Armand had always hoped that his charismatic younger son would lend his energies to the Dann Brothers Insurance

Company where Scott, his older son, was already working and doing well. Armand's father, Morton, had started the business in 1923, calling it the North American Investor and Loans Association. It was still a small operation when he died at age fifty-one in 1948. At that time, Armand and his brother Charles bought the business from their father's estate and renamed it Dann Brothers. In 1955, a third brother, Donald, joined the firm.

The company grew to be one of the leading independent commercial insurance companies in the Chicago area, with more than fifty employees and a 10,000 square foot office. Russell signed on after graduation and started as a clerk filing claim forms.

He was not brilliant by any measure. He wasn't well read or up on current events and he was not a great storyteller or conversationalist unless it came to sports, but what he needed he had—self-confidence, a competitive drive, a tireless capacity for work and an insistent, unmistakable sincerity. He was "out there," as people said, and when he moved into the sales end of the business he quickly became one of the firm's most prolific account executives.

He bought a condominium in the Cambridge Court complex in Northbrook a few minutes from the office. It was a one-bedroom duplex with a spiral staircase and a Ping-Pong table in the rec room. He settled into a comfortable life of working long hours, playing in softball and touch-football leagues, winning tennis tournaments at the country club, calling radio programs to talk sports, seeing all his old buddies and dating the tempting variety of eligible women available to a wealthy and affable guy who bore a slight resemblance to Davy Jones.

In fact he was so preoccupied with the whirl of events that he never did follow up with a call to that cocktail waitress, "Linda," with the cute nose and the great figure. He was reminded of this social error one night several months later when he was cruising with friends at Bennigan's, a popular suburban chain of restaurant-bars complete with ferns, brass railings and a studied variety of ersatz-quaint decor—old street signs, antiquey photographs, flashing stoplights and fiddles and banjos. Bennigan's was a sprawling, Anywhere, U.S.A., hangout, the kind of bar you'd expect to find in a shopping mall. It was very un–North Shore in some respects, but because it was near the interstate and dozens of Northbrook's charmless office buildings it was an ideal meeting spot for young up-and-comers. Russell's group had latched on to two women, one of whom looked a lot like Linda, only it wasn't her, Russell thought. Different hair, slightly different attitude— her sister, probably.

"What's your name?" he asked cautiously.

"Laurie," she said, not letting on that he'd asked her that same question before.

Talk about an awkward moment. Laurie was clearly the prettier and more poised of the sisters, yet technically he had asked Linda out first. Should he say anything? He thought it over as the conversation proceeded and decided not to men- tion that he knew Linda at all—it might spoil his maneuvering, which was going well.

They spoke for a while longer, then Russell asked Laurie and her friend for a ride home even though the friend he'd come with would have been more than happy to take him. During the ride he got Laurie's phone number, and this time he followed up with a call. Several days later he picked her up at her parents' house in Glencoe in his Honda Accord and took her into the city for dinner. Her idea was to go to La Crepiere, a small, casual French restaurant on Clark Street in the trendy Lincoln Park area, but she couldn't remember the name or exactly where it was, so they drove around through the maze of angled and one-way streets looking for a familiar facade. The misadventure only added to Russell's general agitation over the Linda problem.

"I feel really bad," he confessed once they found the place and were seated. "See, I asked your sister out and then I stood her up. Now I'm going out with you, and I thought I should be honest. I mean, it could be terrible if I ever have to meet her."

Laurie shrugged uncomfortably. "Don't worry about it," she said.

Their first date was followed by several more, with Russell

driving down from the suburbs to pick her up in front of her dormitory on Lake Shore Drive for nights of dinner and dancing. But he was still bothered by what Linda was going to think when she found out. "I'm probably going to meet her sooner or later," he began one night. "And I don't know what I'm going to say."

"That was me both times," she said. "You asked *me* out, you goof-head."

Russell was embarrassed but he admired her ability to pull a fast one. He also felt that in getting beyond this first misunderstanding they'd broken through that first awkward layer of caution and reserve and were headed toward a serious relationship. She seemed very impressive at first blush—she said she was a graduate student in hospital administration at Northwestern who was also taking aerobics and working part-time as a research assistant on a book about women in the workplace. She would get all dressed up in the mornings and take a clipboard and a pencil and go out on the streets to interview people.

The project seemed pointless to Russell, who also noticed that when he took one of Laurie's marketing textbooks off the shelf in her room and opened it, the spine cracked as though she had never read so much as a single page.

"Hey," he said lightheartedly. "Aren't you supposed to be reading this?"

"Nahh," she said. "I just study hard the week before the test."

"Yeah, I can understand that," he said. "I made it through that way."

Russell Dann fell in love. Laurie was just about the sweetest, most fetching girl he'd ever met—demure, devoted and, when the lights were out, passionate. She also came from a proper family. By coincidence, at the time that Laurie and Russell were first beginning to date, Russell was in charge of making an insurance presentation to a chain of women's clothing stores for which Norm Wasserman was the accountant. Norm was a successful, friendly man and Russell's father, Armand, spoke highly of him.

By that time Norm had branched out from simple ac-

countancy into other investment ventures and was part of a
trust that owned a 144-unit apartment building in Chicago,
several condominium buildings in the suburbs, a shopping
center in Northbrook and a lucrative chain of currency ex-
changes. Russell pegged his net worth at $3 to $4 million.

He and Norm got along well. They shared an interest in
tennis and finance, and though their interactions were always
superficial and distant by Dann family standards, Russell
realized after a while that Norm treated him the way everyone
in the Wasserman family treated everyone else. They were
proper and very controlled people, with the possible exception
of Laurie, in whom a quiet fire seemed to be burning. Every
once in a while she would lash out in anger or throw little
tantrums with only slight provocation. But the episodes were
always brief, and fifteen minutes later it was like nothing
had ever happened.

Russell's relatives and friends had their doubts about the
burgeoning romance. Russell's uncle Charles thought Laurie
lacked vivacity and was altogether too reserved a companion
for a live wire like his nephew. Bruce Silverman, who'd known
Russell since grade school, found Laurie extremely dull and
thought she had nothing whatsoever to offer. Artie Litchman,
another grade-school friend, was also bothered that Russell,
always the ringleader and rake in their fast, good-timing
crowd, had suddenly been tamed.

Beth Kamin, whose boyfriend, Noah Rosen, was one of
Russell's best friends from the country club, was struck by
Laurie's singlemindedness. Laurie seemed totally wrapped up
in Russell's world to the point of not seeming to have a life of
her own. She hung on him constantly, holding his hand at all
times, kissing him and making almost no effort to socialize
with anyone else.

When Beth and Noah parted company with Russell and
Laurie after an introductory get-together, Beth turned and
shuddered. "That girl's weird," she said. "That girl is really
weird."

•

On a plane to Las Vegas for a wild weekend getaway,
Laurie finally said the words: "I love you."

Russell had been waiting. It was his little rule of dating never to be the first to break down and use the L-word.

"I love you, too," he said.

They stayed at the Golden Nugget, went to several shows, including *La Cage aux Folles*, and lost about $50 in the casino.

•

Russell's older brother and sister were married and most of his contemporaries were either engaged or married, all of which gave him the feeling his time was coming, too. Though Russell acted rebellious at times, deep down he was something of a conformist who was more attracted than anyone knew to the idea of a house, a wife, a big dog and a couple of kids. He figured that, in Laurie, he'd found a woman who would complement him, yet let him be; a woman who would make a good wife and mother. On the surface, everything seemed to fit perfectly, as though destiny meant for them to be together. Friends were starting to give him those dig-in-the-ribs looks and asking, "Well?"

Nine months after they began dating, Russell and Laurie went to Boca Raton to spend the winter holidays with her parents. During that visit they took a long, late-afternoon walk together along South Ocean Boulevard and around the condo building. They talked about how happy they were and what the future might hold, and Russell said, well, he'd been thinking maybe they should get married. They let the idea hang in the air between them for a minute, then Laurie decided, yeah, that would be really cool.

Edith was feeling sick and lying flat on her back in the master bedroom when the happy couple returned. Laurie was giggling and fidgeting, trying to figure how best to phrase the announcement.

"What is it?" said Norm, who was standing by impatiently. "You're late."

"We're engaged!" Laurie said.

"That's great. Congratulations," Russell recalls Norm saying with little enthusiasm. "Now can we go eat?"

•

Dr. Stuart Needler, one of Russell's gang from junior high, heard that Russell was marrying a girl who'd been in

Alpha Delta Pi at Arizona. When he was an intern at the University of Arizona hospital, one of his good friends had been another doctor who used to be in A D Pi, so he called her to ask what Laurie was really like.

"Oh, my God!" said the woman. It was Laurie's Pledge Mom. "Your friend is going to marry her? She was really odd. She wasn't serious about school, all she did was date different guys."

Needler then made the mistake of bringing up the Pledge Mom the next time he saw Laurie. "I spoke to one of your biggest fans," he joked.

Laurie made sure he was not invited to the wedding.

•

In Russell, Laurie found a purpose. She dedicated her whole life for the better part of a year to impressing him and winning his affections. When he gave her a Dann family heirloom for an engagement ring, she felt, for the first time, like a success. Her seemingly aimless life had been leading somewhere after all.

"Look! I'm engaged," she bubbled to her childhood playmate Jeanne Nelson, when she and Russell ran into her working as a salesclerk at a North Shore clothing store. "So how's it going with you? What are you up to? Who have you heard from?"

Jeanne wasn't surprised to see Laurie again after so many years—the North Shore was a small place—but her attitude was startling. In the old days she'd always been so flat and faraway, like she didn't give a damn about anyone. Now here she was carrying on like the two of them were best friends, reminiscing and suggesting they get together again soon.

But the truth was that Laurie really didn't have many friends. Her focus on boys and boyfriends since the early years of high school combined with her lack of social confidence and initiative had left her in the humiliating position of having very few people she even knew well enough to invite to her own wedding.

Russell did not have the same problem. At the time, he was playing on three softball teams, two basketball teams and two touch-football teams. He considered himself friends with not only his teammates, but also with a large number of country club, business and school associates. He could have filled both sides of the aisle easily, but he knew Laurie would find that embarrassing. The only manageable compromise was for him just to invite ten of his very closest friends and explain to everyone else that it was going to be a small wedding.

"We talked about the idea of having a really big blowout," Russell said to Noah and Beth during a strained conversation that took place when he and Laurie invited them over to Russell's town house for an afternoon barbecue by the swimming pool. "But Laurie's parents offered us fifteen grand instead, so we figured it would be a really good nest egg to start out with. Then my folks said they'd give us the money they would have spent on a big rehearsal dinner. We're having less than seventy people."

Noah and Beth nodded, but both of them were puzzled. Russell was doing well financially and Dann Brothers was thriving. The nest egg story just didn't make any sense. They wondered, briefly, if it was Russell's strange way of telling them they weren't invited.

They were offended not to be asked, as were many of Russell's other friends. The boys were all in the habit of standing up for one another, virtually en masse, at weddings. Bruce Silverman, for example, had nine groomsmen. But because Laurie was so limited, she could only find two attendants— Russell's older sister, Susie Taylor, and her brother's wife, Paula. This forced Russell to make a painful draw, and he eventually settled on Paul Zucker and Dick Kahn for groomsmen and, as best man, his brother, Scott.

All along, Russell, being both trusting and oblivious by nature, remained unaware that Laurie was not really a student at Northwestern. He did not figure it out when she announced that planning the wedding was just too much and that she was moving home, dropping out of school and quitting the research project, and it didn't seem strange to him when she then took a full-time job as a receptionist in the printing and duplicating office on Northwestern's main campus in suburban Evanston over the summer.

On her application for that job she lied that she had worked three years at Dann Brothers and that she had an accounting degree from the University of Arizona. She stayed five weeks, then quit a month before the wedding by telling her supervisor that the job wasn't challenging enough.

•

In the interest of good family relations, Russell's sister, Susie Taylor, Scott's twin, agreed to stand up at the wedding, loan Laurie her wedding gown and host the engagement party. She and her husband, Jeff, a wealthy banker, put together a big spread of appetizers and fried chicken at their house in Highland Park and invited five dozen people, most of whom were Russell's friends.

Susie was holding off judgment on Laurie. She seemed nice enough in her introverted way and Susie trusted her brother's instincts, but it did strike her as peculiar that Laurie never made any comment either way about the party or thanked them for hosting it.

Five of Russell's closest friends took him up to the resort town of Lake Geneva, Wisconsin, for a weekend-long bachelor party at the end of the summer. They played golf, drank heavily and spent much of their time in a euphoric daze playing a game on the water called Kill the Skier, in which the object was to pull the guy on water skis through the biggest wake possible to try to make him fall down.

Laurie, meanwhile, was gearing up for the wedding, to be held on September 11, 1982. One of her tasks was to find a rabbi who would marry them. Neither family had strong connections to a temple. Laurie had never been bat mitzvahed and Russell had never been bar mitzvahed—"The only Jewish I know is 'oy vey!'" he used to say—so they had to look around for a rabbi who would do them a little favor.

Another of Laurie's tasks was to practice reading a short speech Russell had written for her to deliver at the rehearsal dinner at Green Acres where she and Russell had first met. In it, she was to say how grateful she was to her parents for all they had done for her, and that she loved them very much.

It was a speech much more in the Dann tradition of open

expressions of family affection than in the Wasserman tradition, and when the time came, Laurie was dumbstruck. She stood, she fumbled, she hemmed. The people around her said come on, it's okay, it's okay.

Laurie sat down. She simply could not say the words.

6

Silly Superstitions

Laurie's bridesmaids wore bright yellow dresses for the wedding, and Russell's friends in attendance wore zany dark sunglasses.

Russell felt like an ice-cream man in his white tuxedo. At the end of the ceremony, he triumphantly broke a glass with his foot in keeping with Jewish tradition, then, because he was a tidy person, he bent down to pick the shards up off the floor.

Rabbi Sholom Singer stopped him with a smile. "It's okay," he said. "You can leave it."

Everyone laughed.

The reception, which included a sit-down dinner for sixty-five guests, was also at Green Acres. Everyone danced the hora, and Russell's friends, half drunk and half stoned, hoisted him in a chair and danced around the room waving him aloft precariously. The band was named Emma after the lead singer, and as Russell was bobbing overhead to the rollicking music it gave him pause to realize that it wouldn't be beyond his buddies to drop him suddenly to the floor, sort of as a joke.

The balance of the festivities was more subdued. Norm, as usual, was congenial and mixed with everyone, but when

Russell went to hug him—his new father-in-law, a member of his family—he stiffened at the embrace.

The Wassermans had insisted on dominating the guest list—taking forty-five spots and giving only twenty to the Danns—but only three or four of those on Laurie's side were actually her friends. The rest were relatives or acquaintances of her parents.

The newlyweds spent their first night together as husband and wife at the O'Hare Hilton by the airport. They flew from Chicago to Atlanta the next morning and, during their layover, Russell became so engrossed in playing Donkey Kong at the video arcade that he failed to remember that they were in the eastern time zone, not the central time zone. They were half an hour late for the flight to Puerto Rico and had to catch a later flight that stopped in Miami. The next day they rode a puddle jumper from San Juan to Virgin Gorda in the British Virgin Islands where they had reservations at the Rockefeller-owned Little Dix Bay resort.

They stayed two weeks on the white-sand crescent bay. Russell spent his days sunning, snorkeling, scuba diving and sailing, but Laurie often preferred to stay in the room. He was surprised once to come back to the room and find her masturbating with the vibrator she'd packed along.

Another time, walking back from the beach they passed a window with the blinds not fully down and through the gap they could see a young couple copulating vigorously. The woman moaned with pleasure. "Hey!" Laurie shouted. "It can't be that good!"

Russell, embarrassed and angry, ran ahead to their room.

Despite her bawdy outburst, Laurie was generally more withdrawn and less self-confident than he had expected, but it was not so bad that he doubted his decision to marry her. It would clearly take time for her to blossom under his care and guidance.

But when they returned home and moved into Russell's town house in Northbrook, the changes he noticed were not for the better. Laurie gradually began adopting superstitions and little rituals to go along with them—something Russell hadn't seen from her before. Every so often she would open the car door at a stoplight and tap her foot on the pavement or walk down a street touching every telephone pole and hopping deliberately over cracks in the sidewalk. She developed an aversion to putting tops and lids back on containers and she refused to let Russell leave for work in the morning until she put her hand on the sofa. "Something bad will happen if I don't," she explained.

"Whatever you say," Russell answered with a shrug. It wasn't so hard to humor her.

Such ritualistic behavior often arises in response to stress and feelings of helplessness, psychiatrists say. It can indicate that a person is attempting to gain a feeling of control over life that he or she otherwise lacks.

Laurie admitted on several occasions that she felt badly outclassed by the other women in her husband's life. Susie, his sister, was poised, generous and outgoing, a former school-teacher and a mother of three. Elaine, Russell's mother, was not only a great tennis player but also a successful commodities broker. Beth, Noah's girlfriend, had a master's degree in business from Northwestern University and was employed as a corporate benefits consultant. These and other formidable North Shore women had set the standard against which Laurie knew she would be judged—she could not be like her mother and still earn the respect of her peers.

In her relationship with Steve Witt, Laurie had turned into her own worst enemy, driving him away with behavior she couldn't control. She'd avoided making the same mistakes with Russell Dann, but suddenly, after marriage, the stakes seemed higher. The pressure of knowing she had to measure up professionally, socially and domestically seemed to bring on and magnify the quirky behavior that had plagued her briefly when she was a child.

The unintended, maddening result for Laurie was that the rituals became part of the problem, making it difficult for her to tend to the normal requirements of life.

One of the first things Russell noticed was the appalling condition of the linen closet. Laurie threw all her clothes—new, old, clean and dirty—inside on the floor, and filled the rest of the space with household objects she picked up while ostensibly cleaning. Russell would open it up to look for something and then have to dance backward to get out of the way of falling debris.

He built her a second closet downstairs, but that one got to be even worse. Pretty soon he was complaining that it looked like a donation bin for the Salvation Army.

Such aggressive sloppiness struck a sharp contrast both to the way Laurie had enjoyed "playing house" with Steve Witt in Arizona, cooking and cleaning for him, and to her own upbringing. Guests of Norm and Edith Wasserman used to remark on the lack of clutter, dirt and dust in the house, and to note that the vacuum patterns were often visible in the living room carpet. The furniture and knickknacks were placed in a studied array as though in a museum or a hotel room. It looked like a house where nobody lived.

From the looks of Laurie's closets, though, you would have thought she was raised by bag ladies. It was particularly upsetting for Russell, who had always been something of a neatnik and had a taste for minimalist decor and strict household organization. Everything had a place for him, or at least it used to.

His initial reaction to his bride's fractured domestic sensibilities was to challenge her gently; sit her down and help her devise step-by-step plans to organize her clothing and keep track of little things in the house. First she was to pick up what was on the floor and put it into piles. Then sort the piles. Then fold what she couldn't put on hangers, and put the hanger clothes in the closet—the fall clothes with the fall, the spring with the spring, the pants with the pants, the shirts with the shirts...

He would be firm and unavoidably patronizing. She would be chastened and compliant. For one or two days afterward things would get a little better as she attempted to put his ideas into practice, then she would once again find herself slipping back into her old, careless ways. She either wasn't listening to him or she just didn't care, he couldn't tell which.

•

Laurie's inattentiveness, lack of motivation and other emerging peculiarities made it impossible for her to keep a steady job. Several months after the wedding she began working as a waitress at Langtry's, a restaurant and sports bar in nearby Glenview that had television sets hanging from the ceiling in nearly every corner. Russell stopped by for a drink after tennis at the club and wondered why he didn't see Laurie, who had told him she was working that evening.

The manager, who knew Russell, came over to the bar. "I...I'm sure you're here because of what happened with Laurie the other day," he began awkwardly.

Russell didn't know what he was talking about, but played along. "Yeah," he said. "But I want to hear it from you."

"Well, there was a table of girls," the manager said. "They were kind of rowdy and they were changing their drink orders all the time, so Laurie, she just blew up. It was a whole scene. A whole to-do. I had to fire her on the spot."

Russell tested Laurie when he got home. "How was work?" he asked mildly.

"Fine," she said. "Everything was great."

"Well, how come when I was over there they told me you got fired?" he asked. "It's not that that's so bad, Laurie, I just wonder why you're lying to me."

She buried her face in her hands and wept. "I'm doing the best I can," she said. "I'm just trying to please my dad. I'm just trying to show him how I can work and do stuff. I didn't want you or anyone to know I got fired."

"You need to be honest with me," Russell said. "Talk to me. Tell me what happened."

But again, Laurie offered no explanations, only excuses.

●

She tried again in the early spring, this time at Glenbrook Hospital in Glenview. She wrote on her application that she'd worked as a volunteer at Northwestern and Evanston hospitals in 1981, though she misspelled the suburb as "Evansten." She listed her last job as having been with Haven Equities, the investment firm at which her father rented office space. She said she was a $5 an hour "computer expert," hired "to program and feed [the] computer." Her reason for leaving: "[I] want to work in a hospital." She claimed to have graduated from Drake University with a bachelor's degree in general studies, with a concentration in liberal arts and home econom-ics. "I have a great insurance and computer background," she wrote. "And I have the training to work in a large hospital corporation."

Her résumé looked good and she was hired. She started in the Admitting/Business Services department and was trained as a full-time patient services representative in central registra-tion. After she completed her three-week training period, her supervisor concluded that Laurie had almost no interpersonal skills when dealing with outpatients in the registration area. Further, her childish, curlicued handwriting was so bad that many of the requisitions she completed were illegible. Yet another problem was that she mishandled cash receipts and caused revenue to be credited to incorrect departments and accounts. She was fired almost immediately, and came home to tell Russell that it was because the workers were forming a union and management wanted to get rid of her before she was eligible for benefits.

When she went to work as a receptionist for Dr. Joseph Granata, a Deerfield orthodontist, she mis-entered payments in the ledger, scrambled files, forgot to write appointments on the schedule and snapped at patients who called. It was her habit to store a ratty, white sweater at the office and put it on as a uniform first thing every morning. Whenever the other office assistant, Debbie, the doctor's daughter, tried to correct Laurie's bad habits or suggest she wear another sweater, Laurie hunched her shoulders like a whipped animal.

But at other times, Laurie sparkled. She spoke of having just received her degree in nutrition from Northwestern and of being married to a wealthy and charming man who treated her like a princess and often took her out to dinner and to parties.

"If you want to meet great guys," Laurie advised Debbie, striking a sisterly note, "go work at a Jewish country club. That's the place to be."

The women had lunch together several times in the first several weeks and appeared to be building a friendship, but after the doctor fired Laurie for being so erratic, she stormed out of the office and never contacted Debbie again.

She fared no better in the Highland Park office of Dr. Albert Slepyan, a dermatologist, where at first she impressed her co-workers as pretty and personable, but then started showing up for work with greasy hair, wrinkled skirts and baggy pantyhose. She twirled her hair nervously as she worked and she was terrible with phone messages. They had to let her go.

On and on it went, job after job. Russell would return home after a long day at Dann Brothers and there would be Laurie, fuming. The jerks fired her again. She'd done nothing wrong. Luck was against her. It was an outrage.

Russell would usually sympathize, but Laurie seemed to like it best when he'd get angry and swear. "Those sons of bitches," he'd say. "How could they do that to you?"

After she'd been through nearly a dozen employers, Russell sat her down for a serious talk about goals, personal directions and her future. "You know," he said, "you don't have to work. I make enough money for both of us. There's no reason you have to put up with all those idiots out there."

"But I've got to do something," she said.

Russell swallowed the bitter response that came to mind— she could certainly start by learning to take care of herself and her belongings. She was barely earning $300 a year after taxes anyway. "Why do you have to have a job?" he said instead.

She shrugged. "You're supposed to have a job," she said, avoiding his eyes. "I mean, people think you should have a job, right?"

"Don't work to try to impress everybody else," he said. "Do something you like. You like to help people, right?" She nodded. "Well, then you should volunteer with a charity," he went on. "There's no pressure, and you're going to get a good feeling. You start your day by doing something nice for somebody else. Help an old lady. I don't care if you make any money, just have a good feeling and do something."

Laurie embraced the idea in theory, but after her initial flurry of interest and activity in volunteer positions, she grew bored and frustrated, then finally quit. She came back home, where she killed her days by shopping, going to lunch with her mom, sleeping, watching TV and worrying that her own failings would destroy the marriage she had wanted so badly.

•

Russell and Laurie often played cards with Noah and Beth, who had joined the crowd and gotten married the summer after the Dann wedding. Laurie was such a careless card player that she and Russell lost consistently at spades and it stopped being fun for him after a while. He hated to lose at anything. So they regrouped and made it the women against the men, a setup that brought out Laurie's competitive side. She and Beth, who otherwise didn't have a whole lot in common, built a friendship on the bond they formed trying to beat their husbands, which they did from time to time. The joke always was that the winning team would get to choose the destination of trips they would take together as a foursome. Laurie and Beth wanted to go to resorts; Russell and Noah, who was a former tennis pro turned investment banker, wanted to go skiing or camping.

The women would occasionally go off together to talk, and it was on one of their walks that Laurie confessed her growing worries about her place in the Dann family. "They're so warm and outgoing," she fretted. "My family is kind of introverted. I mean, they meet my needs, basically, but we don't communicate like the Danns. We don't get together and laugh and have fun. And his mom is so great, and his sister is so great. I just don't fit in."

Beth tried to be upbeat. "I'm sure they accept you," she said. "I'm sure they love you. Give it time."

"I know I should," Laurie said abjectly. "But Russ is the first person who gave me a lot of warmth and a lot of love. I don't even know how to deal with it."

"What do you mean?"

"Well, like, if he asks me to do something tomorrow, I'll really want to do it, and I'll be so nervous that I won't be able to remember to do it that I stay up all night trying to remember to do it, then I fall asleep and sleep all day and forget what I was supposed to do. Is that crazy?" Before Beth could answer, Laurie rambled on. "And I've gotten real superstitious," she said. "Like I'm afraid if I close the cabinets in the kitchen, he's going to stop loving me. It seems like the more time I have, the more I worry."

"Don't," said Beth. "Don't worry. Russ loves you, he's loyal, things will be okay. Enjoy what you have."

And, for stretches of time, Russell and Laurie were able to carry on like healthy, happy suburban newlyweds. He would come home from work and they would have dinner and talk about his day, their friends, the movies. They'd go dancing or down to Chicago to see the White Sox—Russell, always the iconoclast, hated the Cubs primarily because nearly everyone else on the North Shore rooted for them. He cheered and Laurie ate hot dogs and indulged in her passion for people watching. She loved looking at everyone who walked by, examining their clothes, their movements, their expressions. Sometimes she made Russell's friends feel as though they were in a movie and she was the audience.

On weekends, Russell and Laurie would go to Green Acres where he would hit tennis balls with her even though she showed no aptitude for the game. As a couple, they earned the last-place trophy in the club's mixed doubles tournament, and Laurie celebrated by playfully pouring water over his head.

She was no better at golf, though he bought her an expensive set of golf clubs, and his parents chipped in and bought her a handsome leather bag to carry them. She would bend down and push the tee into the ground as though she were planting a flower, then stand, find her ball, bend over again and balance it carefully on the tee. Russell thought it was adorable, especially the way she happily proceeded to flail with her club five or six times before making contact.

•

Susie tried to be as generous as possible in her assessment of her brother's wife but, like everyone around Russell, she was quietly entertaining doubts. Laurie came off as immature and unfriendly, and it became a point of interest at every family gathering whether she would say thank you to the hosts, help out in any way with the cleanup chores or, if she was particularly out of it, say anything at all. Once in a while she seemed normal—other times she seemed impenetrable.

Susie had also been annoyed—but by no means worried—at the way Laurie treated the Taylor children. Susie's kids were Laurie's nieces and nephews by marriage, yet when she saw them at the Green Acres Country Club swimming pool she would walk right past and not even acknowledge them, even if they were clamoring for her attention. Susie had even asked Russell if he would please mention to Laurie that it might be nice if she would say hi to the kids. The next thing she heard, Laurie was furious at her for talking behind her back.

Laurie took virtually every opportunity to try to bring down Susie in Russell's eyes, mentioning how much time she wasted at the club and the fact she had domestic help and was so boring and suburban.

Despite this mutual lack of respect, Susie called Laurie when she needed an emergency baby-sitter for a short time one afternoon about a year after the wedding. She asked Laurie to stay fifteen minutes with Lisa, the infant, while she drove Adam to speech class after preschool. But at the appointed time Laurie hadn't arrived, so Susie bundled Lisa into the car and took her along.

No sooner had she returned than Laurie showed up, trembling and holding her arm in the air.

"I was in a terrible car accident," she said. "You know how reliable I am, but I was in an accident."

"My God, are you okay?" Susie said.

"I don't know," Laurie said. She was on the verge of tears and Susie hugged her and gently guided her to a seat.

"You should call Russ," Susie said.

"No, don't," Laurie said. "Don't. I'll... I'll tell him later."

"Where did it happen?"

"On the highway," Laurie said, referring to nearby U.S. Highway 41. "North of Clavey."

"How's the car?"

"Oh, it's fine," Laurie said. "I didn't really get hit, but I had to swerve real hard."

And sure enough, when Susie walked Laurie out to look at Laurie's Honda Accord hatchback, the one her father bought her the year she was married, there wasn't a mark on it.

Laurie continued to hold her arm in the air and tell the same story to Russell at home and when they went out to keep a dinner engagement with Norm at a Cantonese restaurant. She said her wrist was killing her. It was so bad she acted as though she couldn't even lift a glass of water. Norm didn't express the least concern, but Russell worried all through the meal and out to the car.

"We've got to take you to the hospital," he decided.

"Naw," Laurie said, her arm still cocked tragically.

"If you don't go to the hospital with me, I'll put you over my shoulders and carry you."

She lowered her arm. "Russ, I made it all up," she said.

"Oh, perfect," he said, now not sure what to believe. "Shake my hand, squeeze it really hard."

She took his hand and squeezed. Nothing was wrong with her wrist or her arm.

"Why'd you do it?" he asked.

She shrugged. "I don't know."

•

When Russell and Laurie invited friends over, Russell usually did all the setup and all the cleaning, just as he had written all the thank-you notes after their wedding and assumed responsibility for paying all the bills. When he once put her in charge of the snacks for a party, she got so worried that she wouldn't have the pretzels and potato chips ready in time that she set them out on the buffet a week in advance. They were soggy and stale when the guests arrived.

For a pot-luck luau, she bought generic pretzels, generic hot dogs and generic soda pop. When she agreed to take charge of side dishes for a barbecue, she served rotten potatoes and frozen vegetables, and set out a vase of half-dead gladiolus. Russell was proud of her for at least making an effort, but the little blunders—one simply does not serve guests generic products and frozen vegetables instead of fresh on the North Shore—were in some ways the best measure of how out of sync Laurie truly was.

Russell did almost all of the talking for the both of them when they went out together, but Laurie would make everyone cringe from time to time by coming out of her shell in little manic bursts, laughing loudly and inappropriately at one of her own stories that no one else found amusing.

Sometimes she was her usual, pretty self, but other times she applied her makeup in clumsy blotches, put on heavy black dresses in the heat of the summer and let her hair hang limp in no particular style.

When she went out with groups of women—usually the wives of Russell's friends—she always somehow seemed to leave her wallet behind. The women covered for her and then got word back to Russell, who would discreetly reimburse them.

7

Family

Laurie knew Russell wanted to have children and re-create the vibrant family life he remembered from his own youth, and, for her part, Laurie wanted to fashion a life for a child like the life she never had. He used to say he wanted two, and she had said she wanted one. They even made a deal early on—if Laurie would agree to have more than one kid, Russell would allow her to adopt a lapdog instead of the big dog he wanted.

Laurie went along with the plan in theory, but the reality of little children seemed to confuse her. When she visited her college friend Pearl Gelb after Pearl returned to her parents' home following a broken engagement, she was often brought face-to-face with Pearl's three-year-old niece, Samantha. The girl was always ready to play or jump into Laurie's lap.

"Oh, how darling," Laurie would say, drawing back and keeping her distance. "How cute!" She appeared uncomfortable, the way an awkward teenaged boy looks when handed an infant. All in all, she seemed to prefer the company of Barney, the Gelbs' goofy, seventy-pound Labrador retriever. He would jump into her lap and lick her face, loving her unconditionally. She would sit on the couch and just soak it in.

"I'm afraid to have kids," she confided to Pearl. "I wouldn't know what to do with them. It's such an incredible responsibility."

"You'd handle it," Pearl promised her. "It's an instinct people have."

"Not me," Laurie said.

Over the years Pearl had become an important friend for Laurie—she wasn't particularly beautiful or vivacious, but she was loyal and a link with a simpler and more carefree part of her past. After Pearl had broken up with her boyfriend in Tucson in 1981, Laurie called every day to see how she was doing, and now that Pearl was recovering from another heartache Laurie would always make a special point of inviting her over when she and Russell were throwing a party. Other times she might call and say, "Hey, if you have nothing to do tonight, Russ and I are going out to dinner, why don't you meet us?"

Laurie had also been reaching out to Dhana Cohen, one of the more unfailingly friendly of her former college roommates. She had run into her by surprise at a restaurant in Skokie before the wedding and called her occasionally ever since. Dhana accompanied Laurie and Russell several times to parties, softball games and other casual social events, but she noticed that, just like at school, Laurie was living solely as an extension of someone else. She had nothing to say for herself or about herself, but she kept calling and Dhana, because she was that kind of person, kept calling back.

•

Laurie's friendship with Beth Rosen was more intense but less straightforward. Though Beth seemed to care an awful lot for Laurie and was a good listener, she was still part of Russell's circle and thus competition of a sort for Laurie. During one lunch date at Hackney's, a burger restaurant in Wheeling, Beth spoke of her own dilemmas. "I just don't know what's going to happen when I have kids," she said. "I know I want a family, but I really like my job."

Laurie looked critically at her for a long minute. "You know what your problem is?" she said at last. "Your problem is that you just don't know what you want out of life."

Beth was stunned. Nothing was further from the truth. She knew exactly what she wanted—everything. That was the problem. Laurie had totally turned it around. She was the one who was messed up. Laurie was the one who didn't know what she wanted out of life.

•

Russell found that lecturing Laurie was like talking to a cat—she looked at him, seemed to listen, then went off and did whatever she felt like. The messiness in her closets spilled over into the kitchen, where she started storing pots, pans, plates and cutlery together in any old drawer. Russell was working at the office from seven o'clock in the morning until six o'clock at night, then coming home to find Laurie had done almost literally nothing all day except mess things up.

He tried encouraging her with praise, he tried ranting and raving and he tried threatening to cut off her clothing allowance, but nothing worked for long. She continued a slow, gloomy deterioration punctuated by fits of rage reminiscent of the mood swings Russell remembered from their courting days.

"You don't love me!" she would shout. "I hate you!"

When she quieted down, he would ask her to try to be specific—what was she angry about? What had he done? And it was always something small, like he'd forgotten an errand or come home half an hour later than he said he was going to.

"For that you hate me?" Russell said. "For that you don't love me anymore? What happens when I really fuck up or do something wrong? How the hell do you think that makes me feel?"

Overwhelmed with guilt, Laurie would begin to cry.

"Laurie, Laurie," Russell said. "What can we do?"

"I don't know. I'm sorry. Forget what I said. I didn't mean it."

"We have to do something for you."

"I know."

"Things shouldn't be this way."

"I know."

"Do you think you can change? Do you think you can get better?"

"I don't know. I think so."

•

After about a year and half of marriage it was clear that Laurie wouldn't be able to solve her own problems and Russell couldn't do it for her. She decided to see a psychiatrist, but only if Russell would swear not to tell anyone.

"If that's what you want," he said.

She began going to Highland Park psychiatrist Dr. Robert Greendale on Thursdays. She visited his office three times in the first month and he put her on thioridazine.

Greendale has never revealed his specific diagnosis, but the drug he prescribed is what is known as a major tranquilizer—distinct from such minor tranquilizers as Valium—and is administered for short-term treatment of depression that is accompanied by anxiety and agitation. It is also used to treat psychosis, in which the patient is out of touch with reality.

Russell noticed that the thioridazine, in combination with the birth control pills Laurie was taking, helped flatten out her increasingly unpredictable mood swings. Unfortunately it didn't provide the instantaneous cure for her deeper problems both she and Russell were hoping for. He went with her to one of the early therapy sessions during which Greendale was trying to help her control her ritual behaviors.

Laurie explained that she was troubled by "bad thoughts," and that she used her superstitions to ward off these thoughts and prevent harm from coming to Russell.

"Well, next time Russell goes to work, try not touching the sofa and see what happens," Greendale suggested.

"Hey, Doc," Russell complained, making a little joke out of it. "Couldn't we start with something else besides me?"

Laurie repeated to Greendale some of the things she had told Russell about her feelings for her parents—a confused love-hate having to do with what she saw as a lack of genuine support and affection. She was envious, she said, of happy families.

She did not like therapy—it was difficult and the results were far from immediate. She missed her fourth appointment and called the following Monday to tell Greendale she wasn't coming back. He was so alarmed that he wrote her immediately:

I felt compelled to send you a letter as a follow-up to our very brief telephone discussion today. I am genuinely concerned about your ability to cope with the problems that you have been struggling with. I think it is important for you to realize, if you don't already, that the nature of your problems goes back long before you married your husband and it relates very much to your childhood upbringing. Although your husband certainly demonstrated a tremendous amount of understanding and support in his visit with the two of us in the office, I do not feel that he has the training or certainly the objectivity to function in a professional manner. Furthermore, the use of medication can only result in a symptomatic improvement and not in a definitive cure for the kinds of difficulties that you are experiencing. Medication can also only be appropriately administered under an ongoing doctor's observation and care.

In conclusion, I would hope that you would reconsider your decision about coming in for psychotherapy inasmuch as I feel that it is of extreme importance that you reconsider some kind of professional help.

When Russell read the letter, he was not in the least surprised that Greendale had zeroed in on Laurie's family life as the source of her troubles. He himself had already noticed that Laurie's behavior improved dramatically whenever Norm and Edith were vacationing in Florida. She would begin to feel better about herself and show some small signs of being able to cope with the tremendous pressures she was feeling. The best times were when her mother and father were far away, and Norm would call every Sunday night, like clockwork, and talk for ten minutes about the weather and his backhand.

•

By then, Norm Wasserman was fifty-five and semiretired on the advice of his doctor, who had diagnosed him as having high blood pressure and told him to start taking it easy if he wanted to make it to his golden years. Tennis had become an even bigger part of his life—he would play as early as six in the morning with friends at the Highland Park Racquet Club who wanted to get a set in before going to the office, and

Saturdays he went to Bob Lubin's house in Glencoe to play doubles on Lubin's court. In that foursome he was known as a very cool, collected player who never tired and never lost his temper or swore when things didn't go right. Everyone marveled at what great shape he was in for a man his age.

In July of 1984, he and Edith began trying to sell their Glencoe home. They put power of attorney in Russell's hands so he could finalize a deal if a sufficiently attractive offer were made while they were away on one of the five or six two-week trips a year they were averaging to Florida. Retirement would mean soaking up the sun full-time in paradise, still more tennis for Norm, boating with friends and living off investment income for the rest of their lives. No more harsh winters, no more day-to-day hassles at home.

Responsibilities and expectations had weighed upon Norm ever since his father died when he was young, and he'd become a methodical, purposeful man, very concerned with order and control. When his mother had a stroke and was confined to a nursing home, he visited and took her to lunch every single Tuesday. He planned his trips to Florida up to a year in advance so that they were able to take full advantage of discount airfares. He always had plenty of one- and two-cent stamps on hand so as to be sure to have exact postage and no more on his letters. When Edith asked for the salt at the dinner table, Norm reached for it instantly, even if it was right in front of someone else. If Edith's Toyota was low on gas, he would take it to work and fill it up along the way, leaving his car home for her to drive.

Neighbors and casual business associates invariably found Norm and Edith lovely and friendly. Norm in particular was a good one for small talk and how-do-you-do's. And he was exactly the same way at home. Russell and others noticed that he treated his wife and children with an affectionate but casual regard, as though they were all friends instead of a family.

Laurie complained to Russell that a desire for organization, not love, seemed to rule her father's life. Emotional highs and lows made him nervous, she said, to the point that when a large, old tree fell over in his yard on Sheridan Road once, he seemed nearly paralyzed with anxiety: Who would take care of it? How long would it take? How much would it cost? Who would supervise the work? Would he have to take a day off? Would the company be bonded? How would the removal affect other vegetation?

"He's frantic," Laurie reported to Pearl Gelb. "This is the worst thing that's ever happened in his life. He usually hopes problems go away on their own, and this one isn't going away. I hope nothing bad ever really happens. I don't know what he'd do."

Edith was no help in such situations. She was the kind of person who wouldn't drive at night or in the rain because of her uncertainty as to where to find the lights and the switch for the windshield wipers, Russell remembered. She never worked and had no demonstrable ambitions. As far as he could tell, she spent her days shopping, going to the beauty parlor, watching television, working crossword puzzles and waiting for Norm to come home. He'd pull into the driveway and honk the horn, then neighbors would see her scurry out the door and get into the car. Off they'd go to dinner.

Laurie told Russell that her mother had given her no sympathy when she was a child. She would fall down and hurt herself or come down with a cold, and Edith couldn't be bothered. She scorned Edith as "a zero" behind her back; Edith criticized Laurie's hair and clothing to her face.

Mark had always been her favorite child anyway—people said they could just tell. He had the same angular features as his father, the same aptitude for country club sports and the same reserved nature. After getting his master's degree in advertising from the University of Illinois in 1976, he'd gone on to become the supervisor of marketing and communications for the Minnesota Mining and Manufacturing Corporation in Austin, Texas, where he and his wife, Paula, were rearing two daughters, Amy and Sherry.

Laurie always envied and admired her brother. When they were kids she used to brag about his tennis and swimming abilities to her little friends on Sumac Lane, and as the years went by she came to believe he was the only person who truly understood her difficult but outwardly tranquil family relationships.

Laurie could talk to Mark, though it was hard for her to bare her soul to him when he was living so far away and visited so infrequently. She asked Russell to hire him at Dann Brothers so he could move back to the Chicago area, but Mark never pursued the idea.

•

Russell took the letter from Dr. Greendale with him when he and Norm went fishing at a little lake near the Tri-State Tollway west of Highland Park. During a quiet moment, he produced the letter and read it aloud, laying careful stress on the words *"the nature of your problems goes back long before you married your husband and it relates very much to your childhood upbringing...."*

Norm had no response at first, and bit his lower lip contemplatively.

"What do you think?" Russell said.

"I think," Norm said, "that there's really not that much of a problem here. It's a nonissue. I don't believe in psychiatry. I don't believe in that kind of stuff."

Neither did Laurie. She would not go back into therapy.

•

The remote control for Russell's television broke.

"Can you take it down to the cable-TV office?" he asked Laurie. "Either they'll know how to fix it or they'll give you another one."

She tensed. "Can't you call them?" she asked. "Can't you call them and have them come and pick it up?"

•

When they visited Laurie's parents in Florida, she decided she couldn't step on the rug in the entryway and so tiptoed around it, her back to the wall. She insisted on using only one hand on the handlebars when they all went bike riding, and she damn near fell off going over a bridge.

Russell hoped Norm and Edith would find this startling and troubling, but it didn't seem to bother them.

8

Overwhelmed

Russell thought he had another solution. He and Laurie would move out of the cramped condo and into a real house where she would have more room to store things and less of an excuse to jam everything into the nearest drawer or closet. She agreed enthusiastically, and said that she'd certainly be much neater if she had more space. They began looking in late 1984 after having been married a little more than two years, eventually settling on a five-bedroom house built into a little hillside on Hastings Street in one of Highland Park's less wealthy neighborhoods. The house was conspicuously large, even ostentatious for a childless couple in their mid-twenties, and they were unusual on the quiet, gently curving street of young families and empty-nesters.

But even on their first day in the new house, Russell could see how foolish he'd been to think the shift in address was going to change things. As the movers brought furniture in the door and asked Laurie where the pieces should go, she said she couldn't decide, she had no idea, no opinion. There was no new beginning for her. Rather than concentrate her energies on self-improvement, she brooded on the apparent inequity that had her and Russell paying $178,500 for their house while a family on a street behind them had bought a similar house for $20,000 less.

"Let's walk over there so we can see the house," Laurie suggested to Beth when she came for a visit. "She just had a baby, so we can say we're coming to see the baby, but I want to see if it's nicer than ours."

Beth agreed and over they went. Laurie was polite but frosty to the homeowners, and turned increasingly grim as she realized the house was in better shape than her own.

"Damn it!" she said as she and Beth were walking home.

"What?"

"I'm just pissed, that's all."

"Why?"

"They got a great deal," Laurie complained.

"So did you," Beth said.

"Not compared to them."

"Don't worry about it."

"I didn't like them," Laurie said, her voice taking on a hard edge. "Did you?"

"I don't know," Beth said. "They seemed okay to me."

"They were jerks," Laurie said. Her anger was still building and it stuck with her, not just for days but months and years. She nurtured every grievance, saved it, recalling it frequently, allowing it to grow.

•

"That sure is a great house you bought," Armand said proudly to Russell.

Later, Laurie cursed Armand to Russell's face for his remark. "It's not *your* house," she said, pointing at Russell bitterly. "It's *our* house."

•

Laurie refused to use the "unlucky" back staircase down to the family room and developed an aversion to casual physical contact that was so strong she was unable to simply pass an object to someone else without dropping or tossing it at the last second.

She began scattering trash throughout the house and leaving money in the oven and the freezer, canned food in the dishwasher and makeup in the microwave. As startling as these new unconventionalities might have been to outsiders,

Russell was only slightly put out. After two years, he was worn down, almost immune. His wife was kooky; maybe she was just looking for attention. But when he would try to talk to her about what was happening, she would either be catatonic or defensive.

"Why do you put the makeup in the microwave?" he said, appealing to her tenuous sense of reason.

"Because that's where I put it," she said, reflecting his logical tone. "That's where I know where it is."

"It doesn't belong there," he said. "It belongs in the bathroom. I'll show you."

He put the makeup back in the proper place, but several days later he would find it back in the microwave, or perhaps in the freezer or one of the cupboards, and thus gradually with excuses and persistence did she wear him down still further.

Russell was in way, way over his head. He had married—perhaps hastily, in retrospect—a beautiful, unassuming woman who seemed to share his values and meet his basic requirements. And slowly she had become the victim of some sort of mental condition, a neurosis, a psychosis, something, he didn't know what to call it, he didn't know what to do about it, and so a lot of times he just tried to pretend that it wasn't so bad and he could live with it. He was not a genius. He was not a hero. He was not an idiot. He was just an ordinary guy in trouble.

•

Noah and Russell compromised with Beth and Laurie on a group-vacation destination and they rented a Winnebago van for three-day weekends to Wisconsin and to the Michigan Dunes. On the Michigan trip, however, Laurie trashed the Winnebago the way she was then making a mess of the house—strewing clothes everywhere, not putting the food away, tossing trash aside heedlessly.

Laurie and Beth took a walk on the beach one afternoon while Russell and Noah played tennis. When the women were nearly back, Beth said she thought they should head up a certain path to meet their husbands. "Go ahead," Laurie said.

She then turned on her heels and walked the opposite direction, disappearing for more than an hour.

"Where's Laurie?" Russell asked when Beth appeared at the tennis courts.

"I told her I wanted to go where you guys were, and she didn't come," Beth said. "I don't know where she went."

Later, after Laurie had returned, Russell and Noah went off together. They climbed to the top of a sand dune looking over the lake, and sat down to catch their breath.

After an awkward silence, Russell began, "My marriage is not what it appears to be."

"What do you mean?" Noah said.

"We're having our problems," he said. "Nobody knows about it. You can't really see it from the outside. You can only see it if you live with her. She's not happy. She's not self-sufficient. She doesn't do anything all day long. She has no life. Laurie is just somebody who needs to be taken care of, and I know I have to take care of her forever."

Noah was startled by Russell's frankness, yet he was also reassured that Russell's love was not, as he and Beth feared, blind.

When the two couples returned from the trip, the question became who was going to return the van to the rental agency. Russell pulled Beth aside and asked her if she would take care of it.

"I work," she said testily. "Why doesn't Laurie do it? She does nothing the whole day."

Russell winced. "I just don't think she could handle the pressure of returning it," he said.

It just didn't seem right, Beth and Noah said to each other afterward—this devil-may-care guy being saddled with such a burden. She was sapping the life out of him.

•

Laurie and Russell rendezvoused one afternoon at his parents' house in Highland Park for a visit. They took separate cars, and when it came time to leave, she agreed to follow him home. He pulled out onto the road and had gone several blocks before checking in his rearview mirror. No Laurie. He stopped and waited, and pretty soon she came careening down the street toward him, her car swerving from side to side, racing fifteen miles an hour backwards.

•

Susie, Russell's sister, decided she wanted to give away the last of her baby clothes, so she called him and asked if maybe he'd like to take them and put them away for the day he would be a father.

"That's the furthest thing from my mind right now," he said miserably. "I doubt Laurie will ever be able to raise kids, Susie. She can barely get through the day on her own as it is."

"You're kidding."

He broke down and told his sister everything—about the trash all over the house, the belongings stashed in queer places, the superstitions that ruled Laurie's existence. "She's overwhelmed," he said. "That's the only word I can think of to describe it. She's overwhelmed by life."

Susie gently suggested to him the possibility of a divorce. "It's not such a bad thing," she said.

"I don't believe in it," he said. "I won't divorce her. I won't even think about that now."

"But she's not the person you thought she was," Susie said. "You don't have to feel responsible."

"You don't understand," Russell said. "I do feel responsible."

He became Rusty Dann all over again—his face cut to shreds after a minibike accident, holding it all together. Just holding it together.

•

Russell's mother, Elaine, urged him to break off the marriage as soon as she heard word through Susie that Laurie had psychological problems. "Cut the strings," she said. "It can't get better. There's no shame in divorce."

But Russell prided himself on his determination and his loyalty. Laurie was sick and he was not going to abandon her that easily. "I've got to give it time," he said. "All it will take is some work and some time."

His friend Noah thought Russell was just being naive. "Look, it's great that you're trying to make things work," he said. "I'm that way, too. But you can't change people. Laurie is the kind of girl you can't change and you can't help. She has to help herself."

•

All Laurie Wasserman Dann ever wanted, really, was to be someone else—a girl from a happy family, popular, a good student, a college graduate and a presentable housewife. She had no idea what to do with the person she was, and she simply sank further and further into isolation and despair.

She began leaving food out to spoil on the counter, storing new clothes with the tags still on them in piles in the back seat of her car, and refusing to close cabinets or drawers she had opened. The house was in such disarray that when a friend came over for a walk one day, Laurie couldn't even find one pair of her own shoes. She grabbed Russell's sneakers and stuffed three socks into the toes to make them fit.

If no one stopped by, she would sleep all day in her sweatpants and sweatshirt, even while interior housepainters worked around her. When Russell pulled into the garage after work he would hear her get out of bed and turn on the shower. He would then walk in on a house in predictable disarray.

"What's wrong?" she asked him once, reading the irritation and frustration on his face at the end of a long day.

"What's wrong?" he exploded. "I'll tell you what's wrong. Everybody keeps asking me what's wrong, that's what's wrong. What's wrong is I look all day like something's wrong because I'm so unhappy."

"What are you unhappy about?" She turned meek, frightened.

"I'm unhappy because I get home from work and you're in bed," he said, his big gestures taking in the totality of her dissolution. "Then you get in the shower and I go around picking up all the garbage off the floor and throw it out, then I gotta close every cabinet, every drawer, everything you've touched. Then I have to try and figure out what other trouble you've gotten in all day. Laurie, I don't have a wife. I've got a fucking daughter!"

"These are part of my problems," she said contritely. "I've got to work them through."

Her problems. He'd about had it with her problems. He finally gave her an ultimatum: either she return to Dr. Greendale or he would leave her.

"I'll go," she said wretchedly. "Don't leave. You're the only person who ever cared for me. Even after all the shit I put you through, you were still a pal. We have a great house in the suburbs and we belong to a country club. Where would I go if I lost you?"

"You won't lose me," he said, calming down. "It'll be okay."

But it wasn't okay. Laurie's visits to Greendale were erratic and she was unable to keep on schedule with the thioridazine because it nauseated her. Her own shortcomings and a looming realization that she might have inherited or developed a serious mental illness turned her into an even darker and stranger character. She began staying in bed even when guests would drop by, and at times Russell would find her in an almost zombie-like state, petrified at even the thought of leaving her room.

Russell's patience expired. Their verbal battles over her behavior and her refusal to seek help became more heated and would end when either he grabbed her by the arms and held her until she calmed down or he stormed out of the house in frustration.

The more she felt his anger and despair, the more scared she became that he would reject her, and the further she deteriorated. About the only thing that got any better was their sex life. Making love was one of the few pleasures she had left and the worse she got, the more often she wanted to do it.

She was always kind of an average partner in bed, Russell thought, but every once in a while she'd show him her kinky side. There was the vibrator she took on their honeymoon, of course, then once when they were visiting her parents in Boca Raton she slyly showed him how she could masturbate in front of Norm, Edith and everybody by using the underwater jets in the pool. She also confided to him that one of her big sexual fantasies was to have a dog perform oral sex on her.

•

As Russell and Laurie approached their third anniversary, he asked his brother and father to meet him for lunch. After the meal he said there was something he had to tell them. "I've got some real problems with Laurie," he said, "I'm trying hard to work them out and I don't know if I can. I mean, have you seen the house? I have to come home from work every day and play maid."

Scott was surprised at the news and even a little hurt that he hadn't heard anything earlier. He knew that his kid brother was wrestling doubly hard with the situation because he didn't want to be the first in the family to be divorced. In some respects, Russell's competitive nature was keeping his marriage intact.

"She's seeing a doctor," Russell said. "I'm hoping, you know, that she might get interested in life—working or something. She needs to have some meaning or purpose or whatever. Right now she has trouble hanging on to anything."

He arranged again to visit Dr. Greendale with Laurie, but when he went he concluded that Greendale had little grasp of the severity of Laurie's condition. She apparently hadn't told him about the most debilitating of her superstitions and the way she had become virtually a prisoner of her own emotional helplessness. She was telling him instead of petty concerns and minor gaps in communication on the order of fights over her folding the towels wrong or not sealing the salad dressing in the refrigerator.

"Laurie, what are you talking about?" Russell interrupted. "You're not talking about anything important here. You haven't mentioned any of the things that are really problems."

She hung her head. Greendale turned to her. "Laurie," he said, "you know, we have to get back into it."

She nodded.

Russell exhaled wearily. "Guys," he said, "I'm done. I'm burned out. My family has been telling me to get out of this, and now I'm seeing that you're not willing to help yourself. If you're not willing to help yourself, I can't help you."

Laurie knew the split was coming, so she asked Russell for time to prepare herself. Over the next couple of months she made noticeable but feeble efforts to show him that she could live a normal life. She even did the laundry for the first time Russell could remember, gathering up all the dirty clothes, putting them in the machine, adding soap and setting the dial to the wash cycle. She then neatly folded all the clothes and put them away in drawers—soaking wet.

The strain of the effort was palpable, and by early October of 1985 Russell was too weary to continue. "I'm really tired of carrying the weight," he said to Noah and Beth. "I do everything, picking up the slack for two people. I can't do it anymore. If I knew she was going to doctors and getting better, I could cope with it, but I've tried to help her and now she's not going to her doctor and she's canceling her appointments, and I just can't deal with it anymore. I've got to go on with my life. I want to find someone and have a family, and I don't think this woman is capable of having children and raising a family. She can't get up in the morning and take care of herself. She can't get dressed or clean the house. I can't live my life like this. I can't do it anymore."

"Whatever you have to do," they said.

He decided to ask Laurie for a separation, but went initially to warn Norm and Edith before they took their first big trip of the winter to Florida. He took them taffy apples as a little gift and got right to the point. "It's getting crazy," he said. "I'm going nuts. I don't think it's going to last much longer."

Norm pondered for a moment. "We should still go," he said, speaking to Russell through Edith. "Laurie knows we're supposed to go, and she'd know something terrible was wrong if we didn't go. So we should go and then we can come back if you decide to do it."

"I'll hang on as long as possible," Russell said. For her twenty-eighth birthday a week later he bought her a pink warm-up suit and a bouquet of flowers. She carried the flowers around for several weeks after they died, and virtually refused to take the sweatsuit off. She told Beth she was convinced that Russell would never leave her as long as she had the suit on for luck.

When Russell finally told her he was leaving her, she was devastated but not surprised. "Where am I going to go from here?" she sobbed. "What's going to happen?"

She wept and he held her. They tried to call Norm and Edith in Boca Raton, but they were out, so they called other friends and told them what had happened. In the evening, they finally reached the Wassermans.

Laurie was so torn apart with sorrow that she literally

couldn't speak and handed the phone to Russell. He broke the news.

"Okay, Laurie, hang in there," Norm said when Russell put his daughter back on the phone. "Don't worry about it. We'll be back in a couple of weeks and we'll talk then."

Laurie hung up and fell back into Russell's arms where she sobbed for five minutes.

Russell seethed. No wonder the poor girl was all screwed up! He hadn't calmed down when he called the Wassermans back. "Norm, you son of a bitch!" he said. "You fucking son of a bitch, do you have any idea what your daughter's going through?"

He slammed down the phone. A few minutes later, Norm called back. He and Edith would return the next morning.

9

The Dark Side

After the separation in the fall of 1985, Laurie lived at her parents' house whenever Norm and Edith were out of town and with Russell whenever they were in town. It was an uneasy arrangement in which the lines of responsibility and affection were blurred. Russell continued to give her money, usually $50 and $100 bills, and even wrote her an $800 tuition check to the National College of Education in Evanston so she could go to school and earn the teaching certificate she always said she wanted. She endorsed the check herself and kept the money.

They slept in different bedrooms but still had sex now and then. Russell justified it by telling himself that making love was a way of showing Laurie he didn't hate her, which was important to her self-esteem. She was still trying hard to impress upon him that she could get better, and before they went out to dinner at the Village Smithy restaurant in Glencoe she spent hours getting ready—dressing up, brushing her hair, getting her purse organized—all to show him that she deserved another chance.

"I can be a normal person in the right situation," she told him over dinner. "I think I've learned a lot. This whole experience has been good for me, and now I think I'm ready."

Edith also told Russell that she had talked to a doctor friend and that he had assured her that Laurie's problem was common and if she just got the right treatment, she'd be fine.

But Russell wasn't buying any of it.

•

The pain of separation tore Laurie apart. Her friend Beth, Noah's wife, was shocked by Laurie's appearance when she met her for lunch at the Claim Company restaurant in Northbrook not long after the announcement. She was thin and haggard, and said right away that she wasn't sure if she would order anything—she hadn't been able to eat.

"I don't know how we're going to do this," she said. "I don't know how we can possibly divide everything up. There's so much to do."

Beth was matter-of-fact. "It's easier than you think," she said. "My sister got a divorce, and she and her husband basically took away what each of them owned. When you don't have any kids, it's very easy."

"Oh, no, it's not," Laurie said, suddenly bitter. "It's not going to be easy. I'm not going to let Russ get away with this. I want him to suffer. I want him to know what I feel like."

"It doesn't have to be that way," Beth said. "You can just get on with your life. You have a lot going for you, you know."

"Like what?"

"Like you're pretty, you're young, you've got money," Beth said, counting Laurie's assets on her fingers. "You can get better—work through this problem—and go back to school. You can start dating again. Have you thought about that?"

"No, no, no," Laurie said. "I've got to get this all taken care of. I've got to get Russell. I can't let him get away with this."

"It's not going to do you any good," Beth said. "The only thing that's going to do you any good is to get on with your life. It's over. Forget it."

"I'm going to take him to the cleaners," Laurie went on, ignoring Beth. "My dad and I have been talking to the lawyers, and they think we can really get him, really screw him."

Beth changed the subject. She worried about Laurie, but when it came down to it, her loyalties and sympathies lay with Russell. At the end of lunch she assured Laurie they would speak again soon. But she never did have another conversation with her.

•

Laurie's next idea was that she could get Russell to stay with her if she could convince him she was pregnant.

His first response was to slough off her claim with exaggerated patience, but she saw how the very suggestion got under his skin and she kept on with it. He pointed out that it was unlikely—he had been withdrawing before ejaculation because he didn't trust her to take her birth control pills. But she replied that she'd been secretly collecting his semen and injecting it into herself with a syringe.

Then she said that, actually, she had gone out and slept with a man with Russell's blood type. She had the idea they could go on the Donahue show and have the paternity-test results revealed on national television.

Such conversations invariably turned ugly. "You can't even get pregnant," Russell sneered once. "If you could get pregnant, why would you need these?" He produced a drug-store remedy Laurie bought to regulate her ovarian cycle. "You're never going to have kids. And you couldn't have kids anyway because you wouldn't know how to take care of them. You could never handle it."

She would scream, cry and rage at him. He swore, threw a deck of cards at her, changed the locks on the house when she was out. Several times she called for the Highland Park police to come mediate their disputes, though the department kept no written reports on the calls, as they were resolved without arrests or charges being filed.

He began to have the distinct impression that Laurie was being dragged into what he came to think of as her dark side by some sort of outside force; something like the evil Darth Vader character in the *Star Wars* movie. He went to the library and read magazine articles on mental illnesses—what caused them, how to identify them, what to do for them—and found only a great mystery.

•

In her loneliness and desperation, Laurie took to the telephone and fought back in a new way: for hours every day, she called Russell, his family and his friends, waited for them to answer, and then, after a sinister pause, hung up. When her targets compared notes they figured out who was behind the calls, but how were they going to prove it?

A month after the separation she called Steve Witt's father's pharmacy in Arizona and told the clerk she was an old friend who wanted to get in touch again. The clerk told her Steve was at a hospital in New York City doing his medical residency in dermatology, and she called the hospital immediately. She approached the conversation with Steve cautiously. When she found out he was married, she told him she was married, too—something he happened to already know through a mutual acquaintance. Steve said he and his wife were planning to go skiing, and Laurie said she and Russ were also planning to go skiing. It was all very normal, Steve thought, and he was pleased that she was doing well. A happy ending for both of them after all.

Then Laurie called Dhana, her old Arizona roommate, who had moved into the city and fallen out of touch. "Guess who's getting separated?" she said.

"Who?"

"Me!"

She outlined some of her problems with Russell and continued the litany of complaints in numerous subsequent phone calls and a dinner engagement with Dhana. He hated her, he treated her badly, he was spreading all kinds of weird rumors about her, she was going to get him, Russell-this, Russell-that.

•

As relations were getting worse and worse, the parents and their feuding children held an emergency summit meeting at the Hastings Street house to try to sort out the accusations and counteraccusations that were making an amicable divorce settlement seem unlikely. Norm remained adamant that Laurie was being victimized, and insisted that Russell had attacked her and torn her pajamas.

What about the hang-up phone calls everyone in the Dann family was getting?

"What about them?" Norm said. "We're getting hang-ups, too. You don't know who's doing that."

Russell blew up. "You're ridiculous!" he yelled. "How can you be so stupid? So blind? Such idiots? Don't you see what's happening here? Can't you tell how Laurie's lying to you? Can't you see how much she hates you? Think about this: she says she hates me, but when you come home, where do you call her? Here! And when you're in Florida, where do you call her? At your house. Maybe she hates me, but she hates you more."

Edith looked to Laurie inquiringly.

"That's not true," Laurie said.

"Just get your fucking daughter out of here," Russell shouted. "If you think for a second I'm going to support her anymore, you're wrong. You've got a battle on your hands."

Laurie smiled with self-satisfaction, as though his tirade was proving to her parents once and for all what a jerk this guy really was.

•

Russell's father and Laurie's father, as old business acquaintances, had taken the lead in the divorce negotiations. But progress was slow and tensions high during the first several months, and Armand finally gave Norm a deadline of January 3, 1986, to come up with a mutually acceptable proposal, which they would file in the Lake County court system because Highland Park—where Russell and Laurie had been living—was in Lake County on the border between Cook and Lake counties.

But the day before the deadline, Laurie filed for dissolution of the marriage in Cook County. She told Russell it was because she was living in Glencoe, which is just across the county line from Highland Park. She confided to her lawyer, however, that the real reason was the huge backlog of divorce cases in Cook County, which includes the city of Chicago. She was hoping to drag out the proceedings for two to three years, she said.

Her petition alleged that "Without fault or provocation

on the part of [Laurie], [Russell] has been guilty of extreme and repeated mental cruelty."

That same day, Russell and Scott bundled up Laurie's clothes at the Hastings Street house and took them over to the Wassermans' ranch house by the lake. All the rooms were perfect, as usual, except Laurie's, where every surface was draped with blouses, sweaters, slacks, underpants and socks as well as ordinary household trash. He and Scott laid the clothes out on Laurie's bed in a large, neat pile as she stood by. She declined his offer for further help cleaning up.

"Just get it together," he told her firmly. "Put these clothes on hangers; if you want, I'll come back and help sort them. But make your parents proud."

Instead, Laurie called Norm in Boca Raton and told him that Russell and Scott had stormed the house and thrown everything in her room on the floor.

•

Susie had no doubts about the wisdom of the breakup of her brother's marriage, and she called frequently to reassure him it was all for the best and to help counsel him on how to proceed.

His intention was to make the transition gentle for Laurie, he said, but at the same time he didn't want to have his pockets unfairly picked. In one conversation with his sister he spent a long time outlining various ways to split up the marital assets, several of which were less than favorable for Laurie. He was then surprised when Laurie confronted him about those very plans the following day, asking how he could be so ruthless and unfair.

Russell, in turn, blew up at Susie. "What are you going and telling people about my plans for?" he raged. "These things get around! Jesus!"

Susie yelled back at him. She hadn't told a soul and he was a jerk for not trusting her.

Not long afterward, the mystery was solved when Russell heard an unusual click while talking to a friend on the phone one Saturday morning. "Hang on a second," he said.

Methodically he searched the house, first downstairs, then upstairs. Finally he found Laurie, who was supposedly living with her parents, crouched in a pile of birdseed in her old closet, huddled up to the cordless telephone.

Birdseed! It was one of those tableaux that, under ordinary circumstances, would be so frightening and weird that a person would call an ambulance to cart Laurie away to the asylum, but to Russell it was just another nutty thing, totally beyond his ken.

He called Norm in Florida. "Laurie is in a bad way," he said. "She needs your help."

"I understand," Norm said. "Tell her I'll be back in about five weeks."

"Norm, you can turn your back on this all you want, but it's only going to get worse," Russell said. "It's not going to go away."

•

Laurie found that another good way to get at Russell was to call the post office, identify herself as his wife, and ask that his mail be held for pickup. She would then get it, go through it looking for financial or personal information to use against him in the divorce, and finally either throw the rest away or toss it in the back seat of her car, where she was also leaving spare $100 bills.

Russell would get the hold order removed, but Laurie would either put it back on in a couple of weeks or try to intercept the mailman.

•

Laurie sought a temporary restraining order against Russell on the last day of January 1986. Her attorney charged that Russell had started closing out various bank accounts and that Laurie was afraid he was about to "dissipate, transfer, pledge or otherwise dispose of" various marital assets. At the time, however, Russell was still finding money thrown haphazardly in the back seat of her car.

A week later, Russell's attorney filed a counterpetition for dissolution of the marriage, and the gloves were off.

Laurie contacted Dhana again, and this time they got together for drinks at Great Godfrey Daniels, a restaurant and bar in Skokie. Laurie said she was pregnant and that she was planning to have an abortion. She also said she was very angry because Russell had thrown away all of their wedding pictures and a large quantity of meat that her parents had given to her. The meat she was referring to was freezer-burned beef she had been keeping for more than a year. She eventually sent Russell a bill for it, which he ignored.

She also told Dhana that she was thinking about getting a gun—a strange notion, Dhana thought. But actually, the idea was consistent with a fixation on destruction and violence that had started taking over Laurie's life.

On April 8, just after dinnertime, Laurie called the Highland Park police to the Hastings Street house to report that Russell verbally abused her, spat on her, slapped her on the face, kicked her in the stomach, struck her on the back and twisted her legs. She told the responding officer that she and Russell were separated but still lived in the same house, which was sort of true because she was continuing to sleep there when she tired of her parents. She showed no physical signs of having been assaulted and declined to sign a complaint form. Russell, who was standing by, told the officers he hadn't touched her, that she just said crazy things about him all the time.

A little more than two weeks later, Laurie drove to the Glencoe Department of Public Safety and reported that burglars had torn apart her parents' home on Sheridan Road. She said she had left the house at 10:45 in the morning and returned an hour later to find the TV set sitting on the front steps. She carried the set into the house, she said, and noticed that the interior had been ransacked, so she left.

Officers later went through the house and found two drawers pulled out of a dresser in the den. Laurie told them envelopes containing money were missing. Drawers were also pulled out in her bedroom, where a twin bed in the corner had been turned over. Laurie said a $500, fourteen-karat chain with gold letters spelling out "Laurie" was missing along with $2,130 in cash, various stereo and video equipment, clothing and other pieces of jewelry.

Evidence technicians found no forcible signs of entry to the house, and they noted that most of the mayhem seemed to have occurred in Laurie's bedroom, which was unusual because burglars tend to head straight for the master bedroom. Her wedding photo album had been pulled out of a closet drawer and all of her wedding pictures were thrown about the floor. Pictures of Laurie were ripped up.

The Glencoe detective put in charge of the investigation was Floyd Mohr, who, coincidentally, had once played with Russell Dann on the touch football team sponsored by Dann Brothers Insurance. Russell had been the quarterback; Mohr a lineman. When Mohr's working hours changed, he could no longer show up for games and practices and had to leave the team.

Mohr was thirty-one, a year older than Russell, and he'd grown up in Shrub Oak, a bedroom community of 1,700 residents near the Hudson River in Westchester County north of New York City. His ambition had been to become a forest ranger, and he studied conservation and agronomy for two years at the State University of New York at Cobleskill. But the job he'd lined up fell through and a romance went bad, so in 1975 he decided to take a six-week vacation and figure things out by spending time with his brother, a carpenter who was living in the North Shore suburb of Wilmette.

The vacation turned into a permanent move when he found a job doing groundwork and maintenance for the park district in Highland Park. He was content for a time, toiling outdoors and coaching youth football after work, but one day in 1979 he was browsing through the want ads when he saw that Glencoe was looking for public safety officers—catchall public servants who work as cops, firemen and paramedics. He'd never fired a gun in his life, but the thought of being a fireman appealed to him and he didn't want to work in park maintenance all his life.

He took the tests and was hired. He started with the department as a patrolman in August of 1979 and was quickly recognized as being a different breed of cop, lacking that cynical, bravura exterior common to policemen even in quiet suburbs. He was thickly built but had a soft, gentle voice and a deliberative manner that caused other officers to remark that he had something of the social worker in him. He was a listener and a negotiator, qualities that served him well in

Glencoe. Police there and in other North Shore communities weren't called upon to handle violent crime very often; mostly their jobs entailed mediating neighborhood and family spats, stopping executives and rich kids speeding in sports cars, and investigating property crimes like the Wasserman burglary that were minor in the grand scheme of things but nevertheless traumatic for the victims.

Detective Mohr figured right away that he was being dragged into the middle of a vicious divorce battle. In the first place, too many items had been stolen and too much vandalism had occurred for a crime that had taken, at the very most, an hour. The cables on the supposedly stolen VCR were unscrewed, not cut as they normally would be in a burglary; photographs of Laurie had been needlessly destroyed; and each time she told the story little details changed, such as the time of day she returned. Then when he went to the house to interview her the night of the incident, he found her sitting in a totally darkened house watching TV in the rec room. Why wasn't she frightened? Most people would've had every light in the house blazing.

Any police officer who's been around—especially in well-off areas where a lot of money is at stake in divorce settlements—knows there's almost nothing battling spouses won't do to make each other look bad. Mohr's gut feeling was that the burglary was an inside job and that Laurie had done it in order to gain leverage in court. She told him in their interview that she was under the psychiatric care of Dr. Robert Greendale, and with her permission Mohr called Greendale to see what he knew. Greendale relayed what Laurie had told him, and in this version she didn't actually enter the house upon finding the TV on the stoop, but went straight to the Glencoe police.

Mohr also checked the Highland Park police, who told him they were familiar with Russell and Laurie Dann and had been to their house to calm them down several times.

Just to be thorough, Mohr asked Russell for an interview. Russell agreed, suggesting they make it over lunch at Bennigan's. He even offered to pay, though Mohr declined.

Russell was defensive at first. He said he'd been out at a Chevy dealership in the western suburb of La Grange on business for Dann Brothers at the time of the burglary, and he could prove it. "Come on, we'll go to the house—I'll meet you there," he said. "You can look through, search the whole place, see if there's any of her stuff around."

Mohr said he would probably take him up on the offer. "First tell me what you know about her," he said. "What's she like? If she did it, why?"

"She's a pathological liar," Russell said. "You can't believe a word she says. She made it all up in order to get attention and get back at me."

"Does she read a lot of detective novels?" Mohr asked.

"I don't think so, why?"

"Two pillowcases were missing," Mohr said. "In detective novels, burglars always take pillowcases to put jewelry and other stuff in. If this is a fake, that was a nice touch."

The search of Russell's house turned up nothing, and when Laurie's parents returned from Florida several weeks later, Mohr shared his suspicions with Norm that the burglary was a fake.

"It's possible," Norm said after listening to the litany of inconsistencies. He was extremely cordial, even personable about it. "But I don't think so. I think Russell is behind this, I really do."

"Well, something happened here," Mohr said. "I just don't know what."

"There are a lot of things you don't know," Norm said. "It could be maybe she did it. But you don't have enough evidence to prove she did, do you?"

"No."

"And you don't have enough evidence to prove Russell did it, do you?"

"If I did," Mohr said, "I'd arrest him."

10

War

Not long after the reported burglary at the Wassermans', Russell came home from work to find his shirts drenched with water and Laurie hiding again in a closet.

"This is war," she told him, her eyes narrowing in hatred. "You have no idea what I can do. You have no idea how miserable I can make your life."

"Laurie, let's put this behind us," he begged.

"Why?" she said as she stood. "I don't have any reason to go on living. And if I go, you're coming with me. If I can't have you, nobody can. That's true love."

The threat was barely even veiled. "What are you talking about?" he said. "Laurie, why does it have to come down to this?"

Torment flickered briefly on her face, then her gaze turned hollow and she smiled. "This is the worst thing that's ever happened to you, isn't it?" she said.

•

Laurie went to buy a gun on the fifth of May, half a year into the separation. She walked into the Marksman Police and Shooters Supply in Glenview and explained to the salesman that she needed something for protection. She was friendly, even flirtatious, as she browsed and eventually settled on the heavy artillery—a $275 nickel-plated Smith & Wesson .357

Magnum with a four-inch barrel. It is such a powerful and unwieldy weapon that some police departments don't even use it because many officers have a difficult time passing the qualifying tests.

She also picked out a gun-cleaning kit and two fifty-count boxes of ammunition, then filled out an application for an Illinois Firearm Owner's Identification Card. The card is far easier to get than a driver's license. It requires no examination and no personal appearance—an applicant simply pays $5 and fills out a one-page questionnaire that, in 1986, asked only eight questions beyond the usual particulars:

Are you an illegal alien?
Have you renounced your citizenship?
Are you under indictment?
Have you been convicted of a felony?
Are you a fugitive?
Do you use illegal drugs?
Have you ever been in a mental institution?
Were you dishonorably discharged from the Armed Forces?

Laurie truthfully answered no to each, and the salesman told her to come back after the state's mandatory three-day "cooling off" period.

When she returned for the gun, Eugene Miller, a friend of the Dann family and a former senior vice president of the New York Stock Exchange, happened to be at the shop buying ammunition for a handgun he had purchased to protect his home. He recognized Laurie easily—he lived four doors down from the Wassermans in Glencoe and he'd seen her many times in the neighborhood, at Green Acres and with Russell on social occasions. He said hello to her and she nodded and smiled.

When he saw a salesman showing her how to work her new gun, he recalled conversations he had had with Armand and Elaine Dann about the bitterness of the divorce and Laurie's apparent emotional instability. As soon as he got home he called Armand to warn him. Armand wasn't in so he called Armand's brother Charles, who tracked Armand down on the golf course and had him paged.

Armand was so upset that he immediately called both Jeff Taylor, Susie's husband, and Russell. Russell went directly to the Highland Park police department to tell Detective John Burns and Lieutenant John McKeever that his estranged wife was now armed.

"She's trouble," he said. "Call Floyd Mohr in Glencoe. He knows all about it."

Burns tried to reassure Russell by promising to put an extra watch on his house—which meant that a patrol car might make an occasional pass while on rounds—then he called Floyd Mohr, who was off duty that day. He found him at home in Northbrook, mowing the lawn.

"Yeah, Floyd," he said when Mohr picked up the phone. "What do you know about Russell Dann and Laurie Dann?"

"Why?"

"Well, I've got Russell here in my office saying his wife has threatened him and a witness has told him she just bought a gun at this place in Glenview."

Mohr considered this a serious development and canceled his afternoon plans. He hated guns in principle and thought Laurie, of all people, had no business owning one. After using state records to find her application for a firearms card and confirming her purchase with a source at the Marksman, he telephoned Norm Wasserman in Florida to alert him.

"I'll talk to her," Norm said. "I'll call you right back."

A few minutes later Norm was on the line again. "She's planning to move to an apartment in Evanston," he explained. "It's a rough town. She wants protection."

Evanston is the first suburb north of Chicago along the lakefront and the most socioeconomically diverse on the North Shore. It is only a "rough town" compared to the peaceful villages farther up the train line. "I don't think that's a wise idea," Mohr said. "What's she going to do? Shoot at somebody through a door? Or maybe at a cop coming to help her?"

"I don't like guns either," Norm said. "I'm a very passive person. But she does have a right to have it. You can't take away her rights."

"If she's burglarized, the guy could take it away and use it on her," Mohr said. "Rape her. Shoot her. Kill her."

"Well, I'll be home in the next few days," Norm said. "We'll talk about it then."

But before Norm returned, Mohr called Laurie directly. "It bothers me that you have a gun," he said, trying the gentle approach. "I want it."

"No," she said.

"You don't need it," Mohr said.

"I have the right," she said. "I have the card that says I can have a gun. Don't worry. I'm not going to hurt anybody."

Russell was not so sure. He felt so vulnerable in the Hastings Street house and was in such a hurry to move out that he had Susie find a town house for him on Green Bay Road in Highland Park, and he signed the lease before he even saw the place.

Mohr again called Dr. Greendale for help, this time for insight into Laurie's psyche.

"I can't say anything more unless Laurie agrees to let me," Greendale said.

"But you've got to tell me this much," Mohr said. "She just bought a handgun. Do you think she's violent? Could she be suicidal? Or homicidal?"

"She's got some problems that I can't discuss with you," Greendale said. "And I haven't seen her lately, but I'd say no, I don't think she's suicidal or homicidal."

Mohr was only slightly reassured and he continued to raise the issue with the Wassermans for months, trying nearly a dozen separate times to get Laurie to relinquish the Magnum. He would forget about it for a while, then suddenly think to himself, "God, that girl still has a gun," and call Norm one more time.

Norm finally and unexpectedly appeared to give in—he promised Mohr that he and Laurie had agreed to store the gun in a safe-deposit box at the Harris Bank. He gave the same report during a phone conversation with Armand Dann, who had also been making occasional inquiries.

"Oh, come on," Armand said incredulously. "What possible good would it do to have a gun if you kept it in a safe-deposit box?"

"Whatever," Norm said. "As far as I'm concerned it's fine that she has a gun as long as she keeps it far away from me."

When Mohr asked to look inside the safe-deposit box just to be sure the gun was there, both Norm and Laurie refused.

•

During a heavy spring rain, Russell's friend Artie Litchman was driving down Clavey Road in Highland Park near Hastings Street and slowed when he saw Laurie standing by the wayside without an umbrella. She was picking weeds.

•

The theme of Laurie's complaints to her parents, the police and the lawyers who were handling her divorce was that she was the helpless victim of a demented man. She told a good story, full of indignation and sorrow, and they attributed her occasional weird behavior—she recoiled from shaking hands and once insisted on walking on a busy street instead of the adjacent sidewalk—to the ordinary emotional distress of divorce.

At a June 1986 temporary-support hearing, the lawyers introduced allegations that Russell had physically abused Laurie both during the marriage and the separation. A temporary restraining order issued shortly thereafter stipulated:

1. That Russell was forbidden to transfer or hide marital assets.
2. That Russell was forbidden to strike Laurie or interfere with her "personal liberty."
3. That Laurie's request for exclusive possession of the home was denied.

Russell filed a petition with the court the following month to force Laurie to cooperate in the sale of the Hastings Street house. She had moved back in full-time after Russell left and was wrecking the place while refusing to sign a real estate listing agreement. She never emptied the garbage, let the lawn and bushes grow wild and was so far behind on the telephone and electrical bills that Russell was receiving final shut-off notices in the mail.

The divorce negotiations proceeded slowly and with extreme ill will. Norm's demands were steep: he wanted Russell to support Laurie for ten years with $20,000 a year alimony payments after an initial $100,000 settlement.

Russell's attorneys subpoenaed Laurie's school records from Northwestern in an effort to show that she was an educated woman who had the capacity to support herself, and it was only then that Russell discovered that she hadn't been a graduate student when he met her, that there was no research project and that she hadn't even completed her degree requirements at Arizona.

In light of that, Russell offered twenty-four months of support at $1,500 a month along with the agreed-upon $100,000 payment as Laurie's half of the marital property and five years of medical insurance.

But Norm said no. He told Armand that Russell's offer was unfair in view of how much money he made, and that if he didn't settle quickly, he would see to it that Laurie was put into a mental institution and that Russell would be stuck supporting her for the rest of his life. "If Laurie is crazy," Norm said, "then Russell is responsible. He ruined her."

The rhetoric was escalating, and Russell decided he just wanted out quickly. His bargaining posture softened, and he clung only to two specific demands. The first was for the return of the engagement ring; his father had bought it during a trip to South Africa and it had sentimental value to the family. The second was for Laurie to change her legal name back to Laurie Wasserman and dissociate herself completely from the Dann family. He would pay extra, he said, for the return of his name.

But the ring was important to her, too, she said, and she liked Russell's last name. She used to tell Beth she never liked how identifiably Jewish her maiden name was.

"You just can't tell with a name like Dann," she said. One of Russell's ancestors had apparently felt the same way. The original family name was Weissman.

Once again negotiations stalled.

•

In August, Steve Witt in New York got another call from Laurie. The conversation started out with the expected how-do-you-do's and what's-new's, but then she said she had some-thing serious to tell him—she had a five-year-old daughter he had fathered during their last sexual encounter in Boca Raton just before the breakup in late 1980. She was telling him now, she said, because she and her husband had decided to adopt the child legally, and she wanted him to come to Chicago to see her and sign the papers.

Steve took her very seriously, as did his wife, Barbara, who was so upset by the news and the subsequent back-and-forth conversations with Laurie that she took off to Boston to be by herself for a short time. Steve was ready to fly into Chicago to see Laurie and the child, but in talking further with Laurie he began noticing inconsistencies as to where and when his daugh-ter had supposedly been born. He also thought it strange that she would never allow Russell to come to the phone and that she spoke intermittently about "support payments." He finally did some checking with the likely hospitals and determined that no such child existed.

When he confronted her with the facts, she grew silent. "There is no child, is there?" he said.

"No," she said.

"I know it's not my business," he said, "but I think you should seek professional help."

•

So hard to find my way
Now that I'm all on my own
I saw you just the other day
My how you have grown.
Cast my memory back there, lord
Sometimes I'm overcome,
Thinking about making love in the green grass
Behind the stadium
With you,
My brown-eyed girl.

Still seeking some sort of redemption in her past, Laurie tried to contact Barry Gallup, the boy she had dated sopho-more and junior years in high school. He was a doctor by then, too, newly married and living in Northbrook. She called the only likely Gallup in the phone book and reached his sister-in-law.

"I went out with Barry in high school," she explained. "I thought I'd look him up for old time's sake but I can't find the number. Do you have it?"

"I'm not at liberty to give it out," the sister-in-law said. "Why don't you give me your number and I'll have him call you?"

Laurie hesitated, then gave a number. When Barry got the message he was flattered at first, but his wife made it clear she did not want him to return the call, so he didn't. The next day, Laurie called the sister-in-law back and said she was very anxious to talk to Barry, could she please have the number. Again the sister-in-law refused. Laurie hung up politely, but was enraged. She was never in her life at a loss for tracking down unlisted phone numbers, and when she found Barry's she put him and his parents on the ever-expanding list of targets for midnight hang-up phone calls.

She also contacted the local telephone company office, identified herself as Diane Gallup, Barry's wife, and asked a service representative to disconnect her phone and transfer it to an apartment complex in Glenview. Only a routine callback check to Diane blocked the switch, and when Laurie found out she resumed her hang-up assault for four more days.

•

In September, an anonymous female caller contacted the Department of Dermatology at the New York hospital and claimed that Dr. Steve Witt had raped her in the emergency room. The charge lacked substance—he hadn't even done an emergency room rotation yet—but Steve felt so threatened by it that he arranged immediately to transfer back to Arizona to finish his residency there.

Barbara Witt stayed behind and Laurie bombarded her with late-night phone calls. "You'd better get used to me," she said. "I'll follow you. I'll go to Arizona. I'll be on your doorstep. Steve will have to support me for the rest of my life."

The Witts had their attorney write a letter to Laurie at her parents' address and threaten to bring legal action if the harassment did not cease, and the calls stopped—for a time.

•

An unfamiliar woman's voice on the phone said, "Janie?"

Jane Sterling started. No one called her Janie anymore, not since New Trier High School days back in the 1970's. "Yeah?" she said.

"Your husband is having an affair with someone from the office," the woman said.

The line went dead. It must be some kind of a cruel joke, she thought, like those hang-up calls she'd been getting.

11

The Girl
Next Door

Laurie spent most of the summer of 1986 living with her parents in Glencoe. For social amusement she started keeping company with her neighbor, Dean Pappas, a man four years her senior who was also living at home with his parents. His backyard touched hers, and he and his friends had seen and admired her for years as she walked the family dog or rode her bicycle down the street.

They introduced themselves down at the beach. He was thin, tall and dark-haired, but his front teeth were out of skew and he was not particularly handsome. In her more popular days, she probably would have ignored him, but by then she wasn't in a position to be terribly choosy.

They went out a couple of times—to outdoor concerts and a nightclub called the Snuggery—and she began bringing his family cookies and pies. Their relationship stayed almost totally platonic, in part because Laurie shied away from Dean's touch and in part because Dean sensed that Laurie was emotionally a little unstable and he thought it prudent to keep his distance. She told him she was an instructor at the National College of Education in Evanston, but virtually all he ever saw her do was watch trashy TV for hours on end—*The Monkees* and children's cartoons, mostly.

When she spoke, which wasn't often, she bragged about

all the colleges she had attended and explained her intense fear of her ex-husband, who she was convinced was trying to drive her insane. "When I married him, he knew what he was getting into," she said. "I had problems."

After several dates, Dean started noticing Laurie's strange habits—she pulled hair from his head, played with it against her lips and then dropped it to the floor. She would also pull her own hair out a strand at a time and open doors and pick up silverware with her sleeves instead of her bare hands.

She didn't like to answer the telephone, saying she was afraid Russell was calling her, so she and Dean had to work out a signal—he would hang up after one ring and then phone back right away so she would answer.

Dean saw Norm and Edith several times and found them to be cold. Norm had a strong handshake but a weak personality, he thought. The two of them got together when Edith was in Florida and they watched a television series on the Holocaust. Norm patiently provided historical background to Dean. Laurie stayed in her room the entire time, emerging only to bring the men a plate of cookies.

Edith made no particular impression on Dean—she made him think of a black-and-white photograph.

When he was alone with Laurie, Dean heard Laurie call her father a wimp and her mother a yes person. The only kind words Dean heard her say about her family were for her brother, Mark. "He was the smart one," she said ruefully. "He got out when he could. I'm still here."

Dean's mother, the regal Cassandra Pappas, immediately sensed the depths of Laurie's craving for affection and took pity on her. All the girl seemed to want in life was someone to care about her and ask her opinion about things, which Cassandra did. She became one of the only people ever to have any kind of intellectual relationship with Laurie.

Cassandra used to enjoy sitting out in the yard reading a good book or listening to classical music, and Laurie began stopping by and talking to her when she would go out to walk Edith's poodle. Laurie seemed young to Cassandra, with the unsophisticated air and preppie taste in clothing of a rich college student. Cassandra was surprised when Laurie revealed she was nearly twenty-nine and getting her master's degree at Northwestern University.

For a graduate student, she seemed very limited intellectually, with little experience with great literature and the fine arts. Laurie asked ingenuous questions whenever Cassandra tossed off a reference to, say, the Spanish painter El Greco or the American writer Henry Miller.

"What does *Colossus of Maroussi* mean?" Laurie asked, pointing to a Miller book Cassandra had out one day. "What's it about?"

"It's sort of a travel book about Greece," Cassandra said. "It's interesting and very well written."

"I never heard of it," Laurie said, but with little embarrassment.

"You should read more," Cassandra said. "No matter what it is. Reading helps build you."

"It must be wonderful to have so many books," Laurie said. "You should give me some good books to read sometime."

"Anything you'd like to read about in particular?"

Laurie frowned. "I don't know—something about Egypt, maybe?"

"Egypt?"

"Sure," Laurie said. "That trip you told me about sounded real interesting. The Nile and everything..."

"Have you heard of Lawrence Durrell? *The Alexandria Quartet*?"

"No."

"You'll like it," Cassandra promised. She loaned Laurie a volume of Durrell's opus on love and, sure enough, Laurie came back keen to discuss the book.

"I liked his writing," she said.

Cassandra was pleased. It was just the effect she had been hoping for. "Excellent," she said. "You know, to appreciate his work, you really have to read it aloud. His words have such a beautiful sound."

Laurie opened to a page and began to read. Her voice was soft, high and tentative. She enunciated almost perfectly, but had no gift for inflection. When she finished she lowered the book. "I'm not sure I understood everything in here," she said.

"Well, let's talk about it," Cassandra said. And they did. Laurie wasn't particularly insightful, but she was curious, and she enjoyed talking about books. The women did so off and on that fall, with Laurie figuratively sitting at Cassandra's feet, soaking in new knowledge and enjoying the older woman's vigorous discourse.

"Once in school I had this idea about a James Joyce book we had to read," Laurie remembered. "I brought it up in class, and the teacher said, 'No, that's not the right interpretation.'"

Cassandra clucked sympathetically.

"Mrs. Pappas, how do they know what the right interpretation is, since James Joyce is dead?" Laurie said. "Or in a painting, what makes you think Cézanne or Van Gogh meant a certain thing when they painted something or put a certain thing in a certain place? How do you know he didn't just look at a beautiful scene and then paint it?"

Cassandra laughed. "I have to agree," she said. "I took a great-books class once and they said, 'Why did the protagonist take two shots of whiskey at the bar instead of three?'"

"Because he couldn't afford the third shot," Laurie said.

"I would have said that, too," Cassandra said. "But my teacher, he said, 'Oh, no, that was the Father, the Son and the Holy Ghost!'"

Both women laughed. Cassandra remembered the moment for a long time afterward because it was so unusual to see Laurie laugh or even smile. For a young, pretty girl she had an uncommonly heavy personality, with the shroud of night seeming to hang over her. Looking in her eyes, Cassandra detected a certain aloneness—a "modesty of the soul," as she put it.

"If you want to feel a little happy, you should listen to Mozart," Cassandra said to her gently.

"Is that the kind of music you like?" Laurie asked.

"Yes," she said. "But remember, Laurie—all music is beautiful, and all books."

When Cassandra later related this part of the conversation to Dean, he snorted. "You must be kidding," he said.

"No," she said.

"Every time I go over there, she's watching cartoons or listening to the Monkees."

"What are the Monkees?"

"An old pop music group," Dean said. "They're awful. I think if I hear them one more time I'll go out of my mind."

Both Dean and Cassandra noticed that Laurie asked a lot of questions but never volunteered much about herself. When Cassandra let it drop one afternoon that she'd once had surgery to remove a tumor on her brain, Laurie was fascinated.

"Didn't you wonder, 'Why me? Why did this happen to me instead of someone else?'" she asked.

"I'm more the type who asks, 'Why not me?'" Cassandra said. She laughed. "One thing to remember, Laurie—never lose your sense of humor and your positive outlook."

"Then you must be very religious," Laurie said.

"On the contrary," Cassandra said. "Not if you're talking about the Christian dogma and the Bible. I don't consider myself religious in that sense at all."

"Why not?"

"Christianity is the mythology of our culture in a lot of ways," Cassandra said. "We invented it. If you look at the Old Testament, it's part Babylonian, part Egyptian and part Greek. And all those supposedly Christian things—the virgin birth, the passion story, the disciples—they all have roots in other writings of the era."

"My family's Jewish but we're not religious," Laurie said. Since 1976 the Wassermans had belonged to the Sons of Joshua, a congregation that did not have a temple and met only on Rosh Hashanah and Yom Kippur in the banquet room of the Fireside Inn, a suburban restaurant. Members of the Sons of Joshua were generally older Jews without children at home anymore who were either too busy or too uninvolved with religion to attend weekly services. The price of a ticket for a reserved seat at services was around $100, a bargain compared to annual dues at conventional synagogues, which ran well in excess of $1,000 on the North Shore.

Laurie went on. "I've always thought it was weird that the God in the Old Testament is so cruel and unforgiving, and the

God in the New Testament is so gentle," she said. "I was wondering—"

"What makes you think it's the same God?" Cassandra interrupted. "Maybe the God of the Old Testament was simply a portrayal of the kings of those times, and by the time of the New Testament the kinds of leaders had changed?"

Laurie took this in seriously. "I guess," she said. "It's strange, though, isn't it?"

Dean, meanwhile, was not finding his chats with Laurie nearly so stimulating. They played cards together and watched TV, but more and more he was seeing that Laurie wasn't his type. When the Pappas family had a barbecue, Laurie simply sat in her chair and watched as everyone else socialized. Other times she would do weird things when she was visiting, like getting up in the middle of a TV program and walking out of the house without saying goodbye or even giving the least indication she was leaving.

"My God, what a strange duck she is," Cassandra said.

Dean twirled his index finger in the air next to his ear. "I've got to get her off my back," he said.

At first, like many other men who had come into Laurie's life, Dean had thought she was a delicate flower who would bloom if she were just given enough care. But in the end he found Laurie's vulnerable core unreachable, protected by hard shells that were formed somehow, somewhere—he didn't know.

He finally called it off one night when Laurie's stubborn refusal to talk or show physical affection got to be too much. "I don't want to see you anymore," he said angrily.

She said nothing and her face betrayed no feeling. She might as well have been dead inside.

12

A Cry in the Night

Russell was never sure how it happened, but Laurie got her hands on a key to his town house sometime in the summer of 1986. She was dogging him at the time, tracking his movements and looking into his garage to see if his car was there. He started hanging a dark towel over the garage window in an effort to prevent her from knowing if he was home or if his girlfriend at the time, Patricia Cassell, was visiting him. Patricia, twenty-nine, was a wealthy blonde heiress from Detroit living in downtown Chicago. She was worth millions, Russell told his friends.

Little things—notes and pictures—started turning up missing. Files on Russell's XT home computer mysteriously disappeared from the hard disk drive.

•

A little after three A.M. on Tuesday, September 30, Russell called the operator and had her patch him through to the Highland Park police department. "I've been stabbed!" he cried when the dispatcher answered. "Get over here."

Three officers and an ambulance arrived at his town house several minutes later and saw him standing on the balcony waving them over. Only when they were at the door would he come downstairs to let them in.

He hurriedly told his story: He'd been sound asleep for

several hours that night when he suddenly awoke to the sound of his own scream of agony. He felt a sharp, stinging pain in his chest and jumped out of bed in confusion. Standing there, with his hands on his knees, he tried to figure out what had happened.

He walked around the bed and into the bathroom to urinate, and on his way back he looked in the left-hand mirror over his bureau and saw a reddish-purple wound in his chest just above his heart. He first thought it might have been a broken blood vessel or some outer sign of a heart attack. By the time he got back to the bed he was having trouble breathing. As he stood over the telephone by the nightstand wondering if he should call for help, he looked down and saw an ice pick lying between the bed and the unattached oak headboard.

He knew the ice pick wasn't his, he said, because he'd been using a knife to clear his freezer all summer. Nothing else upstairs had been disturbed, so it wasn't a burglary. The only logical conclusion was that his wife, from whom he had been separated for nearly a year, had tried to kill him as she had threatened she would.

The responding officers were more than a little skeptical. The stab wound did not look particularly serious—it wasn't even bleeding, the hole was just at the spot on his chest where a right-handed person might stab himself if he wanted to make it look like he'd been attacked, and the victim was perfectly ambulatory. Russell said he hadn't seen his attacker, and when he showed the officers an assortment of suspicious items on the first-floor couch, including a ski mask, a flashlight, a glass cutter and an aerosol can of Mace, they figured he could have planted them there as easily as he said he found them.

"Are you sure you haven't had a party here?" one of the cops asked him. "Or maybe a friend who would play a practical joke on you?"

"Are you seeing anybody? A doctor?" another asked.

Russell angrily went through his story again. One of Russell's failings in life, his friends and family agree, is that he's not very articulate, especially when he's worked up. His stories are jumpy, like his personality, and each time he tells them he adds new details and takes old ones out. He doesn't contradict himself, exactly, but the effect on the listener is unsettling. He first said he saw the ice pick under the bed, for example, when what he meant was that he saw it under the bed but in plain sight in front of the headboard.

"What did you have for dinner?" one of the policemen asked, exchanging conspiratorial looks with his compatriots. "Did you have anything to drink? Maybe a little something afterward? Take any pills? Smoke anything?"

"You've gotta believe me," Russell insisted. "You've gotta believe me. She broke in here and stabbed me. Look!"

He excused himself to call his brother Scott to have him come over to help, then he returned to the policemen and their increasingly sly questions. "Can we take a picture?" one of them asked, producing a Polaroid camera.

"Why don't you get the fuck out of here?" Russell said. "Just go. Get the fuck out of here."

The open hostility and mistrust on both sides—fueled partly by the historical resentment many North Shore police officers feel for their overprivileged clientele and partly by Russell's residual frustrations in dealing with Laurie—left them at an impasse. The officers had Russell sign a release to let the ambulance go without him, then they tagged along when Scott drove him to Highland Park Hospital in his Saab.

In the emergency room, Dr. Mart Jalakas found that the pick had pierced muscle tissue and gone one inch into Russell's chest, where it caused a 10 percent collapse of his left lung. He had never seen an ice pick stabbing in his career—such occurrences being rare to unheard of in Highland Park.

After the police told Jalakas how strange Russell's story was and how they thought the stabbing might well be self-inflicted, he went back for a closer look at the wound and noticed several small, linear abrasions that radiated outward from the central puncture. He told the officers that these might be "hesitation marks," the small cuts a person makes in moving a weapon tentatively around on the skin before getting up the nerve to plunge it all the way in, but he wasn't sure.

This offhand opinion all but convinced the officers that Russell was lying. It wasn't until three years later that Jalakas, closely questioned on the matter, admitted that, in retrospect, the wounds were far too symmetrical and regular to have been hesitation marks, and that they were almost certainly caused when the surface layer of skin was momentarily dragged into the wound by the point of the ice pick. He said he regretted agreeing with the police suggestion at the time of the incident.

Highland Park police officer Daniel Dahlberg and Sergeant Edward Armitage stayed in the intensive care unit where Russell had been placed for overnight observation to ask him a few more questions, specifically if he would be willing to take a lie detector test. "Gladly," Russell said. He also pressed on them a set of keys to the Hastings Street house where Laurie was living and asked them to please go look around.

At six o'clock in the morning, Dahlberg and Armitage checked inside and outside the unlocked Hastings Street house. Laurie wasn't home and hadn't been for two weeks, judging by the buildup of mail in the box. They found nothing unusual inside but noted a gun owner's identification card on the floor along with a brown paper bag with money inside.

Two hours later, Dahlberg returned to the hospital, this time with Detective Jack McCafferty, who would become the department's point man on the Dann case. Again Russell was grilled about the attack, and again he told his story with great indignation and minor incoherence. "Look, the only person who would want to hurt me is my wife," he concluded. "I wish you'd find out where she was last night. If she wasn't at Hastings Street, she was at her folks' in Glencoe."

McCafferty wore glasses and smoked a pipe, a combination that gave him a canny, deliberative air. Mack, as he was known, had been working in Highland Park for more than twenty years and was closing in on an early retirement. He, too, had seen a lot of ugly domestic situations and knew how difficult they could be for outsiders to sort out.

When he contacted Floyd Mohr in Glencoe to get background, Mohr told him the story of the strange burglary at the Wassermans' the previous spring and his suspicion that Laurie was responsible.

McCafferty went back to see Russell when he was released from Highland Park Hospital at 1:30 that afternoon, and Russell asked if McCafferty thought the stab wound was self-inflicted.

"I don't know," McCafferty said. "But my opinion doesn't really make a difference."

"Will I have to take a lie detector test?" Russell asked.

"We might ask you to."

Russell smirked. "I'll bet my life Laurie won't take one."

He called the police shortly after he got home to tell them that he had found a pair of Laurie's old gym shoes down where the other bits of evidence had been found, and Detective Burns came over to the town house to take the shoes into evidence.

Three hours later, Russell called Burns again to ask if he would meet him and Scott over at Hastings Street to go through the house.

"We've been over there a couple of times already today and we got no answer at the door," said Burns.

"I want to see if Laurie's there," Russell said.

"There's no answer at the door," Burns repeated. "What do you—?"

"Well, let's just check the place out," Russell said, thinking of Laurie's penchant for hiding in closets.

"All right," Burns sighed. "We'll meet you there."

He and Detective Henry Hoban met Russell and Scott a few minutes later on the porch at the Hastings Street house.

"Did you guys come down here and go through the house today?" Russell asked.

"I personally didn't, no," Burns said. "But I don't know if anyone else did. I don't think so."

"It would seem to me that would be the first thing you'd do," Russell said disgustedly. His lack of regard for the authorities was so palpable that there was no way he would get enthusiastic cooperation from any of the Highland Park investigators. He obviously couldn't stand them. He thought they were lousy cops. They thought he was a horse's ass.

With this mutual ill will casting a pall over all of them, Russell entered the front door and led the way into the foyer. He called out for Laurie.

Two lights were on, the front door hall light and the southeast bedroom light on the upper floor, but no one answered his calls. The men searched through the house and ended up in the master bedroom. The covers were tossed and clothes were scattered on the floor amid Laurie's Firearm Owner's Identification Card, a television, a radio, a humidifier, a pair of brown paper bags and other detritus.

"What's inside that bag?" Scott asked Burns as the men were preparing to leave the room.

"Don't patronize me," Burns said. "I'm probably going to lose my job for an illegal search as it is."

Burns picked up the first bag, looked inside and saw a paper receipt and a small amount of cash. He took the receipt out and saw it was from Eckart Hardware in Winnetka, dated September 22, 1986.

"Where is that receipt from?" Russell asked.

"How did you know it was a receipt?" Burns asked.

"I saw it," Russell said.

"You guys better get out of here," Burns said. "We've already contaminated the evidence."

"What's the matter?" Russell complained, backing out. "Don't they send you guys to cop school?"

"Aren't you going to check that other bag?" Scott asked.

"I said get out," Burns said.

Scott picked up the second bag. "Look what we found in this other bag," he said. "See...we're doing your job for you...look at this!" He presented Burns with a package for a Foley brand ice pick. The package had a price tag of $1.39 and an Eckart Hardware store tag.

"I knew it was her," Russell told Burns. "She did it. This is the ice pick she used. It came from this package. Is that enough for you? Are you convinced now?"

Burns shook his head. "I hate to tell you, but this evidence won't be admissible in court."

"Oh, that's okay," Russell said. "As long as you and I both know that she's the one who did it."

Russell locked the house when he left, and Burns eyed him suspiciously. The stuff with the receipt seemed awfully coincidental, and for a guy who had supposedly been nearly murdered eighteen hours earlier Russell Dann was getting around pretty good. "When was the last time you were over here?" he asked.

"It's been two weeks at least," Russell said quickly. "I couldn't have come back to the house today because you guys had my keys. I want you to remember that."

"Right," said Burns.

In later discussions with the Highland Park police, Russell's contempt for their sleuthing abilities was even more plain. "Either you're too dumb to get your facts right," he said once, "or you're Columbo-smart and trying to trick me. Unfortunately I think I know which is true."

He went on to say that if he ever decided to rob a bank he would be sure to do it in Highland Park. "You guys would never catch me," he sneered.

•

The morning after the search of the Hastings Street house, Detective McCafferty interviewed Norm at the office of Haven Equities in Northbrook. Norm told McCafferty that as far as he knew Laurie was home sleeping the night Russell said he was attacked.

"I'm really getting tired of all these problems," he said dismissively. "My daughter isn't capable of stabbing anyone. If you want my opinion, I think this is all just her husband trying to drive her crazy."

"Okay, but we need your help," McCafferty said. "Laurie's got to cooperate with us better than she did with Glencoe in the burglary case. We need hair samples and fingerprints, and it would probably be a good idea if she took a lie detector test."

"We'll talk to a lawyer and get back to you this afternoon," Norm said. "But I'll tell you right now I don't think she should take a lie detector. I know a guy who used to give those tests and he told me they don't work very well."

"She certainly doesn't have to," McCafferty said. "But we're as anxious as you are to clear this up."

McCafferty then went to Eckart Hardware to interview a salesclerk who said he remembered selling a glass cutter to a striking young woman. He said she wore a pink top, pale blue jeans and no bra. He and another male clerk remembered the sale well because the woman had large breasts and they had joked about it after she left. The second clerk said he remembered selling an ice pick to someone the previous week, but could not be sure it was Laurie.

McCafferty had asked Russell for a photo of Laurie he might show around, but Russell told him he'd destroyed every shot of Laurie he ever owned, including the videotape of their wedding. Only Jeff and Susie Taylor had pictures left—and in all but a few of them Laurie's face had been blacked out with a magic marker. The salesclerk, however, was able to identify Laurie from one of the remaining clear shots as the woman who bought the glass cutter.

The case against Laurie was looking stronger, but everything crumbled on Thursday, two days after the stabbing, when Russell failed his lie detector test at Highland Park police headquarters.

Detective Burns was in charge of the test, which put Russell on edge immediately. He squirmed when Burns hooked him up to the electrodes and could barely contain his resentment. He was the victim here, and yet was being treated like a goddamn criminal. He shrugged, shifted in his seat, tapped his toe and fidgeted through nearly an hour of such warm-up questions as "Have you ever lied to authorities?" and "Have you ever stabbed yourself?"

How was he supposed to answer? He had lied to teachers. He had lied to cops who pulled him over for traffic violations. He'd stabbed himself accidentally with a pen, probably, but...

Burns took note of Russell's apparent discomfort and his constant squirming during the two-and-a-half-hour test, and, though the instrument readings were ambiguous, his summary statement said:

Throughout the course, the subject of the polygraph examination has indicated he is engaged in the purposeful act of non-cooperation. The effect has been to distort the test response. It has been the experience of the examiner that when the subject attempts to distort the polygraph examination record by purposeful non-cooperation in spite of repeated instructions to cooperate, they do so to avoid detection regarding one or more of the underlying investigations.

The next day, McCafferty received messages and phone calls from Susie Taylor and Scott saying they were afraid and wanted to know why Laurie had not been arrested. Susie told him that the whole family was upset that Laurie owned a gun. She had severe emotional problems and had threatened her brother. McCafferty told her he could do nothing; Laurie had the correct identification card and was a legal gun owner.

McCafferty was also contacted by Laurie's divorce attorney, who said he would not allow Laurie to be questioned or tested on the polygraph.

"Floyd," McCafferty said to Mohr when he reached him by phone. "Could she have stabbed him?"

"I don't know," Mohr said. "I'm going through the same thing with this burglary. I'm not a doctor. I'm not a psychiatrist. I don't know for sure."

"Could Russell have done it to himself?"

"I just don't know," Mohr said. "I've been going through it in my mind over and over and over."

That same afternoon, Lake County assistant state's attorney Joe Calina decided he didn't know either—there wasn't enough evidence to charge anyone in the ice-pick incident. If an indictment were to come down, he told McCafferty, it would have to come either from a grand jury or the felony review division.

•

The ice-pick incident remains the only real criminal mystery tucked inside the larger psychological mystery of Laurie Dann's life. What really happened in Russell Dann's town house on the morning of September 30, 1986? Did Laurie try to kill Russell? Or did Russell stab himself in an effort to frame Laurie?

It was certainly not unreasonable for the police to doubt Russell's story. At the time of the incident, Laurie had never hurt or attacked anyone and none of her fingerprints were found on the evidence so neatly left behind.

Russell and Laurie were already known to the police in both Highland Park and Glencoe as a battling couple, and Laurie had tried to implicate Russell in a possibly false crime—the burglary at her parents' house earlier in the year.

Russell seemed to have a clear motive for faking the attack. Laurie had been harassing him and his family for many months and he was very worried that she owned a .357 Magnum. Had she been convicted for stabbing him, she would have lost her permit to own a gun, though no legal mechanism existed to take the gun itself from her.

Then there was the emergency room doctor's hasty, inaccurate statement about "hesitation marks," the suspicious way the Dann brothers found the ice-pick receipt among the litter at the Hastings Street house and Russell's failure of the polygraph test.

Yet in hindsight it's also clear that the Highland Park police allowed Russell's abrasive manner and foul language to get in the way of conducting a thorough investigation that might well have led them to arresting and charging Laurie for the crime.

The ice-pick wrapper and receipt found in Laurie's bedroom could have been powerful evidence against her, but Detective Burns rendered it useless by allowing Russell and Scott into the house.

Highland Park also failed to undertake a thorough canvass of neighborhood residents in the aftermath of the incident. One of Russell's neighbors at the time, Kirsten Mundy, now says she heard a scream at the time of the stabbing followed by the sound of rapid footsteps down the stairs and a loud slamming of the door. Though Highland Park police chief Robert Rash said that a canvass was made, he refused to release any evidence of one. No trace of such an effort appeared in the multijurisdictional task-force file of all police paper on

Laurie Dann, and Kirsten Mundy says she was never interviewed. Similarly there is no evidence that Dr. Jalakas' statement about "hesitation marks" was ever double-checked or referred to a doctor with more experience in forensic medicine.

The Highland Park detectives who worked closely on the case—John Burns and Jack McCafferty—have left the department and are declining to elaborate on what is contained in their written reports. In their silence we are left with Russell's story and a case of attempted murder that is still, technically, open.

But what matters about the ice-pick incident is not who did the stabbing. What matters is that the events in the immediate aftermath of the crime poisoned Russell's relationship with the Highland Park police department and made it even harder for him and for Laurie's other targets to make their case later that she was a truly dangerous woman.

•

Directly after the Lake County prosecutors decided not to proceed with the ice-pick case, Jeff Taylor was in touch with attorney Rick Kessler, a former Lake County prosecutor who had gone into private practice. Kessler, as it turned out, had been in the same junior high school homeroom as Laurie Wasserman, though, like most of her classmates, he had no recollection of her.

Kessler had contacts in the county prosecutor's office, and they assured him that the state's attorney was still sorting through the evidence on the ice-pick case. It was, they pointed out, a pretty unusual story.

•

Russell moved in with his brother and his wife, Ann, for a short time because he feared Laurie would return to his town house and finish the job she started. One night when Scott and Ann were out of town, their unreliable burglar alarm accidentally tripped and Russell grabbed a tennis racket for self-defense and climbed onto the roof.

When he returned to his town house, he installed his own alarm system and started keeping a baseball bat at the side of his bed as he slept. The alarm kept going off and he was never sure why. It seemed to take the police forever to respond. Once, when they finally came around, Russell greeted them with a curt, "Jesus, you guys are such fuckin' idiots, I could have walked to the police department by now."

He slammed the door and the officer began beating on it with his nightstick, trading profanities with Russell.

•

In the aftermath of the ice-pick incident, Jeff Taylor, Russell's brother-in-law, told his brother, Scott, what had happened. Scott Taylor, in turn, forbade his ex-wife, Sheri Lynn Taylor, to have Laurie visit while their children were in the house.

Sheri, a former model, had become friends with Laurie as they shared the pain of their marital breakups, and both women had purchased guns, presumably for protection. Once Laurie could no longer come to visit, they drifted apart.

•

Russell met with attorney Kessler in mid-October and hired him to help build a case against Laurie that might result in Lake County bringing charges against her. One of Kessler's first moves was to meet with Detectives McCafferty and Larry Warnke of Highland Park. As the policemen ran through the evidence for Kessler, they made a special point of emphasizing how hostile and agitated Russell had been to the officers who responded to the stabbing complaint.

"Can't you figure out why?" Kessler said. "The guy had just been stabbed. Take that into consideration."

"Okay, but take a look again at what we've got here," McCafferty said. "A ski mask, shoes, an ice pick . . . but only *his* fingerprints. Hesitation marks on the wound. No visual identification by the victim. Victim going through a divorce. There are red flags all over this one."

Ordinarily, Kessler would've bailed out on the case right then, but his instincts told him that Russell's story was true: why would a rich guy like Russell pop his own lung and then not even claim to have seen Laurie do it? It would be easy to invent a much more plausible lie. The very weirdness of his account worked in its favor as far as Kessler was concerned.

•

In exasperation, Russell called Laurie from his car phone. "I don't even know where to start with you," he said when she answered. "You can hate me. You can hate me for trying to divorce you, you can hate me for anything. But to try to kill me? That's, like, totally gone. You're sick. You need help."

"I know," Laurie said. "What do we do?"

"We've got to get you help," Russell said.

"How?" Laurie said.

Static brushed across their conversation. "Someone's listening in!" Laurie cried. She hung up.

13

Fear
and
Frustration

The harassing phone calls had started again, thirteen and fourteen a day at four, five, six A.M., every call a hang-up. It seemed that Laurie had found a way to control people for the first time in her life, and no one in Russell's circle was safe from her power play, not even those with unlisted numbers.

Some of Russell's friends got together over drinks and discussed the logistics of killing her: Could they do it themselves? Would it be better to take out a contract on her life? They weren't totally serious, but how else could they stop her?

When the Taylors bought a new house in Highland Park that fall, they kept their old phone number in hope that Laurie would never realize they had moved. Just in case, they illuminated their backyard with floodlamps, which they called Laurie Lights.

But Laurie was a clever snoop, and one day she called Russell at work: "Why do Susie and Jeff have my outdoor furniture in their new backyard?" she said, referring to a set of lawn chairs Russell had passed along to his sister. "It's mine. They have no right."

Susie, chilled by the realization that Laurie was on their tail, immediately had the furniture shipped back to her to appease her. She warned her children that if Aunt Laurie ever came to the door, they were not to let her in and instead they should push the emergency buttons connected to the alarm system.

"She is not a nice person," Susie said.

Susie also went to Ravinia Elementary and the Young Men's Jewish Council day-care center where her children were enrolled and alerted them that she had a crazy sister-in-law, and that under no circumstances should anyone ever be allowed to take the children from school without a note from her or her husband.

The administrators raised their eyebrows dubiously.

It was more or less the same reaction Beth Rosen got when, alarmed by a sudden increase in the number of hang-up calls, she went to the Deerfield police station to complain.

"Are you sure it's not children in the neighborhood?" the desk officer said.

"Yes, I'm sure," Beth said. "It's definitely Laurie Dann. Listen, this woman stabbed her husband in the chest with an ice pick, didn't you hear about that? It happened in Highland Park."

"No," said the officer impatiently, looking at Beth as if she were the crazy one. "I didn't hear about it."

Eventually both the Rosens and the Taylors paid Illinois Bell $20 a month to install tracing devices on their lines in an effort to have Laurie arrested and perhaps settle the ice-pick incident at the same time. In early December, the traps successfully tracked two of the Taylors' hang-up calls to the telephone in the house on Hastings Street where Laurie was living.

The Highland Park police took the information and wrote out an arrest warrant for Laurie. On a freezing, blustery December afternoon, McCafferty and Detective Myles Bell went to the house to get her.

"I didn't make any calls," she said as they were leading her away. "A lot of people have keys to this place, you know. My husband has given keys to everybody, and he told me—listen—he told me he was going to have me arrested for making silent phone calls because the divorce is taking so long."

McCafferty was finally glad to get the chance to ask

Laurie about the ice-pick stabbing and other oddities associated with her split from Russell. She and her parents had proven extraordinarily difficult over the months, not returning phone calls, refusing to answer the door and just generally stonewalling.

Laurie insisted that she was home with her parents on the night of the stabbing. She didn't know anything about it.

"What about the ice pick?" McCafferty said. "A week before the stabbing you bought an ice pick at Eckart Hardware, didn't you?"

"Yeah," she said slowly. "I was having problems with the ice maker in my freezer. It clogs up all the time."

McCafferty tried a firmer approach. "Would you be willing to take a lie detector test on that?" he said.

"My lawyer told me not to," she said. "That is, my first lawyer. He's not my lawyer anymore. I'm looking for another one." In fact, Laurie went through a succession of attorneys during her separation, frustrating nearly all of them with her unwillingness to take their advice and strike reasonable compromises.

"Well then, tell me about—"

"I have nothing else to say," she said, suddenly deciding to cut him off. "Just give me the phone. I'll call someone to come bail me out."

•

As usual, Laurie's parents were out of town. She really had no one to go to but her old school friend, Pearl Gelb, and Pearl's mother, Betty. They had helped her through the separation and she had found in them people who would listen to her version of events and seemed to believe her.

"I have nobody else to call," Laurie apologized to Betty when she reached her shortly after four o'clock. "I've been arrested and I need a hundred dollars to get out. Can you lend it to me?"

"My God, of course!" Betty said. She wasn't surprised that the Wassermans weren't around. Laurie was one of the loneliest people Betty could recall ever having met—a tragic figure in a tale gone wrong.

Betty thought of her as a sweet princess in a fairy tale who was supposed to be good and pretty and behave herself so she could grow up to marry the prince. The prince was Russell. Then the story fell apart and the princess had nobody. She had nowhere to go and nothing to do. She was at the edge of a cliff, looking down. All she really needed, Betty thought, was someone to say, "Poor thing, we care."

Betty went to the Jewel supermarket and cashed a check for $100, then drove to the Highland Park police station to get Laurie. On their way back to the Hastings Street house where Laurie had money to repay Betty, Betty could not resist asking what the arrest was all about.

Laurie sighed heavily, as though words were insufficient to describe the full extent of her persecution. "For making phone calls," she said. "They called them harassing phone calls."

"Well, did you do it?" Betty said.

"Yeah, but I didn't ever *say* anything," Laurie said, still aggrieved. "I would just hang up when they answered."

"Why on earth would you do that?" Betty said. "That's the kind of thing a ten-year-old does when her parents go out for dinner."

"Because that Susie Taylor's given me a lot of aggravation," Laurie said tightly. "But can you believe it? She's calling the police for such a stupid thing?"

•

Everything was someone else's fault with Laurie, Pearl noticed.

"My mom and dad don't know how to love me," Laurie complained to her. "I don't think they know how to help me, they won't listen and they don't understand. All they can give me is money. I don't want to have anything to do with my parents. All we do is fight, so I just try not to talk to them. If I call my father, sometimes he just hangs up on me or he says, 'What'd you do now? What kind of mess are you in? Laurie, you're making me crazy, you're giving me a headache. I can't listen to this.' Then it's like he hyperventilates. If I call my mom, she just says, 'Here's your father,' and hands him the phone."

"That's terrible," Pearl said.

"They both had difficult childhoods, and they can't help

it," Laurie said. "They just can't handle life. They don't know any other way."

Norm was very angry with her over the failure of her marriage, Laurie said. When his frustration boiled over he would say to her, "You really blew it. You had a rich husband, you had it all, and you just really blew it. What am I going to do with you?"

Edith, Laurie said, had virtually no personality and had been going through the motions of motherhood since day one. "She hardly says anything to me," Laurie reported to Pearl one afternoon. "Then the other day she tells me, 'You look terrible, why don't you do something with yourself?' Can you believe she'd say that?"

"Well," Pearl hazarded. "Maybe you should get your hair styled or something."

Betty suggested perhaps a little pink lipstick, maybe a new outfit. The sweatsuit was shabby and unappealing, and Laurie seemed bent on wearing it everywhere, covering up her petite but shapely body, one of her best attributes. Pearl went to her house to pick her up for a Halloween party once, and even then she had her sweatsuit on.

"You're supposed to *be* something for Halloween," Pearl said with exasperation. "What are you going to the party as?"

"A jogger," Laurie said.

Laurie would frequently try to leave the impression with Pearl and Betty that she went out on a lot of dates and was very popular, but it was obvious she was simply lying—that her life in fact had no love in it, and no activity other than perhaps making prank phone calls.

Laurie boasted to Pearl that she had gone to numerous psychiatrists and lawyers during the course of the separation, and each time she'd given them a phony name and address. "It's really funny," she said. "I tell them I'm coming back, then I never come back."

"Why are you making up names?" Pearl asked.

"I don't want them to know who I am," Laurie said.

The deceptions bothered Pearl, as did Laurie's habit of staring at people silently in public. Once they went to the Taste of Chicago, a huge food and music festival in Grant Park on the downtown lakefront. All Laurie wanted to do was watch people. Then she would invite herself along when Pearl would go out with a group of friends, and never order her own drinks. Instead she would try to sneak sips from those at the table who weren't looking. And she'd started pulling her sleeves down to cover her hands before she would touch doorknobs.

Pearl spoke to Norm several times about Laurie. Despite all the horror stories Laurie had told about her father, Pearl kind of liked the guy. He was affable, sometimes even jocular, and he obviously cared about Laurie even if he seemed helpless to do anything for her.

"I just think all this has gone a bit too far," Pearl said.

"I know," Norm said. "But I don't know what I'm going to do with her. She's nothing but trouble. Edith and I really appreciate all the help you've given her. I don't know what we'd do without you."

Pearl pulled away from Laurie gradually. At first it was because they didn't have much in common any longer and Laurie didn't really have any interests in life. Then Pearl found herself caught in the middle between Laurie and Russell, with whom she had become friends. The stories of his heartless cruelty were obviously false to anyone who knew him, which meant that Pearl couldn't trust Laurie as a friend anymore.

It was tough, because Laurie needed a friend more than anything.

•

Dhana Cohen was getting crazy, late-night hang-up phone calls, too, but she never put them together with her forlorn friend Laurie, who contacted her every couple of months. She still had the same complaints, only more of them. Russell was trying to rape her. Russell was trying to have her arrested. Russell was burglarizing her parents' house. Then she would change her story: Russell wanted to get back together with her and she was considering it.

Dhana began to use her answering machine to screen her calls, leaving Laurie's messages unreturned. Who was this girl? What did Dhana owe her? They were never such great friends, not in college, not after college. She was tired of being nice to everyone all the time. She had her own problems.

•

"No one wanted Laurie and there was no place for her to go," said Noah Rosen, an investment banker, looking back on the situation later. "If she was a stock, I would have shorted her."

•

Attorney Rick Kessler thought Russell should try to get a court order allowing him to be wired with a secret recording device so he could meet with Laurie and try to get her to confess explicitly to the ice-pick stabbing. Russell agreed, but the county prosecutor in charge of felony review told Kessler he couldn't go ahead because Detective McCafferty had told him there wasn't enough evidence to support a wire. McCafferty told Kessler it was his feeling the prosecutor's office didn't want to proceed with the plan. No one would take the initiative.

For protection, Russell hired Frank Bullock, a private detective who had once been the sergeant in charge of detectives for the police department in Waukegan, Illinois, a gritty industrial city on the lakefront halfway between Chicago and Milwaukee. Bullock was a gumshoe straight out of central casting—a beefy, forty-six-year-old with red hair, a mustache and a tattoo on his left arm. He'd left the force in Waukegan in 1981 after becoming disenchanted with his bosses and he pursued a variety of private security jobs before co-founding MidAmerica Security Investigation Inc.

Russell found Bullock through his attorney, Kessler, who had first contacted Bullock because of his expertise in wiretap law. Bullock's assignment was two-fold: to try to gather additional information to force the police and prosecutors to take a more aggressive position, and to figure out just how much danger Russell and his family might be in.

•

Laurie desperately needed something to do, and began answering baby-sitting ads in the help wanted section of the local newspaper. As long as the children weren't too young, she found she could connect with them and that they simply accepted her for who she was.

She impressed her first few clients with her reliability and maturity, her prices and her gentle manner. The Rushe family of Winnetka, to whom she identified herself as Laurie Porter for no reason she ever explained to anyone, was happy to recommend her to friends—she eagerly took their five children on outings such as a trip to the park on the Fourth of July to see the Winnetka fireworks. The kids adored her, and Marian Rushe was thrilled to have found a sitter who was willing to work weekends.

Laurie at last had found a challenge she could meet. It was as if Laurie Porter truly was a different person than Laurie Dann.

•

Lake County prosecutors dropped telephone harassment charges against Laurie on February 25, 1987, a little more than two months after her arrest. The prosecutors knew that any judge would dismiss the charges in a second because none of the victims had ever heard the caller's voice and that several people, including Russell, had access to the telephone in the Hastings Street house from which most of the calls were coming.

This dismissal outraged Russell and Jeff Taylor, in part because the county didn't even notify them directly. At the same time it confirmed Norm's belief in his daughter's innocence. He directed Laurie's attorney to make every effort to expunge her name from county criminal records so that she would once again have a clean slate.

•

Russell's divorce lawyer filed several briefs charging that Laurie was refusing to enter into a contract for the sale of the Hastings Street house, and that she was doing so only to harass him and cause "a dissipation of the marital estate." He argued that her failure to maintain the house was causing it to go down in value.

In early 1987, the warring sides edged toward a settlement. They finally agreed to split the money from selling the Hastings Street house, then valued at $249,000, as well as other assets worth another $25,000. Russell said he would pay Laurie $1,250 a month for thirty-six months and $10,000 for her attorney's fees. She would keep his name and the engagement ring. As soon as they could get everyone together in court, it would be over.

Laurie's harassing phone calls diminished for a while over the winter, but when spring arrived she returned with a vengeance. Several times a night she would call, five or six nights running, always with the sinister silence followed by the hang-ups. The Highland Park police grew so tired of the same old allegations that they became more and more lax about returning phone calls to the Taylors and others who complained. Jeff and Susie, in frustration, wrote an angry letter to Lake County state's attorney Fred Foreman expressing disappointment at what they saw as Foreman's insensitivity to their plight.

Foreman did not get back to them.

Noah Rosen got so angry one Saturday night that he measured out a cup of sugar and drove with it over to Laurie's neighborhood. He parked three blocks away and crept up on the house; her car was in the driveway. He'd decided to pour the sugar in the tank so she'd never drive the car again, but when he got twenty feet away he had second thoughts—he knew Russell had a detective following Laurie, and one or both of them might take the blame for his vandalism. He went back home and hit on another plan: if she was up until all hours calling people, she must be sleeping late. So Monday at 6:30 A.M. when he arrived at work, he went to a bank of pay phones in the lobby of his building, dialed Laurie's number and walked away with the phone off the hook.

14

A
Bitter
End

Laurie and Dean Pappas had revived their friendship after the rocky end to their dating relationship, and on April 20 she invited him over to her parents' house and asked him to bring over his copy of the Stephen King movie *Christine* to watch on the VCR. She told him not to bother knocking when he arrived because the door would be unlocked, as it always was.

They watched the movie, then Dean told Laurie he was getting tired and should head home. She said she, too, was feeling tired because she was fighting off a cold, and that she was going to take a bath and go to sleep. She didn't lock the door behind him as he left.

Later, in the early hours of the next morning, Laurie related the following tale to police:

> I took a shower and then a bath after Dean left. It was about one in the morning when I got out of the tub, and I heard noises in the other room. So I put on a sweatshirt, underwear and a dress and went into my father's office. Russell was standing there, wearing surgical gloves and going through drawers.
>
> He told me, "I want the fucking ring."
>
> I told him, "It's not yours."
>
> He said, "You don't know what you're going to do with it. It's mine

and it belongs to my family. I want it back." Then he grabbed me by the arm, dragged me into my parents' bedroom and began going through more drawers looking for the ring and swearing at me.

I told him, "It's not there. I don't have the ring. It's in a safe place."

After he realized he wasn't going to find the ring, he threw me onto the bed. He said, "You'll answer me if you're naked."

He pulled off my dress and my panties with one yank, and started saying how much he hated me and how he wanted to see me dead or at least a paraplegic so I would suffer. He pulled out a little steak knife and put it up against my neck and demanded the ring.

I said, "You're not going to hurt me with that."

He said, "I'm not stupid enough to leave any marks. But if you don't give me what I want, I'll make it look like a suicide. And no one will believe you, not even the cops. They think you're crazy."

So he pulled the knife away from my neck and put it in his back pocket. "You're looking pretty good," he said. He reached down and put several fingers inside me, then pulled them out and stuck them in his mouth. He said, "You always were good, Laurie."

Then he started to get mad again and he told me I'd better sign the divorce papers by Friday or else. He pulled the knife from his pocket again and stuck it into my vagina. He said, "You sign the papers or I cut you all the way up, bitch."

Then he unzipped his pants and began to masturbate with his right hand while trying to hold me down with his left. I sat up and grabbed for his groin, but I missed and ripped out some pubic hair.

He yelled out, "I ought to kill you, bitch!" Then he started to leave and said, "The police aren't going to believe you. I'm not stupid, that's why I didn't leave any marks."

Glencoe officers found an eight-inch cut in the screen of a porch door. They also found three bloodstains on the sheet and two clumps of dark, curly hair, which they took into evidence. They drove Laurie to Highland Park Hospital where a doctor examined her and found only a very small scratch on her vaginal wall. Laurie said she was too frightened to sign a complaint.

Again she had no one to call except Pearl Gelb. "Leave

your door unlocked, I'm coming over," Laurie said. "Russ tried to rape me."

"Right," Pearl said. Another damned story. Laurie was just too, too flaky. And when the police dropped her off at the Gelbs', she didn't even have the good graces to appear scared or upset.

"Russ wants to kill me," she complained. "He's got a detective following me, he doesn't want to pay me anything in the divorce and he and Susie are trying to set me up because they hate me."

"I'm sure they don't hate you," Pearl said.

"Russell wants me dead," she said.

"You poor thing, you should write a book," Betty told her. "You could make a fortune. This whole thing would make a great novel."

What she was really thinking was that if Laurie would take the time to write down everything she said was happening to her, she would see how ridiculous it all sounded.

•

Floyd Mohr took the case the next morning when he came in to work, and he called Laurie at Pearl's to ask her to meet with him and sign the complaint.

"I just can't handle it today, Detective," she said. "And I don't know if I'm going to press charges."

Mohr then called Russell, who said he had been home sound asleep at the time Laurie said she was attacked. Hadn't Mohr gotten the picture by now? Russell had once again reached the state of philosophical fatigue and resignation that he'd reached with Laurie during the days when she started storing toiletries inside of kitchen appliances. Nothing surprised him anymore, not even Mohr's apparently chronic inability to sort out fact from fiction. Russell said he wasn't going to answer any more questions until he talked to his attorney.

Russell called Kessler, who in turn had Bullock and Bullock's partner at the detective agency, Marc Hansen, go to Glencoe and meet with Mohr.

Bullock took an instant dislike to Mohr because of the way

Mohr demanded to see identification badges from both men and the way he treated them as adversaries.

"I believe something happened here," Mohr said, adopting an interviewing-school pose by sitting on a table above Bullock and Hansen, as if they hadn't seen *that* trick a thousand times.

"Look, Russell Dann may not be perfect," Bullock said. "But Laurie is the one who's causing all the trouble. She's filing all these phony charges."

"Who says they're phony?" Mohr said. Truthfully, he didn't know whom to believe any longer. It was back and forth, back and forth.

"We can help you," Bullock said. "We want to put an end to this. Laurie Dann has problems that have to be addressed, and Russell can't address them because every time he turns around she's making these allegations."

"I really can't discuss the case with you," Mohr said.

On their way back to the car, Bullock turned to his partner and shook his head. "That guy's hooked," he said. "He believes whatever she tells him."

•

Rick Kessler didn't think much of Mohr either. The men had a face-to-face meeting after Mohr made a request for Russell to come in for questioning. "We just want to talk to him," Mohr said. "Get some facts."

"I'll be happy to bring him in," Kessler said, "but I'll advise him not to answer any questions."

"What are you worried about?"

"That's not the point," Kessler said. "My client is a suspect in this assault, so if you think you've got the evidence, then go out and arrest him. But he's still not going to talk."

"Okay, but I'm going to go ahead and get a warrant for a sample of his pubic hair," Mohr said, a slight challenge in his voice.

"Fine," Kessler said. "You get a warrant, and we'll be happy to comply."

The important result of the two meetings was that Mohr was left with the impression that Kessler and Bullock—like himself—were unsure whether Russell was guilty or innocent. Both Kessler and Bullock have since vigorously denied ever saying anything to suggest they doubted Russell; Mohr, equally vigorously, has sworn that the men were waffling.

Either way, Mohr went forward more sure than ever that the interaction of Laurie and Russell was a screwball, he-said she-said divorce in which no one was totally in the right and no one was totally in the wrong—there was no way to tell from moment to moment.

The knife rape seemed impossible, on the surface. How could a man hold a woman down, insert a knife into her with one hand, masturbate with the other and leave no bruises and only the tiniest scratch? But then, to further confuse him, Laurie took and passed two separate polygraph tests.

•

"If I had more guts, or more balls, I'd hire somebody to take care of Russell for how he ruined Laurie's life," Norm said to Floyd Mohr during one of their conversations about the ongoing travails. "Break his legs or something like that. Now, I'm not like that, but if I was a different person, I would hire some friends to break his legs."

"That wasn't a very smart thing to say," Mohr said. "If, in fact, Russell's legs ever get broken now, I'm going to get you."

"Floyd, you know I'd never do something like that," Norm said. "I'm not stupid. But look at the mind games he's been playing with her, causing her problems. Russell wanted Laurie to be his slave. He was trying to make her look crazy so he didn't have to give her anything in the divorce. He makes a lot, believe me. But after a while I just told her to take whatever he's offering and go—she doesn't even know what to do with money when she has it—but she wanted more."

Norm went on to offer to do Mohr's taxes for him. Mohr said thanks, but his return really wasn't all that complicated.

•

On April 27, 1987, a Cook County Circuit Court judge signed off on the divorce. The marriage of Russell Dann and Laurie Wasserman had lasted a little more than four and a half years, including a year and a half of separation.

The very next day, Laurie told Mohr that she was confused and frightened about the knife rape and she had decided to prosecute so that Russell would never hurt her or anyone else again.

Mohr turned the police reports over to Cook County assistant state's attorney Edward Vienuzis in felony review, then drove Laurie down to meet with Vienuzis at his office in suburban Des Plaines two days later.

During the meeting, Laurie was in rare form. She went over the knife-rape story again; then, prompted for more details by Vienuzis, added that Russell used to force her to have sex, and once tied her legs to the bedposts and inserted the end of a hairbrush into her vagina. On another occasion, she said, he had pleaded with her to masturbate with a banana. She also said that he used to make her watch pornographic movies and go to gay bars with him, and that one time he asked her to insert an unlubricated eight-inch dildo into his rectum.

Vienuzis took it all in, thought it over and made a preliminary decision not to file charges against Russell. The evidence was inconclusive and a jury would never buy it.

•

Any thoughts Russell might have been entertaining that the final decree in his divorce signaled the end of his troubles were rudely dispelled on the morning of May 12 when three Highland Park squad cars pulled him over in what is called a felony stop, one car in front, another behind, hands on holsters.

"What now?" he said, fully out of patience. This was like a bad movie.

"Mr. Dann, you are wanted for questioning by the Glencoe police about an arson attempt earlier this morning," one of them told him.

"You've got to be nuts," Russell said.

At 3:45 that morning, Laurie had called the police to her parents' home in Glencoe and showed them an unexploded Molotov cocktail on a table in the den. She said she had been headed to the bathroom when she saw a candle burning in the den. The candle was the fuse—and a nearby window screen had been cut. The glass that held the flammable liquid, Laurie told police, was part of a set of glasses she and Russell had received as a wedding present.

A bulletin immediately went out that Russell should be stopped for questioning, and, though no one in his family owned a gun, that he might be carrying a Smith & Wesson Model 19 revolver.

"Oh, Jesus," Russell said when this was explained to him. "Why didn't you just call me at home? Am I so hard to reach?"

One of the officers shrugged. "Don't ask me," he said. "All we know is that they want to question you."

"I'm sure I know a lot more about all this than you guys do," Russell said. He called Kessler on his car phone while the police searched Russell's latest car, an Audi 5000, including the trunk. They found nothing, and told Russell to go to the Glencoe police department at nine A.M. for further questioning.

"I'm going to an important time-management seminar today," Russell said. "I'll get in touch with them when it's convenient for me."

•

Norm and Edith were genuinely frightened by what they believed was Russell's escalating campaign to harass their daughter, and they had started to fear for their own safety as well. Through Mohr, they arranged for a hearing with Nancy Sidote, supervisor of felony review for the branch office of the Cook County State's Attorney. Sidote had the power to override the original decision not to prosecute, and Mohr drove Norm, Edith and Laurie to Sidote's office in Skokie for a forty-five minute conference.

The lack of significant injury to Laurie was what stuck out, Sidote told them. Everything was very neat in the bedroom where the attack supposedly took place, there were no fingerprints and given the previous allegations against Laurie—the phone calls and the ice-pick stabbing—she wasn't going to make a terribly credible witness.

Laurie seemed bored and distracted during the entire meeting. "He's a very smart guy," she told Sidote. "He knows how to cover his tracks. So why are we even wasting time talking about this?"

"But we have to do something," Norm insisted. "I mean,

we can accept that this isn't a good case to try, but can't something be done to stop him? Anything? Think of what could have happened if Laurie hadn't found that Molotov cocktail."

Laurie stood up to leave and her father ordered her to sit back down with a sharp, "Just a minute."

"Your only real hope is the pubic hair evidence, which hasn't been gathered and tested yet," Sidote said. "And hair usually comes back, at best, morphologically similar, which means it could come from the suspect, but it could also come from hundreds of thousands of other people."

"That would help," Norm said. "It would let us know in our minds whether it was him or not. Maybe we can't prove it, but at least then we'd know it."

"This just isn't fair," Edith added. It was one of her only contributions to the discussion.

Afterward Norm was very upset when he spoke to Mohr one-on-one. "Laurie's the victim again," he said. "Russell has no right."

"Is she still seeing a doctor?"

"We have her seeing someone new," Norm said. "A Dr. Epstein at Rush-Presbyterian."

Mohr had tried and failed to get Laurie to sign a waiver that would allow him to talk to Dr. Greendale, and Greendale had continued to refuse to help on those grounds. Thinking he might have better luck with the new doctor, Mohr called repeatedly until he finally got through.

Dr. Phillip Epstein also refused to say much of anything. Mohr told him about the burglary, the gun, the knife rape and the Molotov cocktail, and Epstein said coolly, "I wasn't aware of that."

"Well, maybe you'd better be aware," Mohr said. He asked him the same questions he'd asked of Greendale. Do you think she's violent? Homicidal? Suicidal?

"I don't know enough about her," Epstein said. "But I don't see anything that would say she's violent."

"Do you know what you're dealing with here?"

"I'm dealing with someone who had an obsessive compulsive disorder," Epstein said. "She's got problems—chemical imbalances—and we're treating her for them."

•

Frank Bullock followed Laurie around for a while and talked to people who knew her, but in late May he decided he might as well take the direct approach and ring Laurie's doorbell.

She answered the door. He identified himself and gave her his business card, but she wouldn't touch it and simply let it flutter through her hand. She let him in to her parents' kitchen. She had on an old sweater and shirt and a pair of unstylish stretch slacks that reminded Bullock of the clothing he had seen on mental patients. He also noted she was wearing gloves and never took them off.

She offered to show him where she found the Molotov cocktail, and led him through the house. The living room was dominated by a huge pile of clothes.

"What about this sexual assault?" Bullock asked.

"That's my family's problem," she said. "I don't know anything about it. The police didn't believe me anyway."

"You're accusing Russ of trying to burn your house down," Bullock persisted.

"I'm not," she said. "I never said he did it. I never did."

She was physically withdrawing from him. She pulled on her sweater, stretching it out, then wrapped her arms around herself. He shook his head. "What do you want out of all this?" he said. "What good is all this doing you?"

"I don't want anything else to happen," she said. "I just want to get on with my life."

15

Back
to
Campus

After the divorce, Laurie had her cash settlement but little else. She lived at home for a short time, but soon she began planning to get back into a new school setting, her customary way to start fresh. She'd met a lot of men in college, and campuses had been the scene of many of her social triumphs. She also might be able to pick up a few classes and get her life back on track. She was still half a year shy of her thirtieth birthday—too young to give up.

She drove the eight miles south to Evanston one afternoon and walked around the main campus of Northwestern University, a distinguished assortment of brick and limestone classroom buildings, fraternities and ivy-shrouded dormitories bisected by Sheridan Road hard by Lake Michigan. As Laurie walked she posted notices on kiosks and bulletin boards that she was interested in a summer sublet. Derek Christopher, a student in the J. L. Kellogg Graduate School of Management, saw her handbill and called. He was looking to lease his half of an apartment suite on the fifth floor of the Kellogg Living/Learning Center from mid-June to mid-September.

They arranged to meet and she looked over the room, which was connected to another bedroom by a shared kitchen and bathroom along a short hallway. It was a good deal at $334 a month and she said she wanted it. Christopher gave her an informal, one-page lease to sign, and she arranged to move in on June 15 after the conclusion of spring quarter.

When she arrived, she found the other half of the suite occupied by another nonstudent sublettor, Andy Gallagher. He, too, was a North Shore kid still looking to find his bearings. He attempted to be friendly, but his presence enraged Laurie right from the start.

She complained to building manager Marc Boney that she had been under the impression when she'd signed the lease that the other side of the suite was not going to be occupied; that it was and that the occupant was male was more than unacceptable to her.

"He misled me," she said, referring to Christopher, who was working that summer in a New York City investment banking firm. "So I'm not going to keep my side of the agreement. All I want is my deposit and first month's rent back."

"It's between you and him," Boney said. "This is not a university matter."

"But I'm not safe in there," Laurie said. "My suitemate is very strange."

Boney was dutifully concerned. Laurie presented herself well—mild-mannered and tastefully groomed—and he thought of her right away as the damsel-in-distress type. "If I were you," he said, "I'd call Derek and appeal to his conscience, then I'd leave and hope to get my money back."

Laurie said she thought that was probably what she was going to do, thanked Boney for his help and left. Boney, whose office was in another building on campus, didn't hear from or about her again for two months.

Andy Gallagher wasn't exactly thrilled with the setup either, especially when he discovered what a terrible slob his new suitemate was. She left newspapers and food wrappers strewn all over the floor of her room and the hallway, and she heaped dirty and clean clothes together in a huge cardboard box in the center of her room. She left meat dripping in the oven whenever she tried to cook, and she always prepared much more food for herself than one person could eat so that leftovers stacked up unappealingly. Andy, who was into health foods, simply made it his practice not to go into the kitchen very often.

And there were the other oddities: Laurie never used her bare hands to touch anything, so when she opened a door she had to use a towel wrapped around her hands or else pull her hands inside the sleeves of her blouse. Then early in the summer she followed one of Andy's friends into the bathroom and watched him urinate. When he was through, she asked to shake his hand.

She went in and out of the suite a lot at odd hours, but she never seemed to go anywhere. She often said she was going off to play tennis, but none of her partners ever came to the apartment and instead Andy would see her riding the elevators up and down the seven-story building all afternoon or sitting transfixed in front of the TV in the downstairs lounge, often watching without the sound on.

Though Andy didn't care much for her, he came to realize that he was actually one of the only people in the world she talked to. They went out for pizza several times and he listened sympathetically when her goldfish died and she seemed upset. In conversation, he noticed that she often spoke of her brother, Mark, whom she described as her "best and closest friend."

"I could tell him everything," she said miserably. "It was really awful when he got married and moved away to Texas."

Laurie told Andy that she worked in the admitting office of a hospital, but she told another summer resident that she was in the nursing program and still a third that she was an evening student in the hospital management program and that she worked as a hospital administrator at Glenbrook Hospital, the institution that had fired her four years earlier. Over and over again, with bland and convincing sincerity, Laurie reinvented her life, projecting new and better identities onto herself.

To Donna McDonough, a front desk clerk at Kellogg, she was a business student who had transferred from the University of Chicago because U. of C. was "too stodgy" for her—the very story that Russell's friend Noah Rosen often told of his own education.

"You know, a lot of frat brothers are asking me out," she said one afternoon as she used a rag to play tug-of-war with Donna's dog. "Sigma Chi, Kappa Sigma, Psi Upsilon...which one do you think has the best parties?"

Donna wasn't sure, and Laurie went on to speak particularly highly of Psi Upsilon. Scott Freidheim, a popular, handsome soccer star who lived in the fraternity, had given her a ride once when she was having car trouble, and Laurie said she was seriously considering dating him and wondered how it would be if she were known as someone who was dating a Psi U.

Freidheim, however, had all but forgotten even giving Laurie a ride, and was not even to learn her name until ten months later.

Pearl Gelb also heard Laurie's preposterous tales of her own popularity when Laurie called to bring her up to date. "There's tons of parties," she said. "Guys are everywhere. You have to come down and meet these guys. I do a lot of fun stuff with friends."

"Yeah?" Pearl said. "Who?"

"Well, just friends," Laurie said.

Warily, Pearl accepted Laurie's invitation to enjoy her new social circle, but when she walked with Laurie from the main entrance up to her room, she saw that the other residents of the dorm tended to say hello and move away quickly. At the doorway to the suite, Laurie turned and blocked Pearl's progress. "Wait in the hall," she said. "It really smells in there."

Sure enough, when Laurie opened the door, a dank, sickening odor wafted out from the clutter. "What is that?" Pearl asked, wrinkling her nose.

"Oh, it's my fish," Laurie said.

Pearl shook her head. She'd long ago given up trying to figure this girl out. "Whatever," she said.

•

Laurie apologized to Dhana Cohen by phone. They had made plans in the late spring to get together and walk through a street art fair in the city, but Laurie had canceled at the last minute by leaving a message on Dhana's machine.

"It's no big deal," Dhana said.

"Listen, I've moved to Evanston," she said. "I'll give you my new number."

"Okay."

Laurie recited her number—the first three digits, a pause, the last four.

"Uh huh," said Dhana. She wasn't writing it down.

•

Catherine Farago, another of the front desk clerks at the Kellogg Living/Learning Center that summer, thought Laurie might actually be making a pass at her the way she hung around the lounge all the time and stood too close when she made conversation. She wore tight-fitting, summery tops that showed off her cleavage as she leaned over the counter. But she never made any overt suggestions to Farago—she just wanted to be friends.

Farago and other residents noticed that Laurie would change clothes many times a day even though she wasn't going out. One man who tried to befriend her would answer knocks on his door at odd hours to find her standing there asking if he wanted to watch TV with her.

Maintenance supervisor David Campbell got acquainted with Laurie through the prodigious amounts of junk she left behind in the TV room—cookie wrappers, empty pop bottles and other trash—but he went from angry to concerned when he noticed she was wearing rubber gloves as she wandered the hallways. One day he discovered her inside an unoccupied room sleeping so soundly he was unable to wake her. On the carpet near the kitchen was a burned spot several inches wide that had not been there earlier.

•

Laurie was still not happy that she was having to share a suite with Andy Gallagher. She told resident Robert Hollander that she wasn't afraid, though, because she had a gun.

"A gun?" Hollander asked incredulously. "Why do you have a gun?"

"I've had troubles in the past," she said. She didn't elaborate.

•

In early July, Laurie had her father, who was depositing her alimony checks into one of his personal bank accounts, hand-write a sword-rattling letter to her summer landlord. "Dear Mr. Christopher," it said. "This is an unlivable situation for me. You rented this apartment to me under false pretenses...please refund my [money] at once. If I do not receive your check within one week, I will be forced to take you to small claims court. Respectfully yours, Laurie A. Dann."

Andy Gallagher had taken more direct action. Though Laurie seemed more pitiably troubled than actually dangerous, he'd started sleeping with a knife and a baseball bat at his side, just in case. Laurie had started to show a disturbing fascination with meat—her mother would bring groceries to the dorm and Laurie would unwrap the raw meat and put it on a plate in the refrigerator where it would drip down onto the other food. When she put some in the freezer, blood trickled into the ice-cube trays.

Maintenance supervisor Campbell, meanwhile, was finding uncooked slabs of prime-cut beef hidden in peculiar places throughout the dorm. He found the first piece stashed under the carpet in the hallway, then he turned up several pieces stacked on top of each other behind chair cushions in the main hallway and another stuffed inside a chair in the TV lounge. He also discovered fish bones stuffed into the cushions where Laurie had been watching TV and large quantities of spaghetti thrown all over a hallway.

One day housing director Andrew Burke saw that the door to a vacant apartment on Laurie's floor was ajar, went in to investigate and found spoiled food in the refrigerator. The occupants of another room down the hall discovered that a whole chicken had appeared mysteriously in their refrigerator.

From time to time Laurie ate pieces of the meat she was hoarding even though some of it had gone bad. One day Andy came upon her writhing in pain on her bed, barely able to stand. He helped her to his car to drive her to the hospital, but suddenly along the way she told him to take her to her parents' house instead. He turned around and headed toward Glencoe.

Edith was pleasant to Andy when he brought Laurie to the door, but when he said he was worried that Laurie had no direction in life, Edith just shrugged.

When Andy talked to Norm, Norm told him that the real problem in Laurie's life was that her ex-husband was out to get her.

Several weeks later, she was admitted to the emergency room of the Evanston Hospital with severe stomach cramps.

•

Russell Dann also went to Evanston Hospital that summer, but it was no emergency. Detective Floyd Mohr, in his pursuit of the truth on the knife-rape allegations, had obtained a search warrant for a sample of Russell's pubic hair, and the two antagonists met along with Russell's attorney, Rick Kessler, in the hospital waiting area. While Kessler and Mohr sat in an outer room watching marine colonel Oliver North testify during Congressional hearings on the Iran-contra affair, a male nurse snipped approximately twenty-five hairs from Russell's crotch and another twenty-five from his head. The conclusion of the lab report, which came back two weeks later, was just as prosecutor Nancy Sidote had predicted—the hairs were only morphologically similar and thus meaningless as evidence.

But the ignominy of it all! The marital nightmare was legally over, but when would it end? The harassing hang-up phone calls had started again after a hiatus of several months. Susie and Jeff Taylor were so worried about Laurie's persistence that they secured a protective court order prohibiting her from coming near their home—just in case. Beth and Noah Rosen reported Laurie's calls to their local police department in Deerfield and stressed that the woman was in bad need of mental help. They considered installing another tap on their phone and trying to press charges against her, but past experience had taught them that it would be futile and perhaps dangerous. Not only would the evidence not stand up in court, but Laurie would know who had reported her.

Russell moved out of his town house when he learned that Bullock had temporarily lost Laurie's trail. He took a unit in the Americana Apartments on busy Lake–Cook Road on the county line, got an unlisted phone number and had his mail delivered to a post office box so Laurie wouldn't be able to find him. He never drove straight home from work, and always kept a close eye behind him to be sure Laurie wasn't in his rearview mirror.

Then early one morning he looked out the window of his new home as his girlfriend, Patricia Cassell, was leaving and saw Laurie standing menacingly on the sidewalk. He called Bullock at home and woke him up, but by the time Bullock could throw on clothes and get to the house, Laurie was gone.

Then Patricia started getting hang-up calls.

•

In the meantime, Laurie's curious activities in the Kellogg apartments had escalated into the realm of the quasi-criminal. Building personnel kept seeing her wandering through rooms and areas to which she was not supposed to have access, and the front desk clerks caught her trying to break into other people's mailboxes. She was wearing rubber gloves when they stopped her, and she explained in an injured tone that she was just looking for a letter she had been expecting.

One afternoon in August, two male residents were sitting in their room when they heard the lock click on the front door to the suite. When they went to investigate they found Laurie standing in front of their refrigerator with the door open. She told them that she was just checking the room because she was thinking of subletting a similar apartment, and that the front desk had given her a passkey to enter their room.

The residents began complaining, and Derek Christopher, her summer landlord, was starting to raise hell. Laurie wasn't paying rent and he had gotten nowhere in three telephone conversations with Edith, who didn't seem the least bit concerned and kept saying the problem was no big deal. Now he was badgering both building director Marc Boney and the Northwestern Department of Public Safely to have her evicted.

Boney confronted her in her room along with graduate housing manager Daniel Clay and two public safety officers. "I thought you were leaving here back in June," he said.

The room was a riot of clothes and old cookie bags, and

the smell of urine hung heavily in the air. Laurie didn't apologize for the mess or appear the least bit embarrassed. "That was my plan," she said. "But Derek wouldn't give me my money back, and since I'm paid up through the summer I just decided to stay."

"Well, I'm getting a discrepancy between you and Derek," Boney said. "He told me you paid a deposit and one month's rent, but now it's August and he tells me he hasn't received any other money from you."

"Oh, no, no, no," Laurie said. She rummaged through piles of trash and produced several bank receipts, none of which proved anything. She also presented Boney with a copy of a standard Northwestern University apartment lease for the Kellogg Center on which she had underlined the passage stating that apartment residency was limited to people of the same sex. But that only made Boney more suspicious than ever. The lease was obviously stolen and forged, as summer sublease agreements were private arrangements and never involved formal university contracts.

"Something's wrong here," Boney said.

"Oh, come on," Laurie said. "Why are you persecuting me?"

"We're not persecuting you," Boney said. "We just want to straighten this out."

Over the next several days, while Boney was waiting for Christopher to send a copy of Laurie's lease to him from New York, Boney's student manager, Andrew Burke, called to tell him that one of the spare building passkeys was missing, which might explain how Laurie was getting into unauthorized areas so easily.

Boney immediately met with Burke and they went to Laurie's room to demand the key. She wasn't there, but in the process of searching her fetid quarters they found stolen student papers, a luggage cart that was missing from the front desk, a stash of rubber gloves and a large collection of *Penthouse* and *Penthouse Letters* magazines. When they opened up the refrigerator they reeled at the ghoulish sight and smell of thick, dripping cuts of spoiled meat stuffed into every corner.

"We've got a problem," Boney said dryly.

He called a psychiatrist he knew socially and asked him what Laurie's fixation might mean. The doctor told him her behavior was symptomatic of inner rage—the slashing and hiding of meat was symbolic of the way someone would kill a person and hide the corpse, but in such an obvious way that people would find it.

But Boney could not easily evict Laurie for strange expressions of rage or, for that matter, for nonpayment of rent. He knew that tenants' rights laws in Evanston required formal eviction proceedings that would take sixty days minimum. By that time the summer would be over. His best shot, he figured, was to catch her with the passkey and use the threat to press criminal charges as leverage to get her to leave.

•

Laurie's sometime boyfriend at the time was Stephen Greene from the second floor. They'd met while watching TV in the lounge and one day she'd asked him if he would like to go dancing with her in a downtown Chicago bar. He agreed. He was going through a divorce at the time and Laurie was slim and pretty.

She told him she was twenty-nine and had graduated from UCLA with a degree in psychology, but when he said he was twenty-six, she said she was twenty-six, too. As he got to know her better he found her typically moody and indifferent, to the point of rudeness sometimes. Once when they were on a double date, the other girl in the foursome attempted to shake Laurie's hand and Laurie refused, twice. She explained away all her strange behavior by saying she had chemical imbalances because her mother had taken fertility drugs, and she likened her condition to bone marrow disease. She said blandly that she possibly could die quite young as a result of her condition.

They went out for pizza a couple of times and once she came to his apartment to watch videos. She told him she really enjoyed the movie *Black Widow,* a violent thriller, because she was intrigued by the idea of plotting to get back at people.

Once he came home, took off his shoes and stepped on a wet spot in front of the TV. He rubbed his finger in the dampness, and when he smelled it, he realized someone had urinated there. Was it Laurie?

•

She sat down at the typewriter on August 22 and wrote four short, unsigned letters.

The first said: "I want my ring back, you spoiled bitch. But most of all I want it all and I always get what I want. Where there is a will there is a way. What have I got to lose?"

The second said: "I told you I would warn you only once. You are either stubborn or just plain dumb. It is your funeral, I mean choice."

The third said: "This is not blackmail, it is the American way. You just got unlucky. I did some dumb things and even I get nervous, so cooperate and make it easier on yourself."

The last one said: "I am much stronger than you. I can always break you physically and emotionally. I can make mince meat out of you."

She slipped a photograph of Russell and Patricia— apparently stolen from his apartment—into one of the envelopes and mailed all four of the letters to herself.

She would use them as evidence against Russell. She would show them to her father and to the Evanston police when questions came up concerning who was whose victim.

•

Stephen Greene took Laurie to the Lincoln Park Zoo near the lakefront in Chicago two weeks later. They had a pleasant and normal outing until they walked into the elephant house, where the smell of urine was overpowering.

All at once Laurie grabbed him and gave him a passionate kiss. It had never happened before.

"Hey," he said, feeling both pleased and shocked. "Why'd you do that?"

"I just felt like it," she said.

That very afternoon, Marc Boney was out to spring a trap on her. When she'd left on her way to the zoo, Boney proceeded to her room to search for the passkey. He didn't find it, but he did find the room key that Derek Christopher had given her. He knew, then, if she returned and let herself in with a key, it almost certainly had to be a passkey.

At four o'clock, a desk clerk saw Laurie use a key in the front door of the complex, so she stopped her to ask to inspect the key. Laurie held it up, but refused to let the clerk touch it. When the clerk persisted, Laurie left the lobby and went back outside, where Boney and Burke eventually caught up with her.

"Give me that key," Boney said.

"No way," she said.

"The game's over," Boney said. "I know what's happening here. I'm going to do everything I can to get you out of here."

"You can't do this to me," Laurie snarled, staring daggers at Boney. "I want both your names, I want your titles, I want your phone numbers. You're not throwing me out."

"You're caught," Boney said. Her look was sending chills up his back. "That key is university property, therefore you are committing a criminal act. We don't want to prosecute you. We just want you to leave."

"Fuck you," she said and walked away.

When Laurie returned to her room and saw that it had been searched, she filed a burglary report with the Evanston police. Then she got in her Honda, drove five blocks and parked it on a busy commercial thoroughfare. The police noticed her sleeping in the car the next morning.

•

The burglary report put Frank Bullock back on Laurie's trail. He had learned that hang-up calls to Patricia Cassell's telephone had been traced back to somewhere at Northwestern, so he'd left word with contacts in Evanston to call him if Laurie's name ever turned up. After they notified him, Bullock discovered the sickening stories of her behavior at the Kellogg apartments and reported back to Russell and Rick Kessler.

•

Norm called Marc Boney on September 6 in a snit, demanding to know why Boney had singled out his daughter for harassment. Boney said he would meet with Norm and Laurie at three o'clock the next afternoon to explain and to see if they could reach a settlement of some sort.

Boney's plan was to intercept Norm in the lobby before the formal powwow began and try to reason with him—perhaps convince him that Laurie would be better off in a hospital.

"Mr. Wasserman?" he said, stopping a lean, gray-haired man in a short-sleeved button-down shirt. "I'm the building manager you spoke to yesterday."

"Yes," said Norm. He was wary.

"May I speak with you in private first?" Boney, who had put on a sport coat and tie for the conference, pulled Norm aside and spoke in low tones. "Look, I'm not sure what your daughter has told you, but the problems we have here are that there are irregularities with her lease and she appears to have a passkey. We've seen her in parts of the building she should not have access to, and we suspect her of setting a fire in one of those rooms."

"What's happening here?" Norm complained. "I thought a person had rights in this country. I thought a person couldn't just be railroaded."

Boney sighed. "Well then," he said, "I guess we'll just have to sit down here and weigh out the situation."

The formal proceedings took place at a square table in one of the small meeting rooms on the first floor of the Living/Learning Center. Laurie, in a pale green sweatsuit, sat next to her father across from Boney, Burke and two uniformed campus security officers. The university personnel explained that Laurie was behind in her rent and then laid out the case that she was in possession of a master key—the witnesses against her, the circumstantial evidence, the direct evidence. Boney concluded by offering not to press charges if Laurie would return the key, pack up and leave that very afternoon.

Norm looked gravely to Laurie. "Laurie," he said. "Do you have that key?"

"No, Dad," she said.

"Did you ever have that key?"

"No, Dad," she said. "I've never had the key."

Norm turned to Boney, his palms up. "She doesn't have the key," he said simply. "She never had the key."

"What about the time we found you in rooms that are locked for the summer?" Boney asked.

"They were unlocked," she said. "One time I was looking

for some brownies in a friend's room and another time I was looking for my friend Francine."

"But—"

"Listen here," Norm flared. "My daughter hasn't done anything wrong, you heard her. I don't understand what's going on here. I thought people had their rights. What kind of a Nazi are you?"

Boney started. "Look, Mr. Wasserman, I didn't want to bring this up, but you've given me no choice. We've seen your daughter wandering the halls of this apartment building wearing rubber gloves and trying to break into mailboxes. She's been leaving garbage and big, bloody pieces of meat stuffed in strange places all over. I asked her what she was doing here this summer and she said she was a student, but I checked with the registrar and she isn't a student."

Laurie interrupted. "I am a student," she said. "I'm auditing classes."

"Oh, yeah? What classes?"

"Nursing classes," she said. It was almost a guess.

"Well, we don't have a school of nursing here," Boney said, a note of triumph in his voice.

Norm was silent for a moment. Then he took a breath and said, "Laurie has some emotional problems, we're aware of that. Can we drop the subject?"

Laurie became visibly agitated, turned and said loudly, "Dad, you know why I wear rubber gloves!"

Norm said, "We're getting her medical attention."

One of the security officers interrupted. "We can talk about this for hours, but the fact remains that if your daughter doesn't leave, we're going to press charges."

"Okay, okay," Norm said.

The group went upstairs en masse to check the room. The conditions were appalling in almost every regard, but, Boney noted, if Norm was surprised, he did not show it.

He and Laurie packed up the room by heaping her belongings into several large boxes. Norm told the Northwestern Department of Public Safety officer that Laurie suffered emotional disorders. "I don't think you should press charges," he said. "It wouldn't do any good."

Maintenance supervisor Campbell scrubbed down the apartment after Laurie left, and found garbage in all the cabinets above the kitchen sink. Her bed was so badly damaged by urine that he had to toss both the mattress and the platform board into the dumpster. He also saw urine stains on several spots in the carpet.

When Laurie left the building for the last time, Boney and Burke kicked back in the lounge and sighed with relief.

"Man!" said Boney.

"You're not kidding," said Burke. "You know, I wouldn't be surprised if that girl's in the headlines someday. Like a John Hinckley."

16

Laurie
the
Baby-sitter

Laurie Dann had failed at everything. She'd been a rotten student, an awful wife, a disappointing daughter and an unreliable employee. She couldn't even live on her own without getting into vast amounts of trouble. The single thing she seemed to have an aptitude for was child care.

The only trouble she had early on was with Katie and Matt Williamson, who lived two blocks north of the Wassermans on Sheridan Road in Glencoe. In May, the Williamsons came home to find a pair of garage door openers missing and knife slashes on their leather couches and chairs.

Laurie's vague and unapologetic excuse was that a young man who said he was a neighbor had knocked on the door and asked to use the telephone. She said she left him in the kitchen while she went upstairs to get one of the Williamson children to identify the man, but when she came back downstairs he was gone.

The Williamsons estimated the damage at $1,700 and reported the incident to the Glencoe police, who responded to the call but pointed out that furniture does get damaged now and again and said that proving a case against Laurie would be difficult without witnesses.

Detective Mohr called Laurie to the station for an interview, but she stuck to the story about the intruder. "I know

Russell was behind this," she said. "He hired the guy. He sent him over to try to make me look foolish. Why? Why is he trying to make me look bad?" A sob caught in her throat and she held Mohr with steady but moist eyes. "He can have the money. He can just have it."

Her lip began to quiver and tears poured down her cheeks. Mohr sat uncomfortably by, as confused as ever—she was either one of the most tragic victims he had ever encountered or one of the best actresses.

The Williamson family ultimately let the matter drop and simply stopped hiring Laurie. She responded by pestering them for several weeks with hang-up phone calls at all hours.

She proceeded to answer a newspaper ad placed by Joan Hens, a Wilmette resident who was looking for a live-in house-keeper and companion for her eighty-seven-year-old mother, Goldie. When Laurie arrived for the interview, she struck Mrs. Hens as nicely dressed, slim, well spoken and well educated. She said she was recently divorced and very sad about it, and that she just wanted to have a job and a place to live. "When I saw your ad, I thought, 'I can do that,'" Laurie said earnestly. "I thought, 'I'd be good at that.' I could bake for her and be a good friend to her. I know your mother would enjoy having me."

When Hens asked what Laurie's salary requirements were, Laurie said it didn't matter, she would take whatever the family could afford. Hens decided to test her by offering her the ridiculously low wage of $75 a week—more than $200 less than she was actually planning to pay—and Laurie readily agreed. It gave Hens a funny feeling, and when her mother took an instant dislike to Laurie for reasons she could not quite articulate, the matter was settled. Hens made up an excuse and told Laurie she couldn't hire her.

For two or three months thereafter, Hens was deluged with hang-up calls.

•

When Laurie left Northwestern University housing and moved back in with her parents, she began to take on more and more sitting clients. Her failure to thrive alone on campus seemed to mark the end of the dream that she would ever amount to much, so baby-sitting went from an occasional thing she did to make a little spending money to being her sole constructive purpose in life.

She posted handwritten notices on bulletin boards in libraries and grocery stores on the North Shore: "Experienced babysitter, 25 years old, just finished college, living at home in Glencoe, has own car, references, $2.50 an hour. Call me."

"Why are you so into baby-sitting?" Pearl asked reprovingly when Laurie told her what she'd been doing.

"Because I have nothing else to do," Laurie said.

Pam Berman, a Glencoe mother, saw Laurie's ad in the Glencoe Public Library and thought she sounded too good to be true. She called the number and Laurie agreed to come sit for Jennifer, age seven, and Colin, age five, on the nights of September 17 and 18, 1987.

Laurie looked fresh and collegiate in her crew neck sweater and corduroy pants, but she seemed a little weird to Pam Berman. She smiled very strangely and asked a number of unusually direct questions about such things as Stan Berman's medical specialty. Yet the kids had no complaints and everything seemed fine when the parents returned from their evening out.

But the next night, after Laurie had gone home, the Bermans found $50 worth of gourmet frozen foods missing along with a new pair of $40 shoes, a bottle of shampoo and a bottle of perfume. Colin said he saw Laurie take the items from the house, and Stan Berman called the police.

He did not particularly care to press charges, he told the officers. He was worried, rather, that a woman who stole frozen food—as opposed to jewelry—was so emotionally unbalanced that people shouldn't be entrusting her with their children. "Listen," he said. "This woman is going to hurt somebody."

He said he was going to take out an advertisement in the local weekly newspaper warning other North Shore parents about Laurie, but the police cautioned him strongly against it—maybe there would be trouble. Maybe she would sue. And did they really want to put their five-year-old boy through the ordeal of testifying at a trial?

Instead, Pam Berman settled for pulling down Laurie's advertising signs whenever she saw a new one up at the library, which was almost every day.

On September 24, Florence and Bruce Montrose of Glencoe called Laurie to baby-sit for what turned out to be the last time. She had been working off and on for them since May. She told them she'd been married and divorced, that she had been a nursery school teacher and that she was going back to school at Northwestern in the fall. They noticed she wasn't comfortable talking to adults, but that she immediately sat down on the floor with the children, Jennifer and Peter, and began putting together puzzles.

But over the months the Montroses became increasingly uneasy with Laurie and they dropped her to the bottom of their list of sitters to call. One problem was she occasionally had terrible body odor. Another was she would wear long gloves and full winter coats in the middle of the summer, and when the Montroses would come home they would find her in a dark room with the TV blaring and her coat on, ready to bolt out the door. Then they would come upon unwashed pots and silverware she had placed in cabinets and drawers.

The Montroses discovered their custom-made living room cabinetry gouged with a kitchen knife. Then they noticed little things missing, like boxes of rice. But they were never sure Laurie was to blame, and the shortage of sitters on the North Shore meant that they had to turn to her again.

Many employers in the upscale suburbs had trouble filling low-paying jobs. Young people just weren't interested in un-skilled labor, particularly if it meant working nights and week-ends while their friends were having fun. Restaurants solved the problem by boosting their wages sometimes well above the minimum wage to attract workers from distant, less-affluent areas; parents solved the problem by dipping way, way down on their list of baby-sitters.

Laurie was only at the Montroses for a couple of hours in the morning of what was to be her last day, watching the kids while Florence went to Yom Kippur services. After the children were through eating a snack and had gone outside to play, Laurie went into the deep freeze and pulled out hundreds of dollars worth of steak and shrimp, which she stuffed into a large plastic garbage bag. She heaped various gourmet canned goods on top of the meat, twisted the top closed and with considerable effort hauled the bag out to her car. She opened the trunk, put the bag inside and returned to the house.

She then wandered upstairs to the bathroom, opened the medicine chest and withdrew a bottle of Bruce Montrose's prescription tranquilizers. She swallowed a great handful of them, dropped the bottle on the floor and went back down to the kitchen, where the children had left peanut butter and jelly sandwiches half eaten on their plates when they went out to play.

She threw the sandwiches down and smeared the peanut butter and jelly all across the counter. Meanwhile, outside in the yard, a stray dog was romping excitedly with the Montroses' dog, and Peter, then seven, became alarmed when one of the dogs jumped on Jennifer, making her cry out. Laurie let both dogs inside and they tore crazily through the house. One of them had urinated on the living room carpet by the time a neighbor answered little Peter's calls for help and came to take control of the situation.

When Florence arrived home she found every light in the house on and Laurie sitting catatonically in front of the snowing television set.

"She's really a nut," Florence thought.

When she and her husband discovered all the food that was missing and talked to a neighbor who had seen Laurie hauling away a filled garbage bag, they reported the incident to the Glencoe police. A female officer who took the initial report before turning the case over to Detective Mohr, reassured Mrs. Montrose that hers was a common complaint. "I can't tell you everything," she said. "But we're very familiar with Laurie Dann and have reason to be concerned about her whereabouts and what she's doing."

Mohr sought out Norm this time. "It seems strange," he said. "I don't know what's going on here, but she baby-sits in two places and things are missing, things are cut up, people say she acts weird."

"I don't think she'd steal," Norm said. "I really don't know, but I don't think so."

"We can't prove anything," Mohr said.

"No," Norm said. "But I want to take care of it. I'm not going to say she did anything wrong, but I do want to take care of it financially or whatever."

Mohr went back to the Montroses and dropped some heavy hints. They had a difficult court case, at best, and the alleged offenses were only misdemeanor violations anyway. A civil suit would be expensive. Maybe, he said, the Wassermans would offer some form of restitution.

Peter Montrose telephoned Norm and suggested they could work something out.

"There's no way you know she did it," Norm said.

"The neighbor saw her," Montrose said.

"You'd have to prove it in court," Norm countered. "She didn't do it. We didn't see her bring the food home, and she'd have no other place to take it. Why would she steal meat, anyway? My wife hasn't cooked in years."

The discussion went back and forth, with Norm attempting to establish Laurie's innocence before offering to pay the Montroses for the missing food. "I'm certain she hasn't done anything wrong," Norm reiterated. "But I don't want any trouble, and I don't want to put my daughter through a trial." He wrote out and mailed a check for $400 with the appended memo, "in full settlement of all claims."

Shortly afterward, the Montroses received numerous hang-up calls after midnight—the same kind of calls that Northwestern housing administrator Marc Boney was also getting that fall.

A neighbor of the Montroses who used Laurie despite the warnings said that she would wear long plastic gloves while baby-sitting there, that dining room walls and the kitchen table were hacked up with a pick-like object and that the rubber on their telephone extension cord was cut. She not only stole frozen food, but the Tupperware containers the food was stored in.

The family did not report Laurie to the police, however, because they were worried that Laurie might do something to their child in retaliation.

•

Norm remained convinced that Russell was out to get Laurie, and he spoke angrily to Russell's attorney, Rick Kessler, when he reached him by phone. "Stop harassing my daughter!" he said.

"What are you talking about?" Kessler said.

"Bullock works for you, doesn't he?"

"I know nothing about Bullock working for me."

"Someone is following my daughter around," Norm said. He reminded Kessler that Bullock had handed Laurie a business card when he talked to her the previous spring.

"Well, Bullock doesn't work for me," Kessler said. "And if he works for someone else, I'm not at liberty to disclose that."

Norm was equally sharp with Bullock when he reached him. "You're threatening Laurie," he said. "You're harassing her. You're following her."

"Wait a minute," said Bullock. "I am not. I'm a professional at what I do, and I'll tell you exactly what's happening. I'm real concerned because Russell and his family and his girlfriend have started getting these telephone calls again and Laurie is the source. The man has a right to live a normal life."

"No, no," Norm said. "She's the one getting the phone calls. He even sent her threatening letters this summer in Evanston."

"Nope," said Bullock. "He didn't know where she was at. I didn't know where she was at. It was my job to find her. No way could he have sent her letters. There's no way. I'm being quite honest with ya."

Norm calmed down as he listened to Bullock and turned downright polite by the end of the conversation. "The Evanston police have the letters; they're checking them out," he said. "I'll get back to you."

But he never did.

•

Jane Sterling, the attractive ex-cheerleader who had made Delta Gamma at Arizona, continued to haunt Laurie's memory.

That fall Laurie sent her a handwritten but unsigned post-card saying the Ford Modeling Agency was looking for children to attend a picnic meeting of prospective models at 346 Sheridan Road, in Glencoe, the Wasserman home, on an up-coming Sunday afternoon. She should bring her three kids along.

Jane was intrigued but hesitant, and was still undecided about what to do when Laurie called in the middle of the week. She gave a fake name and said she was from Ford.

"I got your note and I'm glad you called," Jane said. "I've been thinking about it, and the problem is that my kids don't have a portfolio or anything."

"Well, you know, sometimes they make the best models," Laurie said. "And we hear your kids are really cute."

"So how did you hear that?" said Jane, flattered. "I'll bet it was Rachel Liss right? Her kids do some modeling."

Laurie shuffled papers in the background. "It could have been," she said absently, as though there were hundreds of references and she didn't bother to keep track. "So, do you think you'll make it?"

"I'll sure think about it," Jane said.

She talked her husband into the idea, and when Laurie called back two days later, Jane said yes, she'd be there. But what should the kids wear?

"Keep in mind we're having ribs," Laurie said.

Whatever Laurie might have been planning for that Sun-day afternoon fell through. She called Jane Sterling in the morning as she was getting ready to leave, and told her she was going to have to cancel the picnic because her husband had just had a terrible accident.

"Oh, God," said Jane. "A car accident?"

Laurie hesitated. "Uh, yeah," she said. "But don't worry. We'll probably reschedule."

•

Tracy Simons of Glencoe called Laurie after seeing her flyer on the bulletin board at Dee Jay Foods less than a block away from the police station. Her references checked out, and Tracy even took the precaution of calling Edith to make sure Laurie was on the square.

"Has Laurie been doing this a long time?" Tracy asked.

"Oh, yes," said Edith. "And she loves children."

That was nice. And Laurie seemed to know kids—during the job interview in the Simonses' library she asked about such things as nap schedules for the one-year-old, the youngest of the three children. Laurie explained that she used to be a preschool teacher at the National College of Education in Evanston, and that she was currently employed part-time in admissions at Glenbrook Hospital. The only thing even the slightest bit out of the ordinary was that she wouldn't take off her peacoat and red leather gloves for the whole interview.

The first time she sat for three hours in the morning and again refused to remove her coat. Half an hour after she left, Tracy discovered the thermostat turned up to 84 degrees. The second time the same thing happened, and Laurie's hair was greasy and she looked spaced out when Tracy returned.

It is perhaps the best measure of the difficulty of finding baby-sitters on the North Shore that Tracy Simons called Laurie back for yet a third job. This time she would be alone with the baby for six hours, and by the time Tracy got to her friend's house where she was having lunch, she was feeling very uneasy about the whole arrangement. On a hunch, she called Glenbrook Hospital. The personnel department said no one by Laurie's name was employed there.

Tracy raced home, thinking her sitter was probably a mental outpatient—it would certainly explain her behavior. She found her sitting alone in her coat and gloves in the family room upstairs with all the blinds closed, the lights off and the heat turned up to 84 again. The baby was asleep in another room.

"Hi!" Tracy said with a false cheer that disguised her terror. "My appointment was canceled. I'm sorry. I hope I didn't ruin your plans."

"Oh, no," said Laurie absently. "I have a lot of errands to do."

Tracy paid her. "I'll call you the next time I need you," she said. "I'll call you soon."

She was worried for several days that if she fired Laurie outright or even so much as hinted there had been a problem, Laurie might come back and take revenge. She had already discovered clothing missing after Laurie's last visit, and it seemed unwise to anger her further.

Using her most apologetic voice, then, Tracy called Laurie and told her that she had decided to go back to work and hire a full-time live-in sitter.

"Well, that's probably better for you," Laurie said.

She didn't seem upset, but for weeks after she attacked the Simonses with hang-up calls.

•

Laurie also sat for the three girls of Mike and Julie Alt of Glencoe. She told them she worked in admissions at Glenbrook Hospital and that she was soon moving to California to further her schooling. Julie Alt found Laurie generally pleasant but moody and always, for some reason, cold. She frequently kept her coat and gloves on, even in warm weather.

Everything went normally the first half dozen times Laurie looked after the Alt girls, who were one, three and five years old, but then one day Julie came home at four P.M. and found the house torn apart as though a storm had gone through it.

"What happened here?" Julie asked.

"One of the neighbor girls had a fit," Laurie said. "She went crazy. She threw things around and wrote on the walls."

As the two women went through the house cleaning up, Julie noticed that some of the orange crayon markings on the wall were much too high for a child to have made and later, when she asked her girls about the mess, they said they had no idea what had happened. They did say, however, that Laurie had forced them to watch a scary movie on TV.

•

Finally, after four official complaints about theft of food and clothing, Floyd Mohr reached an agreement with Norm Wasserman—Laurie would not seek new baby-sitting clients, but could keep working for the families who liked her.

•

Laurie always seemed to know where Russell was, who he was with, what he was doing. He would see her following him. He would pick up the ringing telephone and find no one there. He would leave work and see her standing sentry in the distance.

In the early evening of October 2, 1987, almost exactly a year after the ice-pick stabbing, he finally called the police. He was on his way to his car after work when he once again saw Laurie waiting in the parking lot of the Combined Fitness Center next door to his office building. She wasn't saying anything, as usual, but this time seemed to be extremely agitated—not a good sign in a woman known to own a .357 Magnum.

"My ex-wife is crazy," Russell said, raising the Northbrook police on his car phone. "She's accused me for years of hassling her, so why is she following me now? She says she's so afraid of me, but here she is hounding me."

Northbrook responded with a squad car. Laurie first protested to the officer that she was only there to take an aerobics class, but as the interview continued the notion lit on her that she had been sexually attacked. She told them:

> I parked fifty feet from the east entrance to the building, facing east, and as I was leaving my car, Russell suddenly appeared and pushed me back into my car, making me fall backwards across the front seat and hit my head on the passenger side door. He took off his warm-up jacket and pushed it into my face to keep me from screaming.
>
> He told me, "Don't scream, I have a weapon."
>
> He told me he wanted me out of his territory. Then he said, "But as long as you're here and in a cute leotard, why not watch me masturbate in your face and listen to me talk dirty?"
>
> Then he shoved my head against the car door and started to masturbate.
>
> "If you'd talk dirty, I'd come faster," he said. "Come on, Laurie, tell me how much you like the outdoors, the excitement of being caught. Put my cock in your mouth, you bitch."
>
> When he finished he ran to his car, which was parked in the same lot four cars away, and drove to a different place in the same lot. A guy who works here came over to help me when I rolled down my car window and asked him for help. He saw me in the car with semen on my face. Then I found a roll of toilet paper in my car and wiped the semen off.

She didn't look as though she'd been beaten until later, when she came to the Northbrook police station to complete her statement. At that time she showed off a wound on her head and blood along her hairline. She also produced the wadded up toilet paper that she said had Russell's semen on it.

Both police officers who had come to the scene thought it was likely Laurie had made up the whole story. The parking lot was far too public a place for anyone to risk such an attack, let alone a prominent businessman whose colleagues and family were likely to pass nearby as they left work. That belief was bolstered several days later when Laurie refused to return to the Combined Fitness Center with investigators in order to find the man she said saw her immediately after the attack.

•

The various bizarre fragments of Laurie's life were starting to come together, and Rick Kessler wanted the prosecutors to do something about it. Kessler arranged for a meeting to review Laurie's case on October 27 in the Waukegan office of Mike Waller, Lake County Chief Deputy State's Attorney. At the meeting were Kessler, Waller, Detective McCafferty and private eye Frank Bullock.

Bullock had the new information about Laurie's behavior at Northwestern—ferreting it out of university and Evanston police records was his major contribution—and when he laid it out alongside the other reports, allegations and charges from various sources, the pattern was unmistakable and compelling.

But Waller could only shrug. The facts of the ice-pick case remained as inconclusive and circumstantial as ever, he said. No matter how peculiar she was, she hadn't done anything that could lead to a conviction.

Afterward, McCafferty, who was no fan of Russell's, said to Bullock, "I don't know what's going to happen, but it's going to happen."

•

"You're not going to believe this one," Laurie said to Pearl.

"What now?" Pearl said. The women were having dinner at a Mexican restaurant in Evanston several weeks later.

"I was in this parking lot," Laurie said. "And Russ came

out of nowhere and jumped in my car and held a knife to my throat and then masturbated on me."

"Huh," said Pearl noncommittally. If there had ever been any doubt in her mind that Laurie had gone off the deep end, her fanciful story that evening erased it.

"He wants to kill me," Laurie said.

"That's just not true," Pearl said. She changed the subject.

On their way out of the restaurant, a water glass suddenly slipped out of the pocket of Laurie's coat and fell to the floor. "Oh!" she said, looking up to catch a disapproving glance from the host. "I ... I ... have to go to the bathroom."

Pearl followed Laurie to the women's room and stood by the sink as Laurie sat in a stall for five minutes making no noise whatsoever. When she emerged, she made light clanging noises when she walked.

They went to see the romantic comedy *Made in Heaven* at the Evanston Theater, then Pearl drove Laurie back to her parents' house. As they pulled into the driveway, Laurie bent down and appeared to be gathering handfuls of flatware from around her feet.

"What is that?" Pearl asked.

"Oh, it's just something I left in your car," Laurie said, opening the door after she'd finished gathering up the knives, forks and spoons. "I gotta go. Bye."

Pearl shook her head sadly as Laurie scurried into the house. "This is too weird," she thought to herself. "I've had enough of this girl."

It was the last time they ever saw or spoke to each other.

•

On November 7, Laurie returned to the Marksman and bought a .32 caliber Smith & Wesson Terrier revolver for $245.

17

Taking
Care
of Laurie

Obsessive Compulsive Disorder, or OCD, was one of the most widely publicized mental ailments of the year 1987. Newspapers, magazines and television documentary shows offered scores of features on the related bizarre ritual behavior such as repeated handwashing, hoarding of useless materials, vacuuming of family pets and uncontrollable thoughts of aggression. New research showed that the syndrome was up to sixty times more prevalent than doctors had previously thought, and that one out of every forty Americans had obsessive thoughts or behaved compulsively in some way at some time.

On the bright side, however, people with OCD were never known to be dangerous and many of them could learn to lead outwardly normal lives. Medical science was also coming around to the conclusion that OCD was usually a physical ailment caused by increased neural transmission in specific parts of the brain, and therefore it could be treated by certain types of antidepressant medications. The most promising of the lot was the then-experimental drug clomipramine, small white tablets that suppressed or eliminated the unusual urges of more than two-thirds of all OCD patients. Reporters were guardedly referring to clomipramine as a miracle drug.

"Well," said ABC-TV's Barbara Walters at the conclusion of a *20/20* report on OCD that aired on March 19, "now that we have shown this report, maybe people will know that they can go to treatment centers and finally have an answer. What a relief it must be."

"There's so many people suffering unnecessarily," agreed reporter John Stossel, who was live on the set for the customary debriefing chat at the conclusion of each segment.

"Thank you for bringing this to our attention," Walters said.

"Yeah," said Walters' co-host Hugh Downs. "Really."

"Nice to have a happy ending," said Walters.

"I'll say," said Downs.

The Wassermans were just one of thousands of families for whom the emerging new information about OCD seemed to be very good news. Laurie's numerous idiosyncrasies, such as her preoccupation with good and bad numbers, her tendency to collect junk and her fetish for wearing rubber gloves, all squared perfectly with a diagnosis of this eminently treatable condition.

Norm arranged that year for her to see Dr. Phillip Epstein, a psychiatrist at Rush-Presbyterian St. Luke's medical center in Chicago. Epstein had sent her for cognitive testing to Dr. Allen Hirsch at the Mercy Medical Center in Chicago on September 8. He tested her short-term memory, had her name colors and objects, read, write and draw. She told him she had a need to feel clean and that she had trouble with concentration. Hirsch's only solid conclusion, he wrote back to Epstein, was that Laurie was not good at telling her left from her right. Perhaps, he suggested, she had a motivational problem. He prescribed alprazolam, a central nervous system depressant commonly used to manage anxiety disorders.

Epstein's billing records show that he saw her four times for therapy. He apparently concluded from what he knew that Laurie did in fact suffer from OCD and that she could benefit from clomipramine. It was actually one of three so-called tri-cyclic antidepressants—fluvoxamine and fluoxetine were the others—under investigation for their effectiveness in treating OCD. The drugs acted on the brain to slow the delivery of serotonin, a neurotransmitting chemical thought to be in excess inside the brains of OCD patients, causing them to feel extremely anxious. But Epstein was unable to write Laurie a direct simple prescription for clomipramine. The drug, which was already in general use for the treatment of depression in some seventy countries, was still undergoing clinical testing in the United States and was approved for use only by selected doctors. Epstein, not being one of those doctors, prescribed it instead through the Lud Bock Pharmacy in Montreal. The pharmacy took the order, along with Norm's credit card number, and mailed the pills to Laurie.

Epstein was a Fulbright scholar and a graduate of the University of Chicago Medical School. He had a minor specialty in the treatment of schizophrenia and was recent past chairman of the Chicago Psychopharmacology Task Force, a group formed to advise the city Board of Health on the drug treatment of patients at mental health centers. One of the recommendations of that task force was that doctors be required to chart and document accurately all prescriptions of psychoactive medications and their clinical rationale for the prescriptions.

The Food and Drug Administration has said that Epstein's use of a Canadian connection was a technical violation of that agency's guidelines for the shipment of restricted medications. His writing of the prescription through Montreal would later cause him to be the subject of an investigation by the Illinois Department of Professional Regulation.

Epstein was no stranger even then to drug-related controversies. In 1977, his patient Sheryl Harrington had died in the hospital after overdosing on Darvocet, a narcotic pain reliever. The lawsuit against him filed by Harrington's survivors alleged in part that Epstein failed to monitor her condition carefully and that the prescriptions he wrote were therefore improper. He ultimately settled the case out of court for $990,000.

Epstein was sued again in 1984 by another patient, attorney Susan Des Rosiers, who alleged that he indiscriminately prescribed drugs for her and performed electroshock therapy without her consent, resulting in brain damage and memory loss. That suit was still in the pretrial stage in Cook County Court in late 1989.

After Laurie began getting clomipramine in the mail, she typed up a letter to the OCD Foundation, a self-help organization in Vernon, Connecticut, that had formed in November of the previous year to inform patients of the latest information on specific therapies and refer them to psychiatrists and clinics that specialized in OCD. The letter requested a list of nearby treatment centers, an informational brochure and the name of an "OCD friend" for her.

The foundation wrote back and recommended Dr. John Greist, co-director of the Anxiety Disorder Center and the Center for Affective Disorders at the University of Wisconsin Hospital in Madison. His clinic was participating in several of the trials and was one of twenty-one institutions in the country officially dispensing clomipramine. He had thirty-two patients in the trial group, some of whom were coming from as far away as Indiana to get the drug.

On November 9, Norm Wasserman wrote to Greist that he had a thirty-year-old daughter suffering from OCD who had failed to improve under psychiatric treatment. She was unable to live any kind of normal life. Could he help?

Laurie followed up a week later with a letter to Greist's clinic asking to take part in a clinical trial of fluvoxamine. She noted in the letter that OCD was the cause of her divorce.

Greist agreed to treat Laurie, and Laurie was enthusiastic about moving back to Madison where she had spent the summer of 1977. It was three hours by car away from her parents, and she would once again find herself in a friendly, college atmosphere. Late in November she packed up her Honda hatchback and left Glencoe.

The campus in Madison lies on an isthmus between Lake Mendota and Lake Monona in the gently rolling countryside of south-central Wisconsin. It is more diverse architecturally than Northwestern University, and much larger. Madison is a true college town—though it is also the state capital—populated by tens of thousands of students and well stocked with bookstores, inexpensive restaurants and movie theaters. Laurie rented a room on the isolated far western edge of campus near the University Hospital for her first month, and she almost immediately had her first appointment with Dr. Greist and his assistant, Yoram Shwager, an Israeli graduate student. Greist's records reveal many details regarding the course of treatment Laurie underwent during her time with Greist and Shwager.

Shwager, who was assigned to be Laurie's primary therapist, helped Greist conduct the formal intake interview with her and her parents on November 30. She told him that the ritualistic behavior that troubled her as a little girl disappeared and didn't return until she reached her twenties. Her most prominent obsession, she said, was that something bad was going to happen to her, and she had developed a number of rituals to allay her anxiety. She brushed her teeth over and over, pulled her hair out by the strand, she couldn't touch restaurant silverware and she found herself compelled to go back and touch people who had touched her, even if they had only brushed past accidentally. The numbers 3 and 13 were very back luck for her and so, but to a lesser extent, were 6 and 9.

She took the sixty-six-question Yale-Brown test designed to determine the severity of OCD in a patient. She answered each question with a number from 0 to 4, with 0 meaning "never" and 4 meaning "severe, always."

She answered 4, "severe, always," to forty-two of the questions, including whether she worried that she had hurt somebody after bumping into them; whether she had been constantly frightened that something terrible might happen, such as a fire or a death in the family; whether she had feared contact with body fluids and excrement; whether she had ever been preoccupied with feeling worthless because she had sinned; and whether she had felt it necessary to stop the car and check if she had missed something important, such as having hit someone.

She answered 0, "never," to twenty-two questions, including these:

Have you ever been constantly preoccupied that you will lose control of your temper and hurt someone or kill someone even though you do not think that you are that kind of person normally?

Have you ever had to check potentially dangerous objects like guns,

Laurie Wasserman (bottom right) in her 6th-grade class photo at Red Oak Junior High School. She is the only student not looking at the camera. (*Chicago Tribune* files)

Laurie, here a high school sophomore, on the night of her boyfriend David Gallup's senior prom. (David Gallup)

Laurie as a junior at New Trier High School in Winnetka, Illinois. (David Gallup)

Laurie (bottom row, third from left) at the University of Arizona in 1976 as a pledge at the Alpha Delta Pi sorority. (*Chicago Tribune* files)

Russell Dann and Laurie at their wedding shower.

After the prolonged, bitter divorce, members of Russell's family used Magic Marker to black out Laurie's face in old wedding photographs.

As the relationship between Laurie and Russell deteriorated, Laurie went to the Marksman gun shop and purchased the first of her three guns. (Chuck Berman/*Chicago Tribune*)

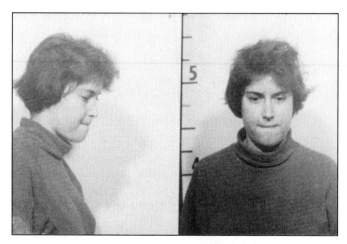

Laurie in a March 1988 mug shot taken after her arrest for shoplifting in a Madison department store. (*Chicago Tribune* files)

Hubbard Woods Principal Richard Streedain, his shirt bloodied from cradling one of Laurie's young victims, talks with parents in the immediate aftermath of the shootings. The list of wounded children is in his left hand. (Ernie Cox/*Chicago Tribune*)

Police lead Laurie's parents, Norm and Edith Wasserman, to command post as armed standoff continues. (Sandy Frankenbush/ *News-Voice*)

Glencoe Detective Floyd Mohr supports a distraught Norm Wasserman. (Val Mazzenga/*Chicago Tribune*)

Substitute teacher Amy Moses shows reporters how she grabbed Laurie's hand after Laurie had pulled a gun in Hubbard Woods classroom 7. (George Thompson/ *Chicago Tribune*)

Police Chief Herb Timm holds up a confiscated juice packet that Laurie had tainted with arsenic. (Chuck Berman/ *Chicago Tribune*)

Winnetka Police Sergeant Patricia O'Connell was one of the first law enforcement officers to arrive at the school after the shooting. She later headed up a multi-jurisdictional task force investigation into Laurie's life and crimes. (George Papajohn)

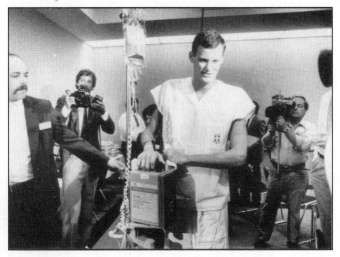

Two weeks after he was shot in the chest by Laurie Dann, Phil Andrew meets with the media in his hospital room (Jose More/*Chicago Tribune*)

Linda and Joel Corwin hold a photograph of their slain son, Nicky. (Courtesy of Linda and Joel Corwin)

knives or medicine over and over to make sure they are in a safe place?

She found middle ground only twice. The first time in answering a question asking if she felt anxiety relating to spending money (3, "moderate/frequently"), and the second time in a question asking if she were ever bothered by sexual thoughts or images of having sex with animals (2, "mild/ occasionally").

Shwager and Greist used the test results to conclude that Laurie's OCD was centered on aggressive obsessions and that her compulsions were a reaction to the fear that something terrible would happen and that she would be responsible. She might have been a candidate for the clomipramine or fluvoxamine trials, but she revealed in the interview that she was already taking clomipramine obtained through Montreal. Greist nevertheless suggested the dosage clomipramine Laurie ought to be taking: one 50 milligram tablet each evening, and if the side effects were mild, two and then three tablets each evening.

Greist believed that the most effective treatment for OCD combined drug therapy with behavioral therapy that required confronting fears and eliminating ritualistic behavior. Shwager had Laurie buy a paperback titled *Understanding and Coping with Anxiety*, by British psychiatrist Dr. Isaac M. Marks. The book outlines strategic steps a patient can take to overcome phobias and anxieties, and it includes homework exercises.

In her first session alone with Shwager on December 3, Laurie created a hierarchy of her problems from easiest— getting dressed, talking on the phone—to most difficult— touching people, shopping. He gave her short lists of tasks and goals along these lines, and Laurie also wrote little instructional Post-it notes to herself, which she put up in her room to help her accomplish normal tasks in a methodical fashion: "Shoes, keys, chair," said one. "Chair, shirt, more than one thing off at a time," said another.

Norm Wasserman and Dr. Greist sat in with Laurie and Shwager for a thirty-five-minute conference four days later, a Wednesday. Laurie said the clomipramine had at first given her a tremor and caused her whole body to go rigid, but those problems went away and didn't come back even when she doubled the dose. Her biggest problem, she said, was lethargy, for which Greist suggested she drink a cup of coffee now and then. He told her to triple her original dose of clomipramine and to begin seeing Shwager three or four times a week for behavior therapy. She agreed to come in Sunday, Thursday and Saturday the following week.

During the Sunday session Laurie practiced touching objects that didn't belong to her. Her hands quivered as she moved, but she was able to do everything Shwager asked her to. She also reported that she'd been able to walk a mile without engaging in her usual rituals of avoiding cracks, and that she felt good.

She and Shwager spoke at length during the next two sessions about her feelings of wanting to hurt herself, and they practiced again having her touch objects that weren't hers. When Greist looked in on the session she complained that the clomipramine was giving her dry mouth and she didn't think it was helping. He suggested she continue trying to increase her dosage until the drug began to have its desired effect.

Just as she seemed to be making progress, it was time for the three-week winter holiday vacation. Shwager handwrote two pages of instructions for Laurie to take with her back to Glencoe. They included:

To Laurie:

* Do not go back to the arrows and the cars in the parking lot.

* Do not pull your hair on Tuesdays, Thursdays, Saturdays and Sundays.

* You can pull your hair on the rest of the week, but only between 10-11 p.m.

* Go out at least three times to either a movie, theater, friends, etc.

* Do not go back to tempting places in your hometown.

To Parents:

* Make sure within two days that Laurie will have an

extension for the telephone line so she can speak from her room.

* Do not watch her closely and do not make any remark or comment about her behavior whatsoever.

* Keep a diary and, every day, at 8 p.m., sit with Laurie and mark, only after she reports, without arguing, the date and hour. How much did she succeed in the instruction she had (in quantity of times); the amount of anxiety she had, between 0 and 100; don't criticize her at all, just remember the effort and trouble she's going through [to follow] my instructions. Send the diary back with her.

●

On Laurie's first day back home, December 20, she suffered a severe reaction to the clomipramine—perhaps related to an accidental overdose—and began vomiting every ten minutes for nearly twelve hours.

Norm called Highland Park Hospital at 4:42 the next morning, and followed up with a two-minute call to the hospital an hour later. At 8:51 A.M. he finally reached a family physician, who prescribed Compazine suppositories. Compazine, like the thioridazine Laurie had been taking while under Dr. Greendale's care, is one of a number of antipsychotic drugs in the phenothiazine class, but one of Compazine's major uses is for the treatment of severe nausea. The *United States Pharmacopeia Drug Information for the Consumer* guide and the *Physicians' Desk Reference* both warn against taking such drugs along with central nervous system depressants such as alprazolam, which Dr. Hirsch had prescribed for Laurie, and lorazepam, which Dr. Epstein had prescribed. The Compazine stopped Laurie's retching but apparently caused her hallucinations throughout the next night, during which she was jittery and agitated.

Norm spoke long-distance to Greist at his home in Madison for seventeen minutes that evening. Greist instructed him to take Laurie off all medication and call him the next morning. But not long afterward Laurie's jaw went rigid and Norm took her to the emergency room in Highland Park where doctors administered benztropine, an antipalsy medication often used to counter severe reactions to phenothiazines such as Compazine. It rapidly relieved her symptoms.

When Laurie came home, she sequestered herself with the telephone and made fourteen quick hang-up calls to homes of people she wished to harass. Her list of victims was expanding, and now included Jeff Taylor's father, Sidney, and numerous friends of the Taylors and Russell Dann. Many of the calls were to unlisted numbers that Laurie had copied from school and country club directories she'd found in the homes when she'd worked as a baby-sitter.

She called Greist early the next morning for a three-minute consultation, during which Greist suggested she try again to resume taking the clomipramine.

On the Monday after Christmas, Laurie returned to the Marksman, where just a month earlier she'd bought a Smith & Wesson .32. This time she picked out a .22 caliber semiautomatic Beretta for $209.15.

Late afternoon the next day she placed two harassing hang-up calls to Russell's office at Dann Brothers. Then in the six hours after midnight she made fifty-five more hang-up calls.

Interspersed among the nuisance calls were daytime efforts to reach several families for whom she had been a baby-sitter, including the Alts and the Hawkins family, Australians who were friends with the Rushes in Winnetka. She also tried to contact Pearl Gelb to see if Pearl wanted to see her, but Pearl never returned her calls.

Laurie then returned to the Marksman after her three-day cooling-off period had elapsed and picked up the Beretta, her third gun. Later that same night she made fifty-nine harassing calls between the hours of eleven P.M. and one A.M. Three nights later came another twenty-eight calls between 1:52 and 2:30 A.M.

Norm was apparently unaware of what Laurie was up to. She had not passed along the instructional note Shwager had written for him and Edith, and his letter to Greist on New Year's Eve was uncharacteristically buoyant.

Norm told the doctor that he and Edith were deeply appreciative of all the help he had given Laurie. He wrote Greist that Laurie liked him more than any psychiatrist she had seen and that the behavioral therapy appeared to be working. Though Laurie was still seriously ill, Norm wrote, she seemed to be taking the first steps toward recovery.

•

The phone harassment over the holidays was so bad it prompted four of Laurie's major victims to ask for a special meeting with Glencoe director of public safety Robert Bonneville, Floyd Mohr's boss. Present at the meeting, held at the Glencoe police department in January, were Jeff Taylor, Jeff's brother, Scott, Noah Rosen and Russell's friend Murray Hyman, who worked with Noah at Goldman-Sachs and was also a friend of Russell's. The men had decided not to include Russell because they wanted to appear to Bonneville as objective and level-headed members of the community with no direct involvement in the divorce case.

Bonneville, who the other men thought looked comically déclassé in his tan corduroy suit, listened politely as they explained how Laurie had been harassing them by telephone and how they felt her behavior was alarming in the context of the ice-pick stabbing in Highland Park, Laurie's problems in the dorm in Evanston and her run-ins with baby-sitting clients.

"She's baby-sitting children in this town," Scott Taylor said, unaware that she had, in fact, gone back to Madison. "And the people sitting here in your office are not the people in the gravest danger. We're careful. We're on the lookout. The people who are in the gravest danger are the people who don't know anything about Laurie. A child in this community is going to be killed unless you do something about her."

Bonneville seemed taken aback at the scope of the problem. He explained that police departments in neighboring villages do not necessarily exchange information, and that the communication problem might be particularly bad because Glencoe and Highland Park are in different counties. "We can't just incarcerate someone for acting weird," he added. "We can all know she did something, but being able to prove it, now, that's something else."

"So society can't deal with her until she actually does spill blood?" Scott Taylor asked rhetorically. "We can't protect ourselves from her until she commits public violence?"

"You guys have to be vigilant," Jeff Taylor interrupted.

"You've got to take it seriously that she's a problem person. This girl is crazy. She has a gun. Something terrible is going to happen."

"She's a ticking bomb," Scott Taylor said. "She's going to kill somebody someday, and I don't want us looking back and saying, 'This could have been prevented if only...'"

"Our hands are tied," Bonneville said. "I know we've only been hearing part of the story, but so has Highland Park, so has Lake County."

"Well, can't you form some sort of North Shore task force or something? Work together? Get the big picture?"

"I don't know about that," Bonneville said. "It seems like a good idea. I'll call Highland Park and talk to them. Don't worry, boys. We've got it under control."

The meeting lasted forty-five minutes, and the men went away frustrated and demoralized.

But they did get some action. Shortly after the meeting, the Glencoe Department of Public Safety issued a news bulletin, published in the local weekly paper, telling parents to obtain a roster of information about their baby-sitters including a list of references, make and model of car and Social Security number.

Such information, the bulletin said, could be useful "for a variety of reasons."

•

Laurie returned to Madison after the holiday break very depressed. She told her graduate student therapist Yoram Shwager that her relationship with her parents was very troubled; he noted that she was back to square one with her OCD, collecting objects, layering her life with rituals and superstitions. Much of her strange behavior was harmless but, as Shwager could tell by looking at the side of Laurie's head, some was not: she'd been worried about wax buildup in her ear canal, and so had soaked pieces of cloth in melted candle wax, wound the cloth around the end of a pencil and jammed it into her ear. Then she set the cloth on fire, thinking it would draw the ear wax out.

Dr. Greist wrote her a prescription for antibiotic boric acid powder capsules to treat the resulting inflammation. She had the prescription filled at the Wisconsin Student Association Community Pharmacy, a counterculture drug store that sold numerous herbs, potions and organic products along with conventional sundries.

Laurie asked at the pharmacy where she could find a massage therapist, and a clerk gave her the number of Jennifer Nehls, another clerk at WSA who worked part-time at the offices of chiropractor Jacqueline Beaudet.

Laurie's first appointment with Nehls was mid-afternoon on February 13. She arrived on time but appeared very tense—her back was rigid and unbending, and Nehls had the impression that Laurie "wasn't really inhabiting her body," as she put it.

During the entire one-hour-fifteen-minute massage Laurie remained tense. She told Nehls that she had just moved to Madison from Illinois, where she'd worked in a hospital. She said she was at the University of Wisconsin to get her degree in hospital administration. "I've had a lot of massages in my life," she said.

Nehls found Laurie false and brittle, as though she were playing an unfamiliar role onstage. She seemed angry, like a misfit determined to show everyone she wasn't really the loser she appeared to be.

Laurie paid for the $35 massage in cash and set up another appointment for a week from the following Thursday. That appointment was for 7:30 P.M., but she arrived an hour early, as the chiropractic office was shutting down for the day. She told the receptionist she had a 6:30 appointment and that she would simply wait for Nehls, who would arrive any moment.

For almost an hour she was alone in the office. She wandered the halls of the building and found the door unlocked at the law firm of Antoniewicz & Gregg next door to the chiropractors. She walked in and stole several sheets of stationery off a desk—material that she would put to use later on. She returned to Beaudet's office, entered the lunchroom area and looked through the cupboards until she found a jar of honey. She took the honey back out to the waiting area and poured it all over the keyboard of the receptionist's computer.

At about 7:15 P.M., Nehls arrived and found Laurie standing in the doorway to the lunchroom.

"What are you doing in here?" Nehls asked angrily.

"I've got a terrible headache," Laurie replied. "I was looking for some aspirin."

Nehls found Laurie a couple of aspirin tablets and then put her on the table for her massage. During the rubdown, Laurie was once again very rigid. She said she had attended a lecture at the university given by a massage therapist. She said the speaker knew nothing about the subject.

"You're a lot better," Laurie said. "I was telling all the people in the lecture there about you. I told them they should come to you."

It was plaintive flattery, sincere but inappropriate, like the gifts Laurie used to take to high school for the popular girls. Nehls changed the subject.

After the massage was over, Laurie sat bolt upright and, after paying her bill again in cash, shot out the door without saying a word.

Nehls shook her head. The woman seemed even more tense than when the massage had started.

As Nehls relaxed in the lounge area, she looked up and saw Laurie walking back and forth in the hallway, her steps choppy, her head down, first thirty feet one way, then thirty feet the other. Nehls thought she might be lost, but decided against offering help because it might embarrass her.

When she left the office later she saw Laurie again pacing in the parking lot, still looking confused. She was making strange, sharp-angled turns and appeared very agitated.

"Are you lost?" Nehls asked. "Do you need help?"

"No," Laurie said, and walked quickly away.

Nehls watched her scurry off. "Oh, God," she thought. "Poor woman."

When a secretary discovered the honey in the computer system the next day, Nehls decided to confront Laurie as soon as possible. But when she saw her next it was from a distance across the pharmacy, and Laurie turned quickly when their eyes met, left the store and never returned.

•

Norm wrote a short note to Laurie in late January on his "from the desk of" memo pad telling her that he was praying that the medication and therapy were working. He asked her to "hang in there and stay out of problems."

He wrote again a week later, expressing disappointment that Laurie did not want him to visit her in Madison on January 31. He said he was eager to see her instead the following week and told her he was prepared to do anything to help her get well. He wrote that he thought about her all the time and was frustrated that he could not do more for her. He closed the letter by urging her to continue cooperating with Dr. Greist and Yoram Shwager.

•

At Greist's suggestion, Laurie increased her dosage of clomipramine to 200 milligrams a day, even though she told him she didn't think the drug was doing her much good. She reported that the new, high dosage helped cut down on the duration of her obsessions, but that it gave her tremors and made it hard for her to remember things. Greist decided to add 600 milligrams a day of lithium carbonate to the pharmaceutical mix to try to help balance her brain chemistry.

The use of lithium salt to even out the highs and lows of manic depression was pioneered in the 1920's by an Australian-born psychiatrist who'd noticed that many of his troubled patients improved when they worked in glass and ceramic factories, where lithium was widely used. Much subsequent research found lithium treatments effective in mood control and the reduction of aggression, but only within a narrow range of blood levels—overdoses caused nausea, fatigue, dizziness and stupors.

Greist was a big believer in lithium and ran the Lithium Information Center out of his office, dispensing information and studies on his use of the chemical to treat both manic depression and OCD.

Manic depression is commonly known to doctors as bipolar affective disorder. In a related ailment, unipolar affective disorder, the patient is often deeply depressed. Psychiatrists frequently treat unipolar disorder with a group of drugs called tricyclics, of which clomipramine is one.

Generally, such drugs are not prescribed to those suffering from manic depression because in lifting a patient out of depression they can go on to trigger frenzied behavior. Specifically, the manufacturer's warning on clomipramine said:

In seriously depressed patients, the possibility of suicide should be borne in mind and may persist. Activation of latent schizophrenia or aggravation of existing psychotic manifestation in schizophrenic patients may occur. Patient with manic-depressive tendencies may experience hypo-manic or manic shifts.

Laurie was also taking birth control pills—known to be associated with depression—as well as lorazepam, an antianxiety medication prescribed to her by Dr. Epstein. The drug is a commonly used tranquilizer in the same drug class—benzodiazepines—as the alprazolam Dr. Hirsch had prescribed for her, and the *Physicians' Desk Reference* warns against using it on psychotic patients or those suffering from depressive disorder.

•

Laurie was lurching through therapy with Shwager. Some days it went well—she was able to realize and articulate that the stress of her marriage had caused her to resort to compulsive rituals. She was also able to speak of the role of her own guilt feelings in her relationship with her parents, and how that relationship now seemed to trigger her "bad" behaviors. Her mood and confidence soared. "I'm ready to get well," she said.

But other times Laurie balked at performing such seemingly simple exercises as touching the same button three times in a row. Three was unlucky. She wouldn't do it, she couldn't do it, she wasn't ready.

Still other times she didn't show up for her appointments at all. Shwager would call her and leave messages, and she would refuse to contact him until he called her father and forced the issue.

•

Law enforcement investigators and medical authorities who have studied Laurie's life have been particularly interested in her pharmaceutical habits in Madison because she took so many different drugs in such a short time. The effects of combined psychoactive drugs on an individual are impossible to predict, doctors say, especially when a diagnosis is not sharp. Psychiatry is an inexact science under the best of circumstances, and the notion that Laurie suffered primarily from OCD came from doctors—Epstein and Greist—who apparently never communicated with each other and who had not treated her at length. They relied for their information on Laurie, a chronic liar, and her father, a man of leonine protective instincts, and they did not consult with Dr. Greendale, who had seen her off and on for several years at the onset of many of her difficulties.

Laurie's interest in guns, her carving up of furniture, her stabbing of Russell, her stealing and her maniacal telephone harassment all suggest a mental condition far more serious than simple OCD—perhaps manic-depression, schizophrenia or borderline personality disorder. It is extremely unusual for individuals with OCD to behave in a dangerously aggressive manner, and, in fact, many of the obsessive fears and compulsive behaviors associated with OCD are caused by a desire to *avoid* harming others. A woman who suffers from OCD may, for example, worry that she has unwittingly run over a pedestrian with her car, so she will circle a city block several times checking and rechecking the same area, looking for a body.

But whatever was the matter with Laurie Dann, the fact remains that the longer she stayed in Madison, the further she swirled downward into madness.

18

The Psycho
Elevator
Lady

When Laurie returned to the University of Wisconsin after New Year's 1988, she moved from her apartment near the hospital across campus to the Towers of Madison, a private, very modern dormitory just a few steps off State Street, the main college shopping strip. It was a $5,800 a year luxury residence hall, "the ultimate in student living" according to advertisements, and it offered weekly maid service, a sun deck, fitness center and twenty-four-hour answering service. The high-fashion high rise ("your ticket to first-class living . . . a step above") was so popular among the sons and daughters of wealthy North Shore Jewish families that it was known across campus as Jap Towers.

Laurie was already familiar with the Towers from her summer there eleven years earlier. It also had a cafeteria that served meals, which was important because she had been trying to eat at the hospital but was so fixated on rituals involved with going outdoors and walking down the sidewalk that the six-block trip from her old apartment was sometimes more than she could endure. The Towers also proved relatively easy to get into for a nonstudent, as the management didn't really check to see if tenants were enrolled at the university as they were supposed to be.

Norm filled out Laurie's housing application for her. He

wrote down that she was a transfer student in the graduate journalism program. For verisimilitude, he shaved seven years off her age.

She was assigned to the vacant half of suite 610, a room like all the others with spare, blond wood furnishings and a shared bathroom. The girl on the other side was Jolie Pollock, a freshman from Highland Park. Jolie, coincidentally, had been friends with one of Russell Dann's cousins in high school, and she recognized the last name immediately. "I know someone in your family," she said. Laurie didn't correct her mistake and continued with the introductions.

She told Jolie she was a sophomore scholarship student and that she'd transferred from Northwestern where she'd been active with Delta Gamma—the sorority that had rejected her at Arizona. She said she had gone to Highland Park High for two years, then transferred to New Trier and graduated in 1986. She added that she had a boyfriend from home who would be visiting from time to time, but that it shouldn't be a problem.

They got along fine, but Jolie could tell that there was something a little off center about her new roommate. Laurie's clothes were out of fashion and her room had no personality— no art prints, no rock posters, nothing on the walls.

In the first few weeks of the semester, Jolie began to pick up on some of Laurie's other peculiarities. She had no social skills, made no friends, had no books, never went to class and never studied even though she claimed to be staying up late working on calculus problems.

She said one night that she was going out with her boyfriend and that they would be staying in a hotel, but when Jolie returned from an overnight sorority function early the next day she found Laurie alone in her room.

Laurie's side of the suite started to smell slightly of urine, and her unwashed, greasy hair often stuck out from her head at odd angles. Sometimes she would run the shower for several hours while lying in her bed. Other times she would wander aimlessly through the halls of the dorm wearing her unflattering sweatshirt, peering into people's rooms, jiggling locked doorknobs and riding the elevators.

All hours of the day and night residents of the Towers would see the elevator doors open and there would be Laurie Dann, just standing in the cab, often having already punched several buttons. She usually looked dazed and she refused to get off when the elevator reached the top floor. "I'm going higher," she said.

Rocky Levy, a freshman, got on the elevator one evening with a group of friends and, as usual, Laurie was standing quietly off to one side. When he saw all the buttons had been punched he turned first to his friends. "Did you do that?" he asked. They said they hadn't. He turned to Laurie. "Did you?"

Laurie flushed with anger. "No!" she said. Her once quiet voice had turned loud and ragged. "What makes you think I did it?"

Rocky backed down. This woman was a real piece of work. He and many other students began referring to her as the Psycho Elevator Lady, a nickname that seemed especially apt when they noticed she never touched the buttons with her fingers but used a pencil or the sleeve of her shirt instead. Kinder residents called her just the Elevator Girl.

Jolie found a note on Laurie's desk that appeared to be a schedule for riding the elevators: "2 in, 6 out, 6 in, 2 out..." The schedule went on to include notations for other floors including B for basement. Her usual practice was to get off the elevator on the fifth floor, walk up to the sixth, ride the elevator down to the second, and repeat the cycle over and over.

It was more intriguing than scary. Late at night, when Jolie and her friends would gather in another dorm room and talk would turn to Laurie, they would say to one another, "God, what is the deal with her?"

•

When Laurie wasn't lurking in the elevators or prowling the halls of the Towers, she usually parked herself in front of the big-screen TV in the lobby. She appeared to be an indiscriminate video junkie, watching movies, cartoons, static, anything. Front desk receptionist Jami Halperin used to shake her head in amazement at the way Laurie would sit in front of the screen all night switching from channel to channel to channel without ever stopping to see what was on.

If other students were watching when she entered the lounge, she would declare, "The TV is mine," and change the station to whatever she wanted to watch. No one wanted to argue with her.

She appeared particularly fascinated by a program called *The Love Connection*, a modern, somewhat risque version of *The Dating Game* in which men and women met each other on one episode, then returned on a later episode to tell the audience what happened on their first date.

Ivy Rosenbaum, a freshman, once sat with Laurie to watch an episode of *L.A. Law*. One of the subplots of the episode concerned the way the prime suspect in the murder of a child went free because the only witness was killed.

"This is so unfair," Laurie said, obviously agitated. "It's just so unfair."

●

Twice each day, just before the cafeteria opened for lunch and again for dinner, Laurie put on gloves and went down to be first in the meal line.

"Why do you wear gloves to eat?" Jolie asked her, trying to sound casual.

"It's the metal," Laurie improvised. "I'm sensitive to hot and cold metal."

Usually they were red, light woolen winter gloves with leather palm pads, but sometimes she chose kitchen gloves or surgical gloves, which she also used when she did laundry. She often wore a red sweatsuit or the pink one Russell had given her before their separation, but once she attracted attention by coming down to eat dressed in pajamas and fuzzy slippers. Another time, when she was in jeans and a sweater, she rode the exercise bike across from the entrance to the cafeteria for half an hour before dinner, then went through the line perspiring heavily.

Inside the cafeteria she placed cutlery on the conveyor belt and stared at it as it traveled down the line; she stood at the head of the food line gazing at the entrees in a puzzled trance; and she used her own fork instead of the community tongs at the salad bar. When other students crossed her path in the serving area, she would sometimes move backwards robotically, pacing out exactly two tile squares; other times she would move only along the lines of the tiles, making 90 degree turns.

Early in the semester she often ate alone, looking forlorn and exhausted at her own table in the cafeteria. Haley Bareck, an effervescent freshman from Arlington Heights, a middle-income suburb northwest of Chicago, noticed Laurie and felt sorry for her. Haley almost always ate with the same chatty group of six young women, and one day she asked Laurie to join their table.

Laurie accepted this gesture of friendship, and she soon became a regular member of the mealtime crew. She listened intently to every conversation and was always quick with questions about boyfriends, classes, dates, jobs and social events that had been mentioned at previous meals.

Sometimes she even took notes on what the women were saying. She told one member of the group that the notes were for a class. "I have to study people and write about them," she said.

She fueled many discussions with her analysis of people and situations, and the other women at the table were quietly surprised that the Psycho Elevator Lady was actually extremely lucid and sometimes very talkative and upbeat.

She cheerfully offered anecdotes about herself—she called them Laurie Stories—though much of what she related was just more of the same old lies about her classes and her boyfriends. The girls wondered about the contradictions in her life—she kept saying she was a freshman, but the journalism project she claimed to be working on would have made her a junior or senior. She also said she used to belong to Delta Delta Delta at Northwestern but wasn't reinitiating because it would cost too much. That was absurd. Tri-Delts were always rich girls.

But some of the Laurie Stories were reasonably close approximations of the truth, such as her account of how she fooled her old boyfriend into thinking she was her own twin sister. Another time she sat down at dinner, laughed cheerfully and said she had been bored that day so she just dropped into a dentist's office. "He removed two wisdom teeth," she said. "And I didn't even have to pay for it."

The other women exchanged smirking, doubtful glances.

"No way, Laurie," Haley said.

"Really," Laurie said. And, in fact, Laurie had walked in unannounced to the dental offices of Dr. Stanley Pollan that day and asked if he could see her. She didn't have an appointment, but another patient had just canceled so he agreed to put her in the chair. He cleaned her teeth, took a full set of X rays and extracted two wisdom teeth.

In the dentist's chair, she told Pollan that she and her husband had just moved to Madison because her husband had been transferred by his company. The treatment wasn't free, as Laurie had told her dinner companions, but she managed to make it so by leaving a false address for Pollan to send his $204 billing statement.

Other times, Laurie lied reflexively, telling her audience what she thought they wanted to hear. When Haley mentioned that she worked summers at the Chas A. Stevens women's clothing store in the Chicago suburb of Mount Prospect, Laurie quickly said that, oh, she worked in the Chas A. Stevens in the suburb of Skokie.

•

One day, Laurie came to lunch carrying a photograph of a lovely woman with long, pretty hair. "This is me!" she said, showing it to the others.

It seemed incredible at first, but upon close inspection the girls could see that the woman in the picture was, indeed, their weird cafeteria friend in better days. Haley and the other girls in turn took in the image with both wonder and pity.

"Your hair..." Haley said, groping for a tactful way to compliment the photograph without insulting Laurie. "It's great. Why did—"

"One day I just felt like cutting it off," Laurie shrugged. "So I took scissors and cut it."

Not only had her hair become greasy, short and uneven, she had started to dye it a dark, unflattering shade of red as the semester went on. At the same time, her face was taking on a rosy cast and she was shoveling in enormous quantities of food. She would eat steadily, not frantically, and go back to the cafeteria line six or seven times during the ninety-minute lunch period and the nearly two-hour dinner period, filling her tray with helpings of each of the four entrees and grabbing dozens of cookies. She stuffed extra cookies into the folds of her sweatsuit and smuggled them along with dozens of pieces of flatware out past student sentries posted at the door.

In order to satisfy her compulsion to eat—probably a side effect of the clomipramine—Laurie had to leave the cafeteria periodically to vomit in the bathroom. A group of Jolie's friends followed her one day, heard her purging herself inside a toilet stall and told the building staff. The staff posted a note at the front desk of the dining room saying, "Please don't let Laurie Dann leave and come back for meals."

•

Laurie bought a cake at the grocery store one day and invited all her dining-hall friends to come to her room and eat it with her. The girls said, well, they might, but then none of them did. They didn't really think of her as a friend in that way.

Laurie often told her dining companions that her long-distance boyfriend was coming up to see her, but the only visitor anyone ever saw was her father, who drove up to Madison from Glencoe several times to check up on her and meet with her therapists, Shwager and Dr. Greist.

Norm frequently returned to the Chicago area from Florida to check up on business interests, leaving Edith behind in Florida. Like many northerners, the Wassermans drove down at the beginning of the winter season in order to have a car at their disposal, drove home in the spring and flew back in between as necessary.

Laurie cleaned up her room for her father, Jolie noticed, and he and Laurie would join the girls in the cafeteria. He was always deeply tanned and never said much. Haley got the distinct impression that he was frightened about what was becoming of his daughter and didn't know what to do about it.

Norm would take Laurie out to the movies in Madison. One night, after they returned from the University Square four-screen cinema, one of the resident advisors asked Laurie if she and her father had enjoyed the film. She said that, actually, they had gone into different theaters and seen different movies.

•

For much of that winter and spring of 1988, Norm and Edith were in Boca Raton, where they kept track of Laurie by telephone and through the mail. On February 21, Norm wrote Laurie a letter from Florida.

After describing his tennis game and remarking on the warm weather, he told her she must have faith that her doctors would come up with a cure for her condition. She also should remember, he wrote, that she could call him or Edith anytime she needed them. Once again, he urged her to stay out of trouble.

Edith also wrote to Laurie, but focused primarily on her day-to-day life in Florida, telling her about the new cleaning lady and VCR. She also told her to "hang in there" because help surely was on the way.

Late in February, Laurie rooted through Jolie Pollock's trash and found an empty Colgate toothpaste box. She took the box across the hallway, set one end on fire and shoved the burning end under the door of the suite occupied by a freshman from Ohio who was part of a small group that had reportedly been teasing her earlier in the day.

The smoke triggered fire alarms and the entire building was evacuated. Damage to the student's carpet and door was minor and no one could really prove who had set the blaze.

Then in early March, Jolie found Coca-Cola spilled onto the keyboard of her new Macintosh computer.

She went to the next room to confront Laurie. "Did you use my computer?" she said. "Do you know anything about why there would be Coke spilled into it?"

"Oh, no," Laurie said, looking up innocently. "I don't even drink Coke."

Not long afterward, Jolie found that her portable stereo had been dropped and was no longer working. She let that incident slide but began locking the door that led into her room. Laurie started doing the same.

When Jolie went home one weekend, she looked through recent Highland Park High School yearbooks to see if she could find a Laurie Dann. There wasn't one.

Rocky Levy told her, "You're going to wake up some night and she's going to be standing over you with a knife."

•

Among Laurie's other favorite haunts were the pay telephones in the lobby and outside the dorm. She didn't have a phone in her room, so the public phones were her only instruments for continuing her campaign against her enemies in the Chicago area.

Early in the spring Laurie called Bruce and Florence Montrose of Glencoe, the couple who had hired her to baby-sit and later accused her of stealing food. "Your children are going to die," she said, and hung up. Shortly thereafter she called Susie Taylor and sang in a falsetto, "Susie, Susie, you're going to die. I'm a psychopath."

She also called Scott Dann in his office at Dann Brothers. "Scott, I need help," she said, making no effort to disguise her voice. "I'm in trouble. I'm sick. If you don't help me, I'll kill your brother."

These and other spoken threats marked a major change in Laurie's behavior—up until then she had never done anything other than hang up on her targets seconds after they answered.

When Elaine Dann, Russell's mother, heard about Laurie's new brazenness, she told Noah Rosen's mother she was convinced Laurie was serious—that Russell was going to end up dead before it was all over.

On March 10, Beth Rosen received four threatening phone calls in a row, beginning at 5:50 P.M. Two of the calls were hang-ups. In two of the other calls, the caller, whose muffled voice sounded a lot like Laurie's, said, "Beth is going to die."

Beth called Director Bonneville of the Glencoe Department of Public Safety. She remembers him saying, "We know all about her. We wish we could do more. She's a very sick girl. We've tried dealing with her father—you could try that yourself, but I don't think you'll get anywhere."

Bonneville suggested that Beth call Floyd Mohr, which

she did. Mohr, however, was not nearly as sympathetic. "You can't positively ID the voice if she muffled it," Mohr said. "So you can't prove the threat came from her."

"I'm pretty sure it did," Beth said.

"Don't worry, we've talked to her psychiatrists," Mohr said, referring to Dr. Greendale and Dr. Epstein. "They say she's harmless."

"So why did she stab her ex-husband in the chest with an ice pick?"

"You can't prove that," Mohr said. "That's not been proven. How do you know Russell didn't set it up himself?"

"Because I'm Russell's friend," Beth said. "I know Russell, and I know he would not stab himself."

"Uh huh," said Mohr.

"I hate to say it," Beth said, "but this is not going to end until somebody really gets hurt."

Mohr sighed. "I can only repeat what the psychiatrist said: 'She's not harmful to herself or others.'"

"Well, I disagree," said Beth. She hung up.

19

Making Plans

As Laurie sank further into her closed, paranoid world, she began plotting to accomplish what she had told her doctors all along was her worst fear: she was going to make something terrible happen.

On Saturday, March 12, 1988, she slipped into a lab across the hallway from Greist's office at the University of Wisconsin Hospital and Clinics Building. A technician saw her looking into a cabinet where chemicals were stored. Three days later, employees discovered arsenic and lead solutions missing from the cabinet, along with a laboratory coat and several beakers filled with stannous chloride. The chemist in charge of the lab was struck by what an unusual sort of theft it was. Such chemicals were only useful for performing mercury level analysis on urine specimens—or for killing something.

Laurie had already been to the Madison City Library and stolen a 1974 book, *Handbook of Poisoning;* a 1962 book, *Poisoning by Drugs and Chemicals;* and a 1977 book, *Poison Antidotes and Anecdotes*. She also took the catalog cards with her so that the books would be less likely to turn up missing.

She went after disguises at Madison's West Towne Mall on March 14, where she shoplifted a pair of white slacks from the Limited Express, a cubic zirconium ring from Prange's department store and four wigs and two hair clips off the mannequins at J.C. Penney. She stuffed her take into the sleeve of the winter coat draped over her arm. Two teenaged boys saw her plundering the mannequins and told store employees, who tailed her as she walked quickly into the mall and toward the exit doors. She began to run when she looked behind her and saw a store detective loping toward her. Outside she scurried behind a wall leading to a truck service entrance, set the coat on the ground and turned around just as the detective caught up to her. He made her pick up the coat, then marched her back to the store office where he called the police.

She told the arresting officers her name was Karen Glass and she lived in Detroit, but she had no identification. She was so hesitant and stumbled so badly when asked to repeat her particulars that Officer Randy Roisum advised her of the extra punishment she could face if convicted of obstruction of justice. He wouldn't charge her for that, he said, if she played it straight from then on.

"My name is Laurie Dann," she said, her shoulders slumping. She said she was a University of Arizona student who came from Highland Park, Illinois.

She bit her lip as she posed for her mug shot down at police headquarters. She was wearing a turtleneck featuring the logo of the Vail ski resort. The police released her on $200 bond, and ultimately the court assigned her to a first-time-offender program. The program required her to admit her guilt and perform community service, but she ducked out on her obligation and left Madison before officials could pursue the matter.

•

Later that week, Laurie tracked down her old college boyfriend Steve Witt, who had left New York to finish his residency in Arizona in order to escape the cloud of the anonymous allegation that he had molested a woman in the emergency room. She called collect and identified herself as Sarah, no last name. Steve refused the charges the first time she called, but several days later decided to see what the caller wanted.

"Stephen Howard Witt," Laurie said, snapping off her words. "You fucking bastard, I'm going to kill you."

Steve hung up and told his wife, Barbara, what he had just heard. "It's her," he said. "She found us again."

Barbara, who had just come home from the hospital after delivering the couple's first child, went hysterical with fear. "She's completely insane," she said. "She's still thinking about you, my God."

The Witts changed to a new unlisted number, but Laurie got it the same way she had obtained the first number, by wheedling it out of a clerk at Steve's father's pharmacy. The clerk also volunteered information about the new baby.

"You don't have to change your phone number," Laurie said to Barbara in her next call. "That won't stop me from killing you. And you might as well take your little baby and throw him in the garbage can. You're messing with some pretty bad feelings here, kid. I'm pregnant because I've been fucking Steve."

The calls started coming in literally by the dozen. Most of them were hang-ups, but every so often she would start in with her threats. "I'm going to move there and I'm going to kill you," she told Barbara. "I know where you are and you don't know where I am."

Laurie's phone calls to her usual Chicago-area victims had become similarly aberrant. She called her old friend Kiki Hyman and said, "Do you still give Murray good blow jobs?" then hung up. At the beginning of April, when Jeff and Susie were vacationing in New York and their kids were home with the housekeeper, Laurie called and told the housekeeper, "Susie is a stinking bitch! Tell her I'm going to kill her."

Several days later, the housekeeper received another call and wrote down the message. "You and your brother are going to be killed. You have to die because you are a bitch." In the next call, Laurie said, "Tell Susie I'm going to get her, and I always get what I want. I'm going to get all of you."

The calls continued when Susie and Jeff returned. Laurie started off muffling her voice or trying to disguise it by screeching, as she did with Steve Witt, but she gradually began using her own voice. "You have to die!" she said to Susie. "You and your bastard brother are going to die."

The Taylors were, by then, seriously frightened. They

warned their neighbors to be on the lookout for Laurie's Honda—unaware that she was no longer driving it after a minor fender bender that wasn't her fault. They called Detective Jack McCafferty of Highland Park to tell him what had been happening and to ask him to tell the department to watch their house.

Jeff Taylor and Russell's attorney, Rick Kessler, made an appointment to see Lake County state's attorney Fred Foreman in Foreman's office in Waukegan.

"I'm disappointed you haven't done anything about my situation," Jeff told the stocky chief prosecutor. "And I find it unbelievable that, given all the facts, you haven't taken action on the stabbing of Russell Dann. This woman is capable of anything."

Foreman, who was accompanied by his deputy, Mike Waller, said that his hands were tied. "All the evidence is circumstantial," he said. "We don't have a case. It would just get thrown out of court."

Waller volunteered to subpoena the telephone records from the Wasserman home for the past six months in order to chart the times and dates of outgoing calls, but even then, he said, making harassment charges stick was going to be tough, given that Laurie was not the only person with access to the telephone.

"Someone's got to put the screws to her," Jeff said. He went on to relate the various stories having to do with Laurie and her obsession with big, bloody pieces of raw meat.

"Let's have a picnic," Foreman joked. "We'll put out some raw meat, and when she comes around we'll capture her."

It seemed funny at the time and they all laughed.

•

On March 26, Laurie saw an article about a spelling bee that appeared in the *Wisconsin State Journal* newspaper and picked out the photo of Jim Remsik, Jr., the ten-year-old champion of Frank Ellis School in Madison. From the parents' name and address listed with his photograph she got the phone number, then she placed a collect call to the family.

Christine Remsik, the boy's mother, accepted the call from "Laurie" because she had a young niece with that name.

"Hi," said an unfamiliar female voice. "I just wanted you to know that I'm going to kill Jim today."

Mrs. Remsik was more confused than alarmed. "Which Jim?" she said.

"Jim your son. I just want you to know that I'm going to kill him today. Have a nice day. Goodbye."

Mrs. Remsik reported the threat to police, implicating her niece, but when her phone bill came later, it showed that the call had come from a pay telephone on Francis Street right by the Towers.

Not long afterward, Laurie mailed two identical, anonymous letters to Arizona. One went to Steve Witt's father's pharmacy, and the other went to the hospital where he was employed. They were typed and addressed "To Whom It May Concern." The letters, which owe a stylistic debt to *Penthouse* magazine, said:

I am a 19-year-old college student. I came to the hospital to be treated for a skin rash on my neck. I was seen by a doctor by the name of Steve Witt. Dr. Witt began to ask me personal questions. "Do you have a boyfriend?" "Are you currently living alone?" Dr. Witt then reached over and touched my chest. I thought it was an accident till the second time. Dr. Witt asked when my last gynecological check-up was, and offered to "examine me." I said NO.

Later that evening the doorbell rang and it was Dr. Witt. He said he was dropping off my prescription. He asked to come in and I said no. The door was open and he pushed his way in. I was alone and scared and screamed. He smiled and ran toward me discarding his clothes. It was a nightmare.

I am currently home. I have to decide whether or not to press criminal charges. What I want to know is if any other complaints have ever been mentioned. He is a sick man.

From this letter you could think I am making this up or I am sick. I am neither one. Let me tell you what I have on my side of credibility. The police were called and I went to the ER to be examined. Sperm was found, and bruises. Finger prints in my apartment, and a neighbor saw a man leave after she called the police because of my screams. I took a lie detector and passed. Dr. Stephen Witt was brought in for questioning. The police are leaving it up to me whether or not to prosicute [sic].

If you still do not believe me, let me inform you of a birth mark Dr. Witt has. On his penis is a freckle or birth mark. How would I know that unless it was shoved in my face?

The fanciful idea of accusing Steve of molestation had perhaps taken root with Laurie on Christmas Day, when the *Chicago Tribune* ran a news story about a plastic surgeon at Cook County Hospital who was accused of molesting a female patient in the emergency room. The doctor in the news story asked the woman about her boyfriends, offered to perform unnecessary examinations on her and attempted to embrace her.

Laurie had neatly clipped the article and taken it with her to Madison.

•

On March 30, Norm wrote Laurie to follow up on a phone conversation he'd had with her the night before. In an apparent attempt to help her overcome her obsession with "good" and "bad" numbers, he emphasized to her that numbers were not lucky or unlucky. "The only thing that will make a difference is when you are 100 percent," he wrote. And, again, he stressed that she must continue seeing her doctors if she was to improve.

Laurie was also getting periodic letters of support from her brother, Mark, and his wife, Paula, whom she was planning to visit in Texas as soon as she was feeling better. Even their daughters, Amy and Sherry, scrawled cards to their Aunt Laurie, inviting her to visit that summer.

•

In late March, Laurie took three pairs of pants into the dressing room at Worth's, a women's clothing store directly across from the Towers, and came back out with only two.

The assistant manager confronted her. "Where's the other pants?" she said. "We gave you three and—"

Laurie interrupted the manager by removing the green pants from inside her jacket and flinging them onto the rack. "I will never shop here again," she said, stalking out. "You people are really rude."

Laurie was so indignant that she brought up the incident

over dinner. When word got back to Jolie Pollock that her roommate was involved in still more oddball activities—crimes, now, even—she finally decided she'd had enough. The quirks had been one thing, but Laurie had clearly become very sick. Despite her occasional deliberate vomiting that had given rise to the suspicion in the dorm that she was bulimic, she'd gained probably fifty pounds and was looking almost pregnant. Her expression was dazed, her conversation often fragmented or listless.

"I'm moving out," Jolie said to Laurie. "There are just too many weird things that have gone on. I don't know how to explain them, I just think I should move out."

Laurie nodded. "Yeah," she said.

And on April 2, Jolie packed up and took her belongings to a vacant room on the eighth floor. Nobody moved in to replace her. Laurie was alone.

•

Her calls continued to Arizona—up to thirty in an hour on one memorable afternoon—and Steve Witt called his old high school friend and college roommate Lou Spivack for advice. Lou was an assistant county prosecutor in Arizona, and calls coming from Wisconsin were out of his jurisdiction. His first thought was that Steve should get an attorney and file a civil suit to stop the harassment, but neither of them could find a lawyer eager to take on a case that would be complicated and financially unrewarding. His second thought was that such calls were felonies under federal law, and he might have luck getting the FBI to investigate and help bring federal charges against Laurie.

So Steve called the FBI. He said he wanted to sit down and outline his problem for them in detail, but the person who took the information over the telephone was brusque and unenthusiastic. Not a big enough problem. Not enough evidence. Maybe if he had taped the conversations...

•

In the middle of April, a group of students at the Towers got together to watch a televised interview with cult slayer Charles Manson. Half a dozen of them gathered afterward in suite 810, dimmed the lights and proceeded to tell their own eerie-but-true stories of murder and intrigue. The door was open and Laurie, who was rambling through the halls again, saw the crowd and asked if she could come in. No one objected, so she plopped herself down at a desk and sat quietly for a time, listening to the vivid and increasingly gory narratives. Then she spoke up. "I've got a story to tell," she said.

It was about a divorcée—a woman out of control—who had harassed her ex-husband for months with various threats, then finally broke into his home and stabbed him with an ice pick. One student remembered later that the husband died at the end of the story; others who were there remember that the husband lived. But everyone remembers particularly how Laurie told the story in a flat, uninflected voice, as though she were relating the details of an unsurprising news event.

"Y'know," one of the boys said, making a collegiate attempt to be cosmic, "there are so many crazy people out there, maybe there's a murderer among us."

•

Laurie had a new nickname: 7-21. She got it late one night when another student walked in on her in the TV lounge. She stood, walked over to the set and began switching back and forth from Channel 7 to Channel 21, 7, 21, 7, 21, as fast as she could punch in the numbers. The other student left and came back twenty minutes later. She was still at it. 7, 21, 7, 21.

"Psycho bitch," he said.

The next day she marched up to him as he waited his turn to shoot pool in the game room. "Don't you ever call me a psycho bitch again," she said, her voice hard and mean. "Or you'll regret it."

•

By then, Laurie had ditched Shwager and Dr. Greist. Her last visit to Greist's office was March 18, after which she began simply breaking her appointments and ignoring Shwager's dogged attempts to reach her by leaving messages at the front desk of the Towers. Shwager had been pushing her hard, forcing her to perform otherwise simple tasks that she found unpleasant and urging her to make lists of goals.

"If you don't take risks, you're not going to make the kind

of progress that will make either you or us happy," he scolded her.

To hell with it. She didn't need the grief. Her life had found another purpose anyway—her plans—and going through therapy was only distracting her.

She continued taking her drugs, however, and in the first week of April she received five hundred more clomipramine tablets as prescribed by Dr. Epstein through the Lud Bock Pharmacy in Montreal, and one hundred more lithium carbonate pills prescribed by Dr. Greist through the WSA Pharmacy in Madison.

On April 10, she, Shwager and her father had a three-way telephone call in which Norm told Laurie to stop breaking her appointments and to go to see Greist the very next day. She agreed, but then didn't show up and didn't call to explain why.

Greist was worried. Laurie's condition was obviously deteriorating and her problems were more serious than he or Shwager could address in sporadic office visits. She needed full-time supervision and intensive therapy as a hospital inpatient if she was to improve and learn to lead a productive life. At the same time, she reacted badly whenever either he or Shwager even came close to broaching the subject. A mental hospital? Her?

"Since you fail to respond voluntarily," Laurie scrawled on the back of one of her mother's greeting cards, "we are forced to seek legal recourse."

To commit a patient involuntarily in Wisconsin, a doctor has to establish in front of a state hearing panel first that the patient is mentally ill—which wouldn't have been a problem in Laurie's case—and second that the patient is a danger either to him- or herself or others. Greist was unsure on that point. Laurie was a very strange young woman, certainly, but he had never known her to speak of violence or make remarks that would lead him to think she was capable of doing any serious harm to anyone. Indeed he had never known of an OCD patient to lash out violently.

But, then again, his knowledge of her life wasn't really all that deep, and maybe there were incidents or episodes that might make a case for involuntary commitment. All he could do was ask Laurie's father for advice, which he did during a face-to-face meeting two days later. It was an unusual step, ethically, since Laurie was an adult, but hers was an unusual case.

Greist explained the situation and probed Norm for specific information that might help him decide whether to try to have Laurie hospitalized against her will. According to Greist, Norm answered quite firmly that Laurie was not dangerous. Greist could not recall Norm mentioning that the police had accused Laurie of threatening and harassing her enemies by telephone for the previous two years, that she was a suspect in the ice-pick stabbing of her ex-husband, that she was suspected of having stolen and defaced the property of her baby-sitting clients, that she had exhibited an eerie fascination with raw meat, or that she owned and had access to handguns.

Norm told law enforcement officials on several occasions that he believed the allegations against his daughter were false and that Russell was behind them. She was not a criminal. She should not be locked up like one.

He came back to see Laurie the following Sunday, April 17, and returned to Boca Raton Tuesday. From Florida, he composed an anguished letter that he told Laurie was "the most important and hardest" he would ever write. He asked for a favor: would she allow herself to be hospitalized for treatment by Dr. Greist? She could not, he wrote, continue to miss appointments with the doctors in the belief that the drugs she was taking would cure her. Hospitalization, he said, was the only way she would recover. In a final, desperate plea, he told her that if she would enter the hospital to be treated, he would give her permission to put him in a nursing home when he grew older. See Greist, he wrote; do it for me.

20

You'll Be Surprised What I'll Do

Susie Taylor answered the phone in early May 1988 and heard Laurie's maniacal singsong on the other end: "Susie, are you all getting together on Mother's Day?" she said. "You shall die."

Mother's Day was the following Sunday, and Susie was so terrified that she didn't even want to walk through the kitchen to the TV room because of the number of windows she had to pass. She had visions of Laurie prowling through the house, hiding on the basement steps, popping out from around a corner, her gun at the ready.

"You've got to do something," she complained to Detective McCafferty in Highland Park. "Anybody who can stand over a sleeping person and stab him with an ice pick is capable of doing anything."

"Well," said McCafferty. "Let's just hope not."

•

The FBI had finally entered the case in Arizona. Steve Witt's friend Lou Spivack had clouted him into a meeting with an investigator by calling the FBI office himself, explaining who he was and dropping the name of an acquaintance, local assistant U.S. attorney Janet Johnson. "This is legitimate," he said sharply.

A few days later, FBI special agent Perry Cole met with

Spivack and Steve and Barbara Witt, and listened for several hours to the disturbing tales of threats and harassments. Laurie had recently been calling to brag that she was going to walk into Steve's dermatology office someday and blow his brains out. They had tried to make home recordings of the calls, they explained, but the little suction-cup microphone they'd used had only picked up their end of the conversations.

Cole set them up with a better taping device—two-party consent for electronic eavesdropping was not needed in Arizona as it was in Illinois—but reassured them that sick people make such calls all the time and ninety-nine times out of a hundred nothing ever comes of it. His response was a great disappointment to the Witts, who felt that they were dealing with an insanely clever and vicious adversary. She had broken through three unlisted phone numbers, she'd learned of their baby not a week after he'd been born and she never seemed to sleep, judging by the way her calls shattered them awake at all hours:

"Fuck you! I'm going to fucking kill you!"

Several days after the FBI meeting, Spivack looked up Laurie's police records from Illinois. He was startled at the variety of alleged offenses but heartened to learn that Steve and Barbara weren't Laurie's only victims. It could only help prod the FBI into action.

He called both Detectives Mohr and McCafferty to share information, and found out the whole story from guns to meat. The lawmen told him, in separate phone calls, that they knew they had a problem with Laurie but they still had trouble knowing how much stock to put in the complaints of Russell Dann and his family and friends. Russell was rude and sarcastic, they said. He was a jerk to people who wanted to help him. If it was just a messy divorce, they didn't want to take sides.

"Well, for what it's worth, we're having this problem here and my victim is totally blameless," Spivack told them. "I'd take this woman seriously if I were you."

The suburban cops agreed to keep in touch with Spivack, and McCafferty even took the extra step of calling Susie Taylor to tell her that big things were happening down in Arizona.

At last! Susie called Spivack at his office almost as soon as she heard. At last someone was taking Laurie seriously. For more than half an hour she told her rambling story to Spivack, sometimes frantically, more often zealously, as if her life depended on convincing the young prosecutor that every last thing she said was true. "We've got to do something," she said excitedly. "You've got to help me."

Russell, when he called several days later, was comparatively subdued. He was through asking for help from the authorities, he told Spivack bitterly. "I've resigned myself to something terrible happening," he said. "I don't expect miracles. I've seen how the cops operate."

"We're pursuing an indictment here," Spivack promised. "All we've got to do is coordinate our efforts and put our evidence together. It's going to happen."

•

Of course as luck would have it, immediately after the FBI recorder had been installed at the Witts', Laurie stopped making threats. For a week or more it was just hang-ups, weird noises and collect calls that terminated at her end before the operator made the connection. But finally, on May 9, the phone rang and it was collect from Laurie. Steve accepted with a mixture of dread and anticipation.

"What do you want?" he asked.

"Stevie!" Laurie began with a whine, her voice high, trembling, cartoonish. It reminded him of the Wicked Witch of the West. "You know what I want."

"What do you want?" he said again, this time trying to sound fully disgusted.

"You know. And I'm going to annoy you until I get it." The threat had an almost pleasant lilt.

"Listen, it's been many years, okay? Why don't you leave us alone?"

"I don't think you understand."

"First of all, I can't even tell your voice. But I assume this is Laurie."

"Of course."

"So what do you want?"

"You know," Laurie said. She was teasing him like a big sister might torment a little brother.

"No, I don't," Steve said.

"Yeah," she said, drawing out the word into two syllables. "I was—you'll see what I'll do."

"Why don't you stop talking in that immature voice and tell me what you really want?" Steve said, a hard contempt in his voice.

"You know what I want. You know what I'm going to do."

"No, I don't," Steve said, trying to draw the threat out of her.

"Yeah."

"No, I don't."

"Yeah," she said. "And I always get what I want."

"Obviously you haven't."

"I will."

"Why don't you tell me—what is your problem? Huh?"

"No problem."

"You know, I think you need to get help."

"Uh huh, I do," she said, the inflection so strangely upbeat it was hard to tell if she meant it.

"Are you getting it?"

"Yeah." Again the whiny indifference.

"I mean seriously," Steve said. "You need help."

"Um hmmm," she said.

"Okay, so you can get on with your life and we can get on with our lives."

"It's not going to be that way, though," she said.

"Why not?"

"Because."

"Because why?"

Her voice dropped lightly into a growl. "Because of who you are."

"And who is that?"

"Mmmmm," she said. Bright again. Nonchalant. "I can guarantee you one thing..."

"What's that?"

"You won't live to see your baby grow up. I promise you."

"Oh yeah?"

"Uh huh."

Steve's voice was dull and nonconfrontational. "So you're threatening my life, huh?"

"No, I'm going to do it."

"You're going to do it, huh?"

"Yeah. I think you deserve it."

"Yeah, and how many other people are you going to take along with you?"

"Does it matter?"

Steve's irritation returned. "Why don't you go get help?"

"I don't want to."

"I think that would be best."

"No."

"Before you get yourself in trouble and other people in trouble."

"I won't."

She was just being a brat, arguing to piss him off. He cleared his throat and waited for her to continue.

"I already have the way to do it to frame Barbie," she said to fill the silence.

"To frame Barbie?"

"Yeah. Take a knife from the place you ate. You know, it'd have her prints on it. And they'll just say she had problems after that..."

"I don't think so."

"You wanna make a bet? I'll give it a try."

"Listen, why don't you go get help and leave us alone. All right?"

"No."

"I think it's been a long time and I think you're having some problems here, okay? I think that with time, you know, you'll forget about whatever happened in the past with anyone you've ever been with, and you can get on with your life. But, you know, making threats about killing me and my family or anyone else is not going to solve your problems."

"It will. It will make me feel a lot better."

"No it won't."

"I'll give it a try," she sang.

"Well—"

"You'll be surprised what I'll do."

"Yeah, well, I've already found out what you'll do."

"You haven't seen anything yet," she said, the darker, ragged tone returning. "That's child's play."

"Well, you're acting very childish right now."

"I know." She was bright again. "What's the difference?"

"Well, I don't think we need to talk anymore, okay? Go get help, I'll talk to you later. Bye."

He hung up the phone and switched off the tape recorder. Bingo.

●

Norm and Edith were vacationing in Florida on that very day, and Edith sat down to write Laurie a Hallmark card. The card was from the company's "Between Friends" series, and the front featured a field of roses and the words "Everything is going to be all right." Inside it said, "I believe in you."

The message Edith wrote on the card was typical of her correspondence with her daughter. She mentioned Mark and how one of her granddaughters had just had her tonsils removed; she related that the weather was fine; she said they had gone to a boat show on Mother's Day; and she described their plans to go for a ride in a friend's red Rolls-Royce. They would be leaving Florida soon, she said.

21

Heading
Home

Steve Witt thought about calling the Wassermans and pleading with them to intercede with Laurie, but he decided against it because he didn't want to tip them off to the FBI investigation.

Instead he bought a gun and put it under his bed.

"The only true solution is for her to die," Barbara told him morosely. "Anything short of that and she'll be hanging over our heads for the rest of our lives."

•

Lou Spivack dictated a three-page letter on May 10 to FBI agent Cole. Writing on official county letterhead, he related to Cole everything he had learned from Russell and Susie about the hang-up calls, the death threats, Laurie's strange superstitions, the Molotov cocktail she had planted in her own house, the ice-pick stabbing and the rituals involving meat. The story, he concluded with a rhetorical flourish, "is frightening, bizarre and, even though we know it to be true, hard to believe."

When Cole read the letter and heard the clear, unambiguous threat recorded off the Witts' telephone, he agreed that it was time to press for an indictment.

•

That spring in Madison Laurie continued to buy *Penthouse* magazines regularly, and she purchased a $15 vibrator from a

Service Merchandise store. In her room she kept a deck of pornographic playing cards featuring photographs of tumescent males in bondage.

Her only known sexual partner during her stay at the Towers was Jesse Roeper, a sophomore with whom she fell into a pattern of loveless intercourse. It started when he offered to give her massages to relieve the tension in her back and neck, and after about the third time, the massages led to sex.

Jesse was a vain, good-looking student from a small town in central Illinois who favored combat fatigues and left copies of *Soldier of Fortune* lying around his dorm room. He thought of himself as a sophisticated lover with European sensibilities—Laurie's poor hygiene never bothered him on the half a dozen occasions they had sex that semester, he said, the way it would have bothered the typical American male.

He and Laurie never saw each other outside the confines of the Towers. Jesse bragged that Laurie was one of at least twenty women he made love to that school year.

A nurse who examined Laurie that spring at the Planned Parenthood office in Madison where she went for a physical exam and a renewal of her prescription for birth control pills noted that Laurie's resting pulse was a frenetic 120 beats a minute. "Very fine tremor," the nurse wrote on the intake form. "Skin is moist and cool. Reflexes extremely reactive."

•

Haley went to a sixth-floor resident advisor, Tonya Neumeier, to ask if she were aware of Laurie's eating habits, her gorging, her vomiting.

"We know about it," Tonya told her. "We're taking care of it. She's seeing someone. The best thing you can do is just be a friend to her. Be there for her."

But the mealtime crew was getting tired of Laurie and her bizarre behavior. As time went on she'd started talking too much, interrupting everyone, dominating their conversations with nonsense about her own life. Just as things were getting really edgy, Laurie offhandedly called one of Haley's friends a bitch.

Haley snapped back in irritation, then laughed as though it had suddenly struck her as amusing that she'd wasted a good retort on someone so pathetic.

Laurie turned on her with a look of intense hatred. "You know, Haley," she said. "Life is hard enough without your dirty looks."

Afterward, Haley didn't know whether to be afraid of Laurie or to feel even sorrier for her. Maybe the situation called for compassion, but Laurie was becoming less and less likable as time passed and Haley *had* at least made an effort. Finally she and the other women started waiting for Laurie to find a table first, then they would go to the other end of the cafeteria and gather around a smaller table where there would be no room for an unwanted guest.

Their purpose was not lost on Laurie, who would proceed to find a seat nearby and turn nearly all her energies into gazing with cool, blank hatred at Haley, often so intently that she didn't touch her food.

"Unbelievable," Haley said, glancing nervously at Laurie and turning away. "She's given up her favorite thing just to glare at me."

Up in her room, Laurie scrawled on the back of an envelope, "Hell on Earth would be having to live with Haley."

•

As spring breezes blew into Madison, Laurie began spending more and more time outside, where she usually wore shorts and mittens. She determinedly skipped lines and cracks as she walked gingerly along the sidewalk, her head down, her face strangely puffy, walking five steps forward, three steps backward, five steps forward, three steps backward. Those who saw her were reminded of the movie *The Exorcist*, in which a pretty little girl is possessed by the devil.

Then a resident advisor found Laurie standing in the stairwell one day, totally nude, opening and slamming the fire door. She approached Laurie and told her to stop. She did, for a while. But half an hour later the door was slamming again.

•

Laurie called Cassandra Pappas at two A.M. from one of the pay phones. "Mrs. Pappas," she said. "You are going to die." She hung up.

Then she left a message on the answering machine belonging to Marc Boney, the building manager of the Kellogg Living/Learning Center at Northwestern University: "You are going to die," she said.

Later she called Julie Alt, one of her old baby-sitting clients, and woke her from a sound sleep: "Your three girls are going to die!" she said. Again she hung up.

Next she mailed a leaking foil pouch of Capri Sun fruit juice to the suburban Glenview home of Rob Heidelberger, the boy who had taken her to the junior prom in high school and then broken off their relationship. The package looked unclean to him so he threw the juice away without drinking it.

•

In her room, Laurie was compiling two separate lists that were apparently related to the murderous plans she was drawing up. The lists included the names of her resident advisor; six residents of the Towers with whom she had had generally minor dealings; five friends of Russell Dann's; a friend of Russell's girlfriend, Patricia; the son of an employee at Glenbrook Hospital where she was fired in 1983; a neighbor of her parents'; her former boyfriend Steve Witt; Northwestern student Scott Freidheim; and the notation "School both Ravinia Clavey Kennedy," a reference to the Ravinia School in Highland Park and the Kennedy School on Clavey Road. Jeff and Susie Taylor's kids were enrolled at both facilities, though the Kennedy School was actually being used at the time by the Young Men's Jewish Council, a day-care center and preschool for 160 children.

At the side of one of the lists she constructed the wording of a mock invitation: "Alumni Party, 620 Lincoln, by your little sisters. Food and Drink. Sunday, May 28, 2:00. Thank you for your hospitality. Congradulations [sic]. Goldman/Sacks [sic] Co." Goldman Sachs was where Kiki Hyman's husband, Murray, worked.

•

FBI agent Cole, assistant U.S. attorney Johnson and Deputy County prosecutor Lou Spivack made a firm decision on Thursday, May 12, to seek an indictment against Laurie in front of the federal grand jury that convened every other week. The next regularly scheduled grand jury session was for the following Wednesday, May 18.

Cole sent out a telex that day asking police departments across the country for additional information on Laurie Dann. In Glencoe, Floyd Mohr just happened to be in the station that afternoon even though he was technically off duty, and he just happened to be at the printer waiting for routine license plate information when the request from Arizona clattered in.

"What's the matter, Floyd?" one of his fellow officers said. "You look like you've seen a ghost."

"You're not going to believe this..." he said. He was beginning to feel that, for some reason, destiny had him on a collision course with this woman.

•

Laurie's last, frantic, threatening call to Steve Witt came on Friday, May 13. On that day, the telex that had arrived at the Milwaukee FBI office was faxed to the Madison office. FBI agent Kent Miller in Madison was asked to find and question Laurie about the threats and to prepare to arrest her as soon as the indictment came down.

The message said she might be armed and should be considered dangerous, but Miller did not note any particular urgency. The telex did not list an address for Laurie and the only phone number they had for her traced back to the office of Dr. John Greist. Miller looked for Laurie's name in the public and student telephone directories, found no listing, and left word with the Madison police department to let him know if they came across her. The person he talked to at the Madison police did not tell him or did not know that the department was that day circulating a memo prompted by the FBI report that listed Laurie's address, down to her room number.

Miller secured an appointment with Greist for four o'clock that afternoon. Greist, after carefully checking Miller's credentials, told him that Laurie was under his care, but that he could say nothing else because he had to respect her right to confidentiality.

Miller argued that this was important. He told Greist that Laurie was not only wanted for making vicious threats, but that she also owned a .357 Magnum and was a suspect in the ice-pick stabbing of her ex-husband. Greist said he was surprised by the information and he had not thought she was dangerous, but he could add nothing else until he talked to the University of Wisconsin legal staff. He tried unsuccessfully to reach the proper attorneys that afternoon and reported to Miller he would have to get back to him on Monday.

•

Chicago FBI agent Rob Daniel went to the Highland Park police department that afternoon and asked for a file photo of Laurie to aid their investigation, which was now active. They were waiting for the federal indictment to come down before arresting her in Madison.

McCafferty called Susie Taylor to tell her that Laurie had been located and was under FBI surveillance. When Susie contacted Lake County chief deputy state's attorney Mike Waller and asked if Laurie might be indicted locally also, Waller told her to wait for Laurie to be arrested on the federal charges, at which point his office would probably have more luck getting an indictment in Illinois.

She agreed to wait.

•

Saturday was the last day before summer break for most of the students in the Towers. Official checkout time was Sunday at noon, and everyone was packing, saying goodbye and exchanging addresses. Laurie found company that night with Jesse Roeper, her occasional sex partner.

They had finished having intercourse and were watching TV in his room at about 8:30 when the fire alarm went off. Jesse decided to leave the building, just to be safe, even though the alarm had been going off frequently the last few weeks of the semester.

"You staying?" he asked Laurie.

"Yeah," Laurie said. "It's probably nothing. You go ahead."

Laurie was right—the alarm had been triggered by three guys smoking pot who thought it would be funny to blow smoke into the detector. Jesse came back a few minutes later and Laurie was still there in front of the TV as though nothing were amiss. She left two hours later when Jesse's roommate returned from a date. The next day, the roommate discovered that someone had used a knife to slash up a pair of shorts, a suitcoat, slacks, three T-shirts, a short-sleeved shirt, two polo shirts and a textbook.

He figured the total damages at $300, and when he called the police he made it clear that Laurie Dann was the only person who could have done it, even though he had no witnesses. Jesse said he never knew if Laurie thought the clothes and the textbook belonged to him and she was trying to punish him for leaving for the summer, or if she were simply jealous of his friendship with his roommate.

The next night, student staff member Dixon Gahnz was checking the hallways and utility rooms to be sure that garbage was cleared away and that everyone who was supposed to be out of the building had vacated. At nine P.M. he looked inside a fifth-floor garbage room and saw, to his horror, that Laurie had burrowed into the refuse and was curled up in a ball in a corner. She was wrapped in a plastic bag and dripping with sweat.

"What are you doing in here?" he asked when he could compose himself.

She stirred. "I'm, uh, just looking for things," she said. She stood, shed the bag and rushed from the room into a stairwell.

Gahnz walked after her, but she'd vanished. He looked for her for a few minutes, then went downstairs and told several co-workers what he'd seen. They decided to call a mental health help line, got nowhere, and went off to search the building for her. When they were unable to find her, they went to her room and pounded on the door for several minutes, then opened it with a passkey. Inside they found a stinking hovel, a toilet filled with excrement, a carpet soaked with urine, garbage everywhere and, in the middle of it all, Laurie, apparently naked, sleeping soundly under a blanket on a bed without a sheet.

What could they do? They left the room and found building manager William Levy, who decided to call the Madison police department and Norm Wasserman to explain what was happening. Madison officers Mike Koval and Therese MacKenzie responded—by then it was nearly 10:30—and when they heard the name Laurie Dann, they contacted FBI Agent Miller at his home.

Miller declined to come out that evening, but told Koval and MacKenzie that Laurie was under a psychiatrist's care. The officers proceeded to check the suite and found no weapons, no suicide notes and nothing to indicate any danger. Officer MacKenzie talked to Laurie as she lay on her bed. She was groggy but said she was okay, she didn't need a doctor. The room was only a mess because she was moving.

And, indeed, she was. Shortly after the officers left, she threw a few of her belongings into a couple of suitcases and spent the rest of the night in a nearby International House of Pancakes restaurant. She caught an early Greyhound bus out of Madison that took her back to the North Shore.

Agent Miller waited until the next afternoon to come to the Towers to question Laurie, but by then, of course, she was long gone, as were all the residents. In her room were fragments from a troubled life—a threatening letter addressed to Steve Witt on the stolen letterhead of the Antoniewicz & Gregg law firm, a copy of a 1933 book, *Famous Feats of Detection and Deduction*, and a pair of newspaper clippings.

The first was from the May 12, 1988, *Wisconsin State Journal*. Under the headline "Police Trace Threats, Attacks to Victim," the article described how a nineteen-year-old Madison woman with a history of mental illness had reported numerous assaults, harassing phone calls and vandalisms to police for the previous year and a half. This harassment, all of which the woman had apparently fabricated, included an incident in which she stuffed a teddy bear full of raw liver, then stuck it to her door with a knife, and another incident in which she smeared her own door with shrimp sauce that was supposed to look like blood.

The second clip was an Associated Press story out of New York from the February 24, 1988, *Chicago Tribune*, and it described how a man suffering from OCD was cured after he shot himself in the mouth. The headline said, "Failed Suicide Provides Patient with a Cure."

Laurie also left behind numerous pages from a writing tablet. The notations within were written at all angles and in a sometimes illegible scrawl.

The first page was a sheet stolen from Russell Dann's town house: a note from his girlfriend, Patricia, telling him what clothes to bring on a weekend trip to Detroit. The note was addressed "Hi Bud," with a flower dotting the "i."

The remaining pages, all in Laurie's handwriting, relate to her relationship with Russell. To read them is to peek into a twisted, paranoid mind: "hate pain... get through to you... abuse. spit, hurt, spat... why gun. question of safety... baglady, scum paraplegic... Threw away wedding tape.... terrified I was helpless. I'll deny it. suffer forever.... Harm children to pay a bill."

The police also found pages covered with obsessive doodlings that focused primarily on the numbers 5 and 7 and the letters P, H and S.

Also in the room was a brown mailing envelope addressed to Dr. Greist containing a V-8 juice box stamped "Sample," a slip of paper with Northwestern student Scott Freidheim's name on it, and a photo of Laurie and Russell standing side by side, beaming.

•

Dr. Greist spoke to university attorney Gail Snowden Monday, according to his psychiatric records, and asked her what steps, if any, he should take given what he now knew about Laurie. He and Snowden agreed that since Steve Witt had been informed of the threats and Greist had learned of them only through the FBI and not Laurie, he could do nothing. They discussed the possibility of contacting Norm Wasserman and telling him that Laurie hadn't been showing up for treatment and was being sought by federal agents. But he decided such a move would be "problematic"—it would violate Laurie's confidentiality because, in his words, "there had been such a long gap" in his contact with Laurie and Norm.

That "long gap" had been under five weeks. He had seen

Norm exactly thirty-four days earlier, and received a phone call from Laurie twenty-six days earlier.

•

The figurative net that was tightening around Laurie broke open on Monday when Steve Witt said he was backing off on the effort to seek the federal indictment. He and his wife had talked about it over the weekend and decided they didn't want to go it alone against Laurie. They envisioned her being arrested, posting bond and flying immediately to Arizona with her gun in her suitcase.

"Why should she have it in mind that it's just us who's after her when it's really everybody?" he said. He had spoken with Russell to exchange horror stories, and figured it would be best to wait at least two more weeks and try to coordinate the indictment with other charges back in Illinois. Janet Johnson told him that yes, this might not be a bad idea since it would increase the possibility that she would be held without bond.

Monday evening at a little past eight P.M. Laurie called from Glencoe to her brother's home in Austin and spoke for eight minutes.

At noon the next day, Laurie called the Young Men's Jewish Council, one of the schools on the list she had compiled in Madison. Shortly afterward she called Ravinia Elementary, the other school. At both places she asked what time the children arrived in the morning.

She proceeded to drive to the Jewish school and went to the office, where she questioned a young staff member about when the children came to school and when they left.

Starting at 7:05 that evening, she got on the phone and began making nuisance calls. At 8:51 she reached Dr. Gail Levee in Los Angeles, a friend from the dorm in downtown Chicago where Laurie had been living when she first met Russell. Laurie was a bridesmaid for Gail in 1983, but the two fell out of touch after that, and the short call was a surprise. Gail said she would be coming to visit soon, and Laurie said they should get together if their schedules allowed for it.

"Life is beautiful," Laurie added. "I've got a package I'll be sending you. Look for it."

She took a break from the telephone at 9:47 P.M., then

got back on at 2:35 A.M. and made twelve quick hang-up calls in the next seven minutes.

The next morning, Laurie mailed the Levees a package of Rice Krispies treats laced with arsenic. She enclosed a chipper note on her father's business stationery—"I'm going to be in Glencoe when your [sic] in town. Look forward to seeing you guys. I was going to send you coffee cake, but I was making Rice Crispy [sic] treats for school and decided to send some. Enjoy." For the return address she put the Towers in Madison.

Then she took a drive down to see Marian Rushe in Winnetka and set up a little outing on Friday morning with her children Patrick and Carl.

•

Wednesday was also the day Norm and Edith arrived home from Florida.

Meanwhile, Russell was in something of a panic. The FBI had told him—and virtually no one else—that they had lost track of Laurie in Madison and they didn't know where she was. Agent Miller kept going back to the Towers faithfully, every day that week, and each time she was still gone.

•

Thursday night at 8:45 P.M. Laurie telephoned Jane Sterling, the woman she had envied when Jane was a cheerleader at New Trier and then came to despise after Jane snubbed her during sorority rush at Arizona. Jane was then living in Glenview with her husband, David, and their three young children.

"I'm from the Ford Modeling Agency, remember me?" Laurie said.

"Oh, yes," said Jane. "How's your husband?"

"He's good," said Laurie. "Remember we were going to reschedule that get-together? Well, it's going to be tomorrow morning at Hubbard Woods Elementary School in Winnetka at nine o'clock. Coffee and doughnuts. Bring whichever of your kids don't have to be in school. Can you make it?"

"Sure," said Jane. "Two of the three will be free, and—oh, no wait. I just remembered. I can't go. I have bowling Friday morning and it's the last week and I'm the president of the bowling league and I have to hand out prize money and stuff. I can't come. I'm so sorry."

Laurie took it well. "Well, I'm sorry, too," she said. "I've been thinking about you."

"Keep me in mind," Jane said.

"Okay," said Laurie.

Then she and her mother spent several hours in the kitchen making yet another batch of Rice Krispies treats. Laurie was so happy, Edith noticed, happier than she'd been in a long time. She was really psyched for the carnival.

22

Free Samples

Lights were burning early at the Wassermans' on the morning of May 20, 1988.

Laurie had awakened shortly after five o'clock, just before sunrise, to begin her final preparations for the day. The demons in her past—her parents, her ex-husband and his relatives and friends, her tormentors in Evanston and Madison, the men who hadn't loved her, the men who had loved her badly, the women who had shunned her, her baby-sitting clients and her doctors—they would all feel the bitter sting of regret. They would never underestimate her again.

She had seen Kiki Hyman's car around the corner in her parents' driveway the night before, so at 5:35 A.M. she called the house and woke Kiki up. "Is Donna there?" she said, asking for Kiki's mother.

"No, she's not," said Kiki, still groggy and unable to figure out who was on the line.

Laurie slammed the phone down. Her bedroom at that hour was a veritable pantry of fruit juice packets, Rice Krispies treats and popcorn. For approximately the next fifty minutes, as Glencoe awakened to a gorgeous spring day, she loaded her syringe with the arsenic solution she had stolen from the labs at the University of Wisconsin and carefully injected the foil pouches of juice with the poison. Some of the pouches she then placed into long, brown envelopes onto which she had written "Free Sample" and the addresses of "Dr. Greist," no first name; Russell Dann; Peter Smith of Wilmette, a former baby-sitting client and Rushe family friend; and others. The rest of the pouches went into a plastic garbage bag.

Her movements through the North Shore suburbs in the following two hours have been reconstructed by examining the addresses she visited and talking to the people who saw her en route.

At about 6:30, she walked next door to a house owned by William and Iris Garmisa, friends of Norm and Edith's, and left a poison juice pouch in the mailbox. Then she returned home and, because her Accord was still in the body shop, loaded up her father's Cressida with supplies. She put her handguns, incendiary chemicals and ammunition in the trunk, placed the poisoned food in containers on the passenger seat and threw in an extra garbage bag.

She proceeded south on Sheridan Road from her parents' house, driving five blocks to Woodlawn Avenue, where she turned right. Halfway down the 200 block she stopped at the home of former baby-sitting clients Sam and Debi Oakner and dropped off a leaking container of Hawaiian Punch.

She drove west on Woodlawn half a block, then south on Glenwood Street to where Old Green Bay Road and Scott Avenue come together. There she placed six padded envelopes in the mailbox—the letter carrier who picked up the envelopes later that morning remembered one of them was wet.

At 6:45, she headed one block southwest on Scott Avenue to Green Bay Road, which she took north through Glencoe and into Highland Park. She turned left into Charal Lane, one block south of Clavey Road in the neighborhood where she and Russell had lived before their separation.

Steven Lapata on Charal Lane heard his screen door open and close at 6:55. When he went to investigate, he found a juice pouch between the doors, leaking through a pinprick hole near the top center. He checked with his neighbors, who said they had received nothing. Lapata's wife, Jodi, had known Laurie slightly when she lived nearby, but it seems possible that Laurie mistook the Lapata house for the house two doors away that had angered her several years earlier when she was convinced that the owners had gotten a better deal than she and Russell had.

She drove back out to Green Bay Road, turned right, then took her next right onto Stonegate Drive. A block and a half down the street she left juice at the home of John Eilian. He knew Laurie through a friend.

She headed west another block and turned right onto Hastings Street. She placed Hawaiian Punch in the rack under the mailbox at the house of Steven Sider in the 100 block. Sider did not know Laurie personally, but he was a close friend of Jeff and Susie Taylor's. She then slipped a juice packet between the screen door and the front door of the Kalish house in the 300 block. She and Marla Kalish had not been close, but they had talked over the back fence from time to time.

Her last stop on the block was at the house of another former neighbor, Steven Jazinsky, where she placed a juice pouch in the mailbox.

She then returned to Clavey Road and drove west a mile to U.S. Highway 41 south, which took her to Winnetka. She was carrying a slip of paper with an address on DeWindt Road, and she arrived at that address at a little past seven A.M., left a juice pouch in the mailbox, rang the bell and walked quickly away.

Homeowner Nancy Mowry answered the door and saw a woman getting into her car and heading away. Mowry didn't know Laurie—had never seen her before—and police investigators later chased down numerous leads, old baby-sitters and family ties trying to figure out why Laurie had made such a special point and gone so far out of her way to leave poison at the Mowrys' and even carry a special note with their address. Ultimately they discovered that Henry Angston of Winnetka had owned the house up until 1984. He had four children, one of whom was at New Trier when Laurie was, another of whom attended the University of Wisconsin at the time Laurie took summer school classes there and a third of whom once dated Robbie Dann, Russell's first cousin. One of them had evidently, at some point, slighted Laurie in a way she never forgot or forgave.

Seven blocks from the former Angston house, she left Rice Krispies treats and a juice pouch in the front door of the Freidheim residence on Indian Tree Road. Scott Freidheim was the Psi Upsilon fraternity brother at Northwestern upon whom Laurie had fixated during the previous summer after he gave her a ride.

A block up the road she left juice at the home of Murray and Kiki Hyman. Then she returned to Green Bay Road and drove south into Evanston. She turned east on Central Street and proceeded past Dyche Stadium to Sheridan Road and the Northwestern campus. At around eight o'clock she left a few plates of Rice Krispies treats sitting on the landing of the stairs at the west entrance of the Alpha Tau Omega fraternity house on Lincoln Street. Alpha Tau Omega was on her list because, the previous summer, the brothers had forced Donna McDonough to give up her puppy. McDonough, who rented a room at the fraternity for the summer and was employed as a desk clerk and hall monitor at the Kellogg Living/Learning Center, brought the puppy to work several times, and Laurie grew very attached to it.

Fraternity member Scott Myers read the note, which was signed, "To the ATO's, with love, your little sisters," and he brought the goodies into the dining room for the other brothers to enjoy.

At 8:30, Laurie entered the east door of the Psi Upsilon house next to ATO on Lincoln Street, and, on a bench in the foyer, set three paper plates of Rice Krispies treats laced with arsenic, a juice pouch, an open bag of Jolly Time popcorn that later tested positive for a high concentration of lead, which masks the presence of arsenic, and a bottle labeled "Arsenic." She left a note signed, "Love, your little sisters. Enjoy." The note seemed odd to the residents because they referred to sorority women as "daughters," not little sisters. The bottle, which actually did contain arsenic, seemed at the time like a silly and not very funny joke.

She also left Rice Krispies treats at the Kappa Sigma fraternity house on Sheridan Road, and in the vestibule of Leverone Hall, headquarters of the Kellogg business school.

Laurie returned to Green Bay Road and, slightly ahead of schedule, turned north toward the Rushe house in Winnetka.

•

The very first day that a young boy gets to ride his bike to school is a big day indeed, and as Laurie Dann drove with stone-faced purpose into Winnetka after leaving her trail of poison through the North Shore, eight-year-old Nicky Corwin was hurrying to pull on his Chicago Bears souvenir jersey, sweatpants and gym shoes for school, running late but excited.

He had been studying bicycle safety and the rules of the road for the previous two weeks at school, and that morning he and his second-grade classmates at Hubbard Woods Elementary would be taking both outdoor and indoor tests. If he passed, he would be allowed to ride the five blocks to school every day for the rest of the year. It was such an epochal event—like getting a driver's license would be for a teenager—that he and a number of his classmates had actually dreamed about the test the night before.

His older brother, Michael, eleven, was astride his own bike waiting at the edge of the driveway.

"Go on ahead!" their mother called. "Nicky will get there."

"It's okay, Mom!" he called back. "I really want to wait. I want to ride with Nicky."

It was, in many ways, like a scene from a corny 1950's TV show. The Corwins lived in a red brick and white stucco house on the corner of a street shrouded by towering oaks. Nicky was a mop top with bright, hazel eyes, freckles across his nose and a gap-toothed grin. Although Linda Corwin held a master's degree in public affairs, she was a full-time mother to Nicky, Michael and Johnny, a five-year-old. She also did free-lance business writing on the side and was a member of the local school board.

Her husband, Joel, was a corporate lawyer in a Chicago firm, commissioner of the local junior baseball league and the former chairman of the Winnetka Caucus, a town-meeting style assembly held in lieu of primary elections in order to select candidate slates for local elections.

Joel Corwin met the former Linda Weissman in 1966 when they were in high school and attending special summer classes at Northwestern University. He was from Evanston and she was from Waterloo, Iowa. Both "cherubs," as the summer students were known, were studying journalism.

They corresponded after the summer and continued to stay in touch when Joel went off to Yale and Linda returned to Northwestern for undergraduate studies. Their romance blossomed again when Joel came home to visit his parents, and after Linda's sophomore year she married Joel and transferred to Yale to be part of that university's first coed class.

They graduated in 1971 and went to Ithaca, New York, where Joel went to Cornell law school and Linda worked as a feature writer for the *Ithaca Journal*. But Linda was homesick for the Midwest so they moved the next year to Minneapolis, where they both continued their studies at the University of Minnesota.

Joel graduated and landed a law job in Chicago. Linda was still two courses shy of her master's degree, but finished up at Loyola University in Chicago. When their first child, Michael, was five weeks old they repaired to the suburban tranquility of Winnetka—a village that usually ranks in the top twenty-five in the nation in household income and has more people listed in *Who's Who* per capita than all but four communities in America.

The town was settled in 1836 and named after the American Indian word "winnet," meaning beautiful. It offered just the right combination of good schools, low crime, serene surroundings and friendly neighbors.

Nicky was born at Evanston Hospital on April 9, 1980, at 2:48 A.M., just three minutes after his parents drove up to the emergency room door. The delivery, Linda later remembered, was totally painless. She said that she was always grateful to Nicky for that, and joked that perhaps that was why she got along with him so well.

His athletic prowess showed itself early—he was already throwing a ball with accuracy by the time he was just a year old—and as soon as he was able he climbed trees and jungle gyms absolutely without fear. He went on to excel in soccer, baseball and football, and set a school record for his age group in the forty-yard dash with a time of 6.9 seconds.

His athletic grace was matched by an artistic talent and academic aptitude already heralded by his teachers, who had started to speak of him as someone they expected to read great things about one day. His elaborate drawings and colored marker creations hung in Dax frames around the Corwin house, and his storage area at school was filled with little storybooks he had both written and illustrated.

But what set Nicky apart from many other pint-size whiz kids was a certain humility; the sense he seemed to have that his special talents gave him special obligations. Instead of lording his abilities over the other kids he became their helper and leader, and was known as much for his sense of fair play and camaraderie as his skills. In the first grade he'd been voted "most supportive" by his classmates for his conduct on the athletic field and in the classroom, and his teacher used to leave notes for substitutes that said, "Nick Corwin is a great helper."

His room at home had a Chicago Cubs poster hanging on the wall above the bed, a Michael Jordan poster against the far wall and a Chicago Bears pennant on the bulletin board to go along with ballplayer wallpaper and a toy basketball hoop hanging from the top of his closet door. Though he was short for his age at just under four feet, he was determined one day to be a professional athlete.

In the fall, he and Michael played football in the backyard against his dad and brother, Johnny. Winter drove the games indoors, where Linda would take over as quarterback and make the boys use a Nerf ball. The Corwins had taken trips together to California, New York, Florida's Walt Disney World and Arizona; one of Linda's favorite holiday photographs showed the three Corwin boys standing by a rail at the rim of the Grand Canyon. Nicky, in the middle, is looking up affectionately at his older brother while draping his arm protectively around his younger brother.

He was the center of the family, Linda said. When they posed for a studio photograph, Nicky sat right in the middle. Similarly, when his second-grade class at school posed in informal array out on the playground for its annual group photo, he was sitting out in front of everyone, even the teacher, all by himself, grinning hugely.

But for all his poise and independence, he still liked to crawl in bed with his mom in the morning after his father got up. Joel Corwin tried to leave the house early for work so he could come home early in the evening, and on the morning of May 20 his last glimpse of Nicky was of the boy curled up against his mother, both sleeping contentedly.

For Mother's Day earlier in the month, he had written a card for Linda titled "My Great Mom":

> *My mother's freckles are pretty as a rose*
> *And when they show, her teeth shine like the night moon*
> *Her skin is as soft as a blanket*
> *When she smiles, her lips are like a beautiful rainbow*
> *Her blue eyes sparkle like a bright diamond*
> *My mom's hair is as wavy as an ocean....*
> *She is loving because when I do something bad she still loves me.*
> *She is concerned because when I get sick she tells me not to go to school.*
> *With all these things I think my mom is the best mom anyone could have.*

"My favorite color is blue," Nicky had written in the introduction to the journal he kept at school. "My favorite letter is N. My favorite number is 3." He recorded that he could do five chin-ups, that he dressed as pro football player Willie Gault for Halloween and that he wore his black sport coat to the spring sing.

He also listed the other things he was most thankful for: "Mom, Dad, little brother, older brother, house, bed, money, doctor, grandma, school, my friends, my life, and me."

•

He raced for his bike, a black dirt-bike model that once belonged to Michael, and streaked down the concrete driveway to join his brother. It was such a perfect day to ride your bike; such a perfect day to be a kid.

23

Fires

The scene at the Rushe household that morning was, as always, a sharp reminder to Laurie Dann of what she never was and never had. Marian was thirty-five years old, married, a mother of five great kids, outgoing, involved. Her children were self-assured and talented. The whole family had that characteristic Irish Catholic zest; the kids were always running off to soccer practice, hockey games, dance lessons or something, getting the most out of life. Their happiness, and Marian's achievement, was an insult.

The Rice Krispies treats Laurie left behind on the counter were, like the others she had distributed that morning, laced with arsenic. Similarly the orange tint to the milk was the result of several drops of arsenic solution she had surreptitiously poured into the jug.

After leaving the Rushes' with the two boys, Laurie drove west on Tower Road, a major east-west artery through Winnetka just a block from their house. Tower took them to U.S. Highway 41, a limited-access expressway that serves the North Shore. She headed north to Clavey Road in Highland Park, then proceeded east and north to Ravinia Elementary, a classic, dark brick, three-story school for 280 students in Highland Park, where she arrived shortly before nine A.M. Jeff and Susie Taylor's nine-year-old boy, Brian, attended the school, and their other son, Adam, was a former student.

Laurie parked the car out front and told Patrick and Carl to stay put, she had to pick up something inside and would be right back. She removed a yellow plastic Herman's Sporting Goods bag with a drawstring top from the trunk and carried it into the school, the glass jars and bottles inside tinkling against one another.

Upon entering the school through a south door she almost immediately came upon a cardboard refrigerator box that had been cut up and decorated to look like a house. The box was all that was left of "Cardboard City," a social studies project in which the second-graders earned play money for doing their homework, then purchased toy houses with mortgages from third-grade "bankers." It was a perfect exercise for the children of the well-to-do, and, Laurie thought when she came upon the house, the perfect hiding spot for her bomb.

She placed the bag down on the hallway floor inside the playhouse and set fire to the drawstring. The sealed bottles contained such stolen flammable liquid compounds as heptane, butanol, etching acid and pyradine, as well as several nonflammable chemicals, just for the hell of it. Laurie had calculated that when they ignited together they would cause an explosion that would rip through the school and saturate it with noxious gasses.

The bag began to burn and Laurie backed away toward the door.

Fifty feet away, second-grade teacher Paul Grant was leading a line of his students to the library. They'd been noisy and uncooperative that morning, the way kids will be when it's warm outside and they must be inside. It had taken him two extra minutes just to get them ready to go. As Grant looked down the hallway he saw a woman he did not recognize stagger back into the exit door, hit the crash bar noisily and run away down the sidewalk.

Strange. What was her big hurry? Grant and all eighteen students filed past the cardboard house. Two sharp-eyed boys near the end of the line—Ben Wigdor and Chet Evans—

happened to look into a window and see the flicker of the flame. Grant, as an adult, was much too tall to have seen inside as he passed.

The boys raced ahead and caught up to Grant as he and the head of the line reached the main office area. "There's something burning in the box!" they said.

Grant smiled. "Well, then, call the Cardboard City Fire Department," he said.

"No!" they said. "Something's really burning!"

"Class, go on ahead to the library," said Grant, still calm. "I'll be right with you."

He and Ben and Chet walked back to the house. Grant bent down, opened the door and saw flames eating the top half of a plastic bag.

•

Laurie jumped back in her father's car and sped off. At a stop sign she passed the Mickey Mouse cup filled with arsenic-laced milk into the back seat and told the boys to drink. They took it from her and both had a taste. It was awful—sour or spoiled, they thought. Without saying anything, they set the cup aside.

Laurie drove them half a mile southwest to the Young Men's Jewish Council, a modern, one-story day-care center on Clavey Road in Highland Park, just around the corner from the Hastings Street house where she and Russell had lived together. Laurie knew that Lisa Taylor, Jeff and Susie's five-year-old, was enrolled at the center, though she probably did not know that Lisa was an afternoon student and not due to arrive until 12:45 P.M., three and a half hours later.

When she pulled into the west parking lot, Laurie told the Rushe boys they should come with her to pick up something from the office. Then she picked up a plastic garbage bag from the passenger seat and pulled it on, sticking her arms and head through holes she had cut.

"You look funny," said Patrick, the older of the two boys.

"I do?" Laurie said. She removed the absurd disguise and left it in the car. The boys threw the Mickey Mouse cup out onto the grass while Laurie went around to the trunk and withdrew a red plastic gasoline container. Carrying the gas can, she led the boys toward the main entrance to the school.

She put the gas can down on the sidewalk in front of the entrance, then led Patrick and Carl into the building—they were her cover. School director Jean Leivick, who had seen Laurie approaching, went to the foyer to intercept her. Laurie explained that her children—she nodded at Patrick and Carl—were going to attend a summer program at the school and she wanted to look around. Leivick let her go, and she led the boys from classroom to classroom, looking in the doors.

Lisa Taylor wasn't there. Laurie returned to the front of the school, where she sent Patrick and Carl off to play on the swing sets and picked up the gasoline container again. When she tried to reenter the school, Leivick stopped her.

"You can't bring that into the building," Leivick said, gesturing at the can.

"I'm out of gas," Laurie explained in mock distress. "And I've got the two kids with me."

"Do you need help putting the gas into the tank? Is that it?"

Laurie hesitated. "Um...yes," she said. Leivick accompanied her back to the Toyota and helped her pour the gasoline in.

Right about then, in Evanston, a brother at the Alpha Tau Omega house was taking a big bite of one of the Rice Krispies treats found on the doorstep that morning. They tasted nasty, he thought. He threw the rest of the plate into the dumpster.

At the Ravinia School, Highland Park police officers and firefighters had been summoned after teacher Paul Grant had blown out the fire in the cardboard house. They were examining the vicious combination of chemicals that had been in the plastic bag and wondered if, considering the heavy Jewish population in the area, they had an anti-Semitic terrorist action on their hands. Off-duty officers were called in, just to be safe.

Russell Dann, meanwhile, was having an unpleasant morning. His dentist was digging around in his mouth giving him a root canal. He hoped it wasn't going to ruin his whole day—he had a date to see the White Sox play the Detroit Tigers at Comiskey Park that night.

•

Nicky Corwin's regular teacher at Hubbard Woods was taking a personal day Friday, but the sub was Miss Moses, who had filled in a lot that year and even knew all the kids' names.

She took them outside right at nine o'clock for the first half of the bicycle safety test, the riding part. The gym teacher was supervising the entire obstacle course and Amy Moses was watching over the figure eights. As each child finished he put his bike back in the rack and scampered out onto the playground, where Moses hoped they all would burn off some of the nervous energy that had been building all week.

Everyone passed the test. Moses then had to get them all together and lead them back to the classroom for the written half of the exam. Before getting down to it, she led a group discussion about how excited and anxious they were about the test and what a big accomplishment it was going to be to win the right to ride to school every day...for the rest of their lives, if they wanted.

•

Laurie summoned Patrick and Carl, belted them back into the car and drove south from the Young Men's Jewish Council school through residential Glencoe to a neighborhood where she had done a lot of baby-sitting.

First she stopped at the home of Paul Lederer on Bluff Street, where she left fruit juice in the mailbox. The packet was marked "Sample" in blue ink, and the foil was sticky to the touch.

Two blocks south and half a block west on Milton Street, she stopped in front of the home of Julie and Mike Alt. She left them poisoned juice, trying to make good on her earlier, anonymous promise to murder the three Alt girls.

She returned to Bluff Street and headed south, stopping to leave a juice packet in the mailbox of Willard Boris. Boris worked out at the Combined Fitness Center in Northbrook, where Laurie used to take aerobics classes.

Farther down Bluff Street she left a juice packet in the

mailbox of Burt Gutteman. She then threw another juice packet on the front lawn several doors away, where homeowner Jackie Coleman later found it.

Laurie turned left on Park Avenue and stopped in the middle of the 500 block to leave juice in the mailbox of David and Rosemarie Hawkins, former baby-sitting clients and close friends of the Rushes'.

Laurie's connection with the Hawkins family was apparent, though her reason for wanting to kill them remains mysterious. But for some of the other targets—Paul Lederer, for instance—the connections have been impossible to determine. Any one member of the family at some unknown time either did something to Laurie or didn't do something for her, said something, looked a certain way, failed to wave hello, appeared to flaunt something, honked a car horn in anger—anything.

But whatever her tangled motivations at that moment, Laurie was done, out of poison. Patrick and Carl were still very much alive, prattling away in the back seat, so she decided to take them back home and deal with them there.

She drove side streets through residential neighborhoods toward the Rushes'. She no doubt figured that all hell was breaking loose at the Ravinia School, with a huge explosion, a savage blaze and the hallways strewn with dead and dying children. Someone might have seen her driving away. The police might well be looking for the car—a white, late-model Toyota Cressida with a couple of kids in the back seat.

A little past ten o'clock, she arrived back at the Rushe house and ushered the children inside. "I'm sorry," she said to Marian, who was surprised to see her back so soon. "I had the wrong date for the carnival. I took them to the park instead."

Patrick and Carl did not appear particularly bothered by the change in plans, so Marian took it in stride as well. She invited Laurie to stay and keep the children company while she did laundry.

Laurie was carrying a pack of matches from a Mexican restaurant in Evanston and a brown shopping bag rattling with bottles. She set the matches on a tabletop in the hallway near the front door and carried the bag with her as she followed Marian and the children down a central staircase to the basement laundry room.

"So," said Laurie, making an effort to sound casual as she set the bag down next to the coffee table. "Are Mary Rose and Robert coming home for lunch?"

Marian shook her head. "They're on a school field trip down in Chicago today," she said. "I don't expect them back until late."

"Oh," said Laurie. Another hitch.

She stood up, hoisting the plastic bag. "I have to get something from the car," she said.

Patrick and Carl were bored with the laundry routine and seemed ready to follow Laurie up the stairs, but Marian had a glimmer that Laurie was engineering some sort of surprise going-away gift for them. "Stay here," she told the boys.

Halfway up to the landing, Laurie pulled out a large flask filled with gasoline and poured it on the carpeted treads at her feet. She opened a second container and set it on top of the spill, then made a quick move to the front hallway to retrieve her book of matches. She returned to the basement stairs, tore a match free, struck it and touched the lighted end to the soaked fibers. Flames danced up off the stairs in a silent flash of blue and orange.

Marian Rushe was occupied with the laundry when she heard the smoke detector go off. What could that mean? She was still trying to puzzle it out when she heard a sound coming from the stairwell that reminded her of a gas grill being lit—woof! The second container of gasoline had ignited.

"Oh! Fire!" Laurie called out. She hurried to the back door and locked it, the better to impede rescue efforts, then locked the front door behind her as she hurried out.

By the time Marian rounded the corner and reached the bottom of the stairs to investigate, the fire was furious, creeping down toward her with black, choking smoke, melting light bulbs in the ceiling as it advanced. She cried out to her boys, gathered them up and led them toward the far corner of the basement away from the fire. In the back of her mind, she worried for Laurie. She had called out, but was she okay? Had she escaped?

The southeast window, six feet high against the wall, offered their only way out. Every other window in the basement had been sealed with glass bricks to guard against flooding. It wouldn't open easily, so Marian snapped a leg off an old baby's crib and broke the glass with several smart blows. Using her hands, she pulled shards and fragments out of the frame, cutting her hands and arms badly. When the opening was relatively clear, she hoisted Patrick on her shoulders and boosted him so he could crawl through the opening and into the window well. The boy then pushed out the grate protecting the well and escaped into the yard. Carl wriggled out behind him.

"Go get help next door!" she shouted.

Getting herself out would not be so easy. She had no light and the smoke was moving toward her in a pernicious cloud as it filled up the basement. She yanked on the frame of the window until it gave way, then broke free. She looked around in a panic for old suitcases and anything else she could pile up to make a platform for herself. When that was done, she climbed upon the rickety pile and pulled herself through the opening into fresh air and daylight.

She was bloodied but safe.

•

Detective Floyd Mohr in Glencoe wasn't scheduled to work until three o'clock that afternoon, but to get a jump on his paperwork he'd come in early and headed out in his blue, unmarked Ford Fairmont on a follow-up call. He was signaling to turn north onto Vernon Drive at 10:21 A.M. when he heard the report of a fire in Winnetka on his police radio and shook his head sympathetically—what bad timing. Winnetka was short-handed, he knew, because most of the department was at that moment attending the funeral of retired firefighter Lawrence Carney, who had been killed by lightning the preceding Sunday while fishing on Lake Michigan.

Mohr figured that the men on duty could probably use an experienced extra hand, so he knocked his blinker from a right-turn signal to a left-turn and headed south toward the fire fifteen blocks away.

When he arrived at the Rushe house, smoke was swirling

ominously out of the north gale vents in the attic. He asked what he could do to be of assistance, and Winnetka fire captain Gary Lindeman, who was in charge, told him to help a policeman drag a hose over and make a hydrant hookup, which he did. They opened it up when they got the signal.

"Floyd," the cop said, "do me a favor: Stick around, and if the guys need air, switch bottles for them."

Mohr nodded. He would do whatever he could.

24

Murder
of
Innocence

After Laurie left Marian Rushe and her two youngest children to burn alive in their own basement, she threw a spare flask of gasoline into the garbage can by the door, opened the trunk of her father's car and removed her three handguns. She placed them on the passenger seat next to her and drove four blocks south and east to Hubbard Woods Elementary, a one-story brick school with homey, white wooden window frames that sits unobtrusively in the middle of a graceful, residential neighborhood in north-central Winnetka.

She parked the Toyota on Chatfield Road at the front of the school so it faced west, toward Interstate 94 a mile and a half away.

It was 10:25 A.M. The doors, as ever, were unlocked and unguarded. Like most schools, Hubbard Woods had a policy that all guests should report to the main office first, but it was hardly ever enforced, and no one even saw Laurie as she circled halfway around the outside of the building, pushed through the double doors at the back entrance by the gymnasium and slipped quickly into a boys' bathroom. There she probably looked in a mirror to be sure that her guns were tucked safely into the waistband of her shorts and that her T-shirt fell over the bulges to hide them. When the weapons were appropriately concealed, she reentered the hallway. The school had 325 students, but fully a third of them, including the elder Rushe children, her likely targets, were off on "cultural enrichment" field trips to ethnic neighborhoods in Chicago that day, so foot traffic in the halls was particularly light.

Kindergarten teacher Phyllis McMillan, whose classroom was next to the bathroom, happened to poke her head into the hall at just that moment to check on her snack group. Kindergartners were allowed a snack break every morning, but because the classroom was carpeted they had to eat in the hall. McMillan sent them out two and three at a time, which necessitated a spry vigilance on her part. When she saw Laurie pass, McMillan thought she looked like a nanny, but she had never seen her before. It was quite unusual that she should be emerging from the boys' bathroom.

As Laurie continued north up the hallway toward the principal's office by the main entrance, she passed Ann Hardy, a teacher who was on break and standing in the doorway of her classroom while her students were in gym class.

"Hello," Hardy said.

Laurie didn't answer and kept walking, past the small wooden coat carrels, the wall murals, the gaily decorated doorways, the knee-high drinking fountains.

McMillan hurried over to Hardy. "Something very strange just happened," she said. "I don't know that woman. She just came out of the boys' bathroom. I've got to stay with my kids, but would you mind checking on her?"

"Sure," Hardy said. By the time she looked up, the woman was gone. She went toward the front of the school and reached the T in the hallway, looked both ways, and again saw nothing. Just to her left, through a set of doors and into the west corridor, she knocked on the wooden entrance of the bathroom where the word "Boys" was written only three feet off the floor.

"Can I help someone?" she called.

No answer. Hardy waited, heard nothing, and went back to report to McMillan. "She must be gone."

When Laurie heard Hardy's footsteps receding, she resumed breathing. She stashed her Magnum and a bag of ammunition in the left-hand sink where she could come back and retrieve them, then left the bathroom and entered the corridor again.

Her plans at that moment had taken on a freeform quality. Ahead of her across the hall from the bathroom was the closed door of Classroom 7. Seven, the little black number high on the left frame. Seven was one of her lucky numbers.

At a little past 10:30, she opened the door and walked in. Twenty-four children were sitting at tables and desks grouped around the room listening to Amy Moses brief them on what they would have to know for the written portion of their bicycle safety test and explain to them how they would be taking it in small groups, discussing the questions among themselves and trying to agree on the right answers.

On one wall was a bulletin board labeled "The Writing Place," where the regular teacher, Amy Deuble, tacked up short stories and compositions. Other bulletin boards featured the "Jelly Bean Book Club" and the "Person of the Week." Way up on the west wall were a series of silhouette cut-outs of all the kids, companion pieces to the hand-tracing cut-outs on the south wall. The room had a computer terminal up front and, more traditionally, the alphabet running across the top of the main blackboard, a height chart in the corner and a flag hanging over the door. Throughout, art-project flower decorations hung from the ceiling like tinsel off a tree.

Laurie walked over and stood next to Moses, who was three inches shorter than Laurie and forty pounds lighter.

Moses interrupted her lesson. "May I help you?" she said politely.

"No," Laurie said.

"Are you here to observe?" Moses asked. Hubbard Woods was informal in this respect. Parents felt free to drop in anytime and students from Northwestern or the National College of Education in Evanston frequently came to watch teachers in action. Laurie looked, from her medical school T-shirt and unkempt hair, as though she were a student, but she didn't answer the question and instead simply sat down at a table in the front of the room. Moses continued with her lesson, but she was bothered by the hard, lifeless expression of the stranger, who should have been engaging the children with a look or a smile or something.

She gave Laurie a copy of the test she was about to hand out in hopes of getting her swept up in the excitement both she and the kids were feeling about Bike Day. She wanted to show by example what teaching was all about for her—enthusiasm, loving and caring. She herself was a former textbook editor and an aspiring writer who had decided in mid-career to become a teacher. While subbing at Hubbard Woods that year she was also working on a master's degree in education and specialty reading. Her life was finally going well. Just that Monday, in fact, she'd concluded her sessions with a counselor who had helped her through the end of a seven-year marriage.

Laurie maintained eye contact when Moses directed remarks her way, but she didn't seem to be picking up on the overall mood in the class. Her face remained blank as her mind roiled with conflicting impulses, plans, strategies.

After several minutes, she stood suddenly, dropped the bicycle information on the floor and left the room.

•

She headed back out into the hall, where she saw Robert Trossman, six, at a drinking fountain. He was returning from the reading lab to his first-grade class after completing a standardized test that he'd missed the first time it was given. Suddenly she found her courage.

"Don't you have to go to the bathroom, little boy?" she said.

Robert was too confused to cry out. Laurie dragged him by the arm into the boys' bathroom, withdrew the Beretta from her waistband and fired virtually point-blank. She was so nervous that her first shot missed and slammed into the tile right between two urinals. With the second shot she hit him in the right upper chest with a bullet that exited through his lower back, and he dropped to the floor.

As she turned to leave she saw to her surprise that two other little boys had walked in behind her and seen what had happened. She pointed the Beretta at them and pulled the trigger, but the gun didn't fire. They fled.

Laurie knew she could not turn back, and doubtlessly figured that the big gun—the blue-steel .357 Magnum—would slow her down. She left it and the ammunition in the washbasin where she'd placed them earlier, and headed back down the hall in the direction she'd come.

The two young witnesses ran wildly across the hall to their teacher, Mary Lind, who was in charge of special education programs in the classroom right next door to Classroom 7.

"Mrs. Lind! There's a woman in the bathroom with a gun!" they said.

Lind had heard the percussive popping sounds and assumed they were part of a science experiment in another class, but, when she thought of it, what the boys were saying might be true, improbable as it seemed. She dropped the papers she was holding and ran across to the bathroom. There she found Robert on the floor, bleeding from the chest. "I've been shot," he cried. "Am I going to die?"

Lind told one of the boys who had been in the bathroom with Laurie to stay with Robert, and she turned and ran, screaming, toward the principal's office. "Call the police! Call the paramedics!"

•

Laurie had returned to Classroom 7 with fury and resolve. The kids were sitting in small groups talking over the questions on the test and Amy Moses was answering the question of a child who had come to the front of the room.

"Put the children in a corner," Laurie ordered.

"What?" she said.

"Put the children in a corner," Laurie repeated.

"No," Moses replied, more surprised than frightened. "What are you talking about?"

Laurie drew her revolver. "This is a gun," she said. "And I have another one."

Moses saw the tiny pistol and thought it looked like a toy. One of the boys on the far side of the room thought the gun meant Laurie was an "Officer Friendly," one of the policemen who visited the school from time to time to give safety tips.

"It's real," Laurie said, reading the doubt in Moses' expression. "I'll show you.'

Amy suddenly realized by the tone of Laurie's voice that the gun was real and that she needed to do something to protect the children. Instinctively she grabbed Laurie's right wrist and began wrestling with her. "What are you doing?" she demanded.

During the first, brief struggle, Moses forced a pair of live .22 caliber rounds to eject from the Beretta. She managed to pull Laurie several feet over to the door of the classroom and called out into the hall, "There's a woman in here with a gun. She's going to shoot the kids. Get help!"

The only person in the hallway was a teacher's aide from the resource center who, in an improbable twist of fate, was suffering from an ear infection and was nearly deaf that day because of medicated plugs she was wearing.

Laurie broke free and pulled the .32 out of her shorts, drawing like a gunslinger. She waved her weapons at the children. "Get in the corner," she said.

They were struck motionless by a combination of fear and confusion. "Why?" one of them asked.

Laurie didn't wait. She moved quickly up to a group of three children against the east wall and held her gun out. Expressionlessly, she pulled the trigger. The sound, Moses remembered, was strangely ordinary, like the popping of a cap.

When the first child, eight-year-old Mark Teborek, went down, Moses thought, "They're filming a movie and they forgot to tell me. They just forgot to tell me."

The bullet had hit Mark on the left side of the neck and exited through the right side of the chest. He fell at the front of the classroom.

Laurie walked swiftly past the students who were sitting along the east wall of the classroom, toward the door that led outside. She fired her guns as she went, point-blank, while Amy Moses screamed, "Get out! Get out of here!" to the children.

Nicky Corwin turned away from Laurie toward the blackboard as she came at him. The bullet hit him in his left upper back, penetrated his left lung and pulmonary artery and exited through the right side of his chest. He fell facedown atop a large throw pillow that leaned against a blackboard.

Peter Munro, an eight-year-old with a blond crew cut, held out his hand to try to stop the bullet, but it ripped through the hand, hit him in the abdomen and exited out the lower back. He fell near Mark Teborek.

Lindsay Fisher, also eight and an avid soccer player, took a .32 caliber bullet in the right upper chest. It ricocheted downward off a bone and lodged in her lower left hip.

Laurie's last victim as she walked through Classroom 7 toward the exit door that took her outside was Kathryn Ann Miller, seven. The bullet hit her in the left side of the chest, hit a rib and exited through her stomach.

One little girl lay down motionless on the ground underneath a table when she saw her classmates begin to fall. She was pretending she was hurt, and when she saw Nicky a few feet away from her she thought he was doing the same thing.

And then the madwoman was gone, leaving behind a room filled with blood, screaming children and the acrid smell of gunpowder.

She ran back to the Toyota, guns in both hands. She drove quickly half a block west on Chatfield Road, the tiny lane that passes in front of the school, and swung hard into a right turn on Gordon Terrace. But at the intersection a police squad car was blocking the way ahead of her, its mars lights revolving. How quickly she was trapped!

Actually, Officer Rich Carlson was on the corner by coincidence. His humdrum assignment that morning was to clear traffic for the Carney funeral cortege as it came out of Sacred Heart Catholic Church at Tower Road and Burr Street a few blocks east.

But Laurie must have thought the roadblock was already there for her. Instead of doubling back toward the more densely populated area east of the school where she could have found another route out to the highway, she pulled a U-turn in a blind panic, a bystander reported, and sped off down Hamptondale Road, which signs identify as a dead-end street. She successfully navigated a spot where a big tree seems to sprout from the pavement and the road narrows considerably, but in swerving to miss the big tree she temporarily lost control of the car, oversteered her way back and sideswiped a sapling on the parkway. At the end of the road she sped past a "Street Ends" sign and a stone monument reading "1200," indicating that the pavement from there on belonged to the sprawling Tudor home hidden back among the trees.

The driveway formed a complete but small circle directly in front of the house, and Laurie was going far too fast to make the full turn successfully. The car swept wide and ended up with its back end lodged on a large rock. From the distance came the sound of sirens, one, two, three, more.

She reloaded the Beretta and the Smith & Wesson, then improvised a new costume—she took off her shorts and wrapped her midsection in a light blue plastic trash bag. She got out of the car, slammed the door behind her and took off on foot through the undergrowth in the opposite direction from the school.

The engine of the Toyota was still running. On the plush, maroon seats she left behind a pair of white shorts with a candle in the pocket, two packages of boxed matches, eighteen rounds of .22 ammunition, one box of .32 caliber ammunition with six rounds missing, a box of .22 caliber ammunition with twenty rounds missing, a can of gasoline and Styrofoam strips soaked in an accelerant.

She also left behind a travel guide opened to the page about Missouri, and a slip of paper with the home number of Scott Taylor, Jeff's brother and her friend Sheri's ex-husband. The paper also had the home and office telephone numbers of her former psychiatrist, Dr. Robert Greendale.

25

A
Shooting?

School secretary Eva Mendelson had lunged for the telephone as soon as she'd heard Mary Lind's screams coming from down the west hallway. She knew school policy—call for help first and ask questions later.

At 10:41 A.M., Winnetka police department dispatcher Bill Saunders picked up the 911 emergency line and heard a frantic call for help. "We've got a shooting at Hubbard Woods School! A child!"

His voice broke with incredulity: "A shooting?"

"Yes!"

"And there's an injury there, ma'am?"

"Yes!" Mendelson said. Another voice in the background added, "Urgent!"

"Okay, where's it at, please?"

"Hubbard Woods School on Chatfield Road."

"Okay," said Saunders. "We'll get somebody on the way. Can you hang on one minute please? Don't hang up!"

Saunders put Mendelson on hold and called for Winnetka ambulance 71 to respond. He got no immediate answer, so, thinking the ambulance was already at the fire on Forest Glen South, he called for Glencoe ambulance 81.

But paramedics Michael Roeder and Lee Fanslow in Winnetka 71 had heard the call and were already on their way.

Almost immediately, however, they found themselves caught
in funeral traffic out of Sacred Heart Church, so they decided
to attempt a back route, around and through the residential
streets.

•

Mary Lind turned as soon as she saw help had been called
and began running back to the boys' bathroom to tend to the
wounded boy. As she ran, she heard a fusillade of shots fired
in Classroom 7.

First-grade teacher Alice Horevitz, who was in Classroom
11 across the hall from Classroom 7, was annoyed by the
disruptive popping sounds. She had just gathered her students together on a rug to listen to a girl read a report she'd
written called "Science in Sweden." The noise reminded her of
bursting balloons, and Horevitz figured the screaming was just
second-graders whooping it up because it was Bike Day and
they'd all passed their tests.

Then she heard the sound of running in the hall and still
more screaming, this time unmistakably hysterical. The door
to her classroom opened and her student Robert Trossman
staggered in holding a test booklet in front of his chest. He
had made the ten-yard walk from the bathroom unassisted.
"I've just been shot by a crazy girl," he said.

The children who had escaped Classroom 7 raced straight
for the office of principal Dick Streedain. Streedain, too, had
heard the unusual noises and screams, and in the back of his
mind thought perhaps a door had slammed on a child's arm
or leg. After Mary Lind had sounded the alarm, Streedain
placed a quick call to his superintendent, Don Monroe. Monroe
happened to be two minutes away at Washburne Junior High
School, where young Laurie Wasserman had taken special
education classes nearly twenty years earlier.

Amy Moses ran into the hallway yelling, "Call the police!
Children have been shot!"

She and Streedain passed each other as he headed toward
Mary Lind's classroom, where shooting victim Peter Munro
had run to hide. Streedain was almost there when he heard
Alice Horevitz call out for help.

She had set Robert Trossman on a cushion, removed his

blood-soaked aqua sport shirt and lifted up his T-shirt to get at his wounds. Her other students hid in a cubby corner behind a group of desks, wailing, whimpering, crying uncontrollably.

"She shot me," Robert moaned, remaining coherent and relatively calm as his teacher tended to him. "Why did she do it?"

No sooner had Streedain looked in on Horevitz than another teacher grabbed him by the shoulder. "We have several more children shot across the hall," she said.

Streedain's first thought was similar to the thought that was on the minds of school officials in Highland Park that morning—terrorists were on the loose. "Be sure the school is secure," he ordered.

In the hallway, a teacher handed Streedain the limp body of Lindsay Fisher, who had run from the classroom after being shot and fallen before she could get to the office. The right shoulder and arm of her yellow T-shirt were drenched with blood. Teacher's aide Jacqueline Slavick was cradling Kathryn Miller, who'd made it all the way to the office before collapsing, her white shirt spotted and spattered with blood. She and Streedain carried the girls to the two, tiny front steps at the main entrance to wait for paramedics. They heard far-off ambulances wailing and time stood still as the color drained from the faces of the little girls.

It was 10:45. Officer Rich Carlson, who had left his post directing traffic and run to the school, saw the bloody scene and radioed in that two children were down. Three minutes later, Sergeant Jimmie Brewer of Winnetka, the second on the scene, radioed in that he had five victims down. No, wait. Six victims down.

Amy Moses was back inside Classroom 7, trying to administer first aid to Mark Teborek and calling out for more help. Mary Lind had also rushed to the classroom and, holding Nick Corwin's arm, soothed him. "It'll be okay," she said. "It'll be okay. Hang on." She thought she had a pulse. Later she realized it was just her own hands shaking.

•

At the scene of the fire at the Rushe house, Floyd Mohr heard his hip radio crackle. "Did they say a shooting?" he asked Winnetka animal warden Craig Tisdale, who was also helping fight the fire.

"Yeah," said Tisdale, as puzzled as Mohr. "At Hubbard Woods School."

"I'm getting over there," Mohr said.

•

Winnetka police sergeant Patty McConnell was waiting at the drive-up window of the Winnetka Bank on Spruce Street with her partner, Bob Kerner, when she first heard reports of shots fired at the school. They were in their Chevrolet Caprice unmarked sedan, putting their paychecks in the bank at the end of a fairly slow morning in which they'd traveled thirty miles round-trip to northwest suburban Palatine to arrest a man wanted for passing bad checks, put him in lockup, then met for coffee with two detectives from nearby Northfield. She was in sweatshirt and jeans, her undercover grubbies.

"Winnetka units, we have a report of a shooting at Hubbard Woods School."

McConnell thought first of a BB gun incident or, at the worst, a teacher involved in a dispute with her husband. A Winnetka cop never thought in terms of murder. There hadn't been one in the village since 1957, when a twenty-nine-year-old hitchhiker shot and killed patrolman Robert Burke for no apparent reason, then turned the gun on himself. The previous year, 1987, had been typical—Winnetka had a total of one reported sexual assault, three robberies, three assaults and three cases of arson.

But a shooting? Perhaps there was some mistake. McConnell and Kerner sped to the school. There they pulled up at the curb, jumped out and ran for the entrance, where they saw Streedain and Slavick, covered with blood, holding the bodies of two unconscious children.

Streedain looked wanly up at McConnell. "There are more inside," he said.

•

Winnetka police chief Herbert Timm, who had been at the Carney funeral, heard the chorus of sirens and ran to a pay phone at a drugstore to call the department to see what was happening. Busy. On his second try, the dispatcher said, "Please hold."

"Just a minute," Timm barked. "This is the chief. I want to know how bad this fire is."

"My God, Chief!"

●

Superintendent Monroe drove up to Hubbard Woods literally seconds ahead of the first ambulance, Winnetka 71, which pulled in around the back of the school just before 10:47, six minutes after the first call had come in. A teacher waved paramedics Fanslow and Roeder around to the outer door of Classroom 7.

Glencoe ambulance 81 was half a minute behind and pulled up to the main entrance. Jacqueline Slavick struggled to her feet and handed Kathryn Miller to Don Monroe. He and Dick Streedain ran to meet the ambulance from Glencoe.

In Classroom 7, Roeder raced for Nicky Corwin, and Fanslow went for Mark Teborek. Everyone was yelling and screaming. *The principal had been shot. Kids were shot all over the school.* Everything was happening at once. Roeder called on his radio for more help.

●

Laurie Dann, wrapped in plastic and running hard, had cut down a path through a break in the trees and bushes at the back of the driveway at 1200 Hamptondale Road where the Toyota was inextricably snagged on a rock. After twenty feet she found herself in yet another driveway leading to yet another enormous house. A ten-foot stockade fence rose up to her right and looming trees blocked the sky all around. She was lost inside a thicket of adjoining estates built into the forest—there were no streets visible and no clue which way led to freedom.

She pushed through a gate in a chain-link fence to get to the backyard of the second house. The address of the home was 6 Kent Road, but Kent Road was more a semiprivate access drive than a real street, so the number was no clue as to where exactly she was. Laurie pounded on the back door, and when no one answered, she grabbed a spade lying by the side of the house and shattered a pane of glass on a porch door.

The commotion brought a barking dog to the window inside, and Laurie took off again.

She ran about another fifty yards under a canopy of trees down the curving, asphalt driveway, turned left when she got to the street, then took another hard left into the driveway of 2 Kent Road, an eight-bedroom stucco mansion so shrouded by vegetation that it is almost impossible to photograph except from the air. A high wall extended from the plane of the front of the house across the side yard to a large combination coach house and garage. A black wooden gate led from the front yard into the back, and by that gate, on the driveway, eighty-three-year-old Vincent Wolf was sitting in the sun in a lawn chair, attended by a nurse.

"My car broke down, I need to use the phone," Laurie panted, running by. She entered the backyard through the gate and turned right into a door that led directly into the kitchen. It was unlocked and she burst in unannounced. Ruth Ann Andrew, fifty, Vincent Wolf's daughter and a former schoolteacher, was washing a few dishes at the sink, having just returned from the Lawrence Carney funeral. She was still dressed for the occasion in a calf-length black skirt, a white blouse and black beads.

Ruth Ann was talking to Phil Andrew, twenty, the fourth of her seven children. He had just come home the day before from his first year at the University of Illinois, where he was a member of the 400-yard medley relay and 400-yard freestyle relay swim teams, and she was waiting for him to get ready to go shopping with her for dress clothes for his summer job at the Cook County State's Attorney's office. He was still dressed in his morning attire of a white T-shirt and red gym shorts.

Laurie, drenched with sweat, was wearing only her Arizona College of Medicine T-shirt and the trash bag, which she held together in front with the same hand that was carrying both guns.

At first Phil thought she was a neighborhood baby-sitter who had gotten the worst of a water-pistol fight.

•

The first media call into the Winnetka police department came from all-news radio station WBBM-AM at 10:51 A.M., a full two minutes before Lindsay Fisher and Kathryn Miller began the thirteen-minute trip to Evanston Hospital in Glencoe ambulance 81.

•

Robert Trossman's mother, Janis, appeared unexpectedly at the entrance to the school in the immediate aftermath of the shootings.

"How did you get here so quickly?" Streedain asked.

"What do you mean?" she said, surveying the chaos.

Streedain realized the timing of her arrival was only coincidental. "There's been a terrible tragedy," he said. "Several children have been shot, and Robert is one of them. He's in Mrs. Horevitz's room. You need to go comfort him."

He took her hand and led her quickly to her son.

•

Teacher Mary Lind was still hovering over Nicky. "I've lost the pulse!" she cried to Winnetka paramedic Michael Roeder. "I had his pulse! I lost it!"

Roeder knelt down and saw immediately how bad it was. "DOA," he said.

Lind didn't move.

Roeder stood. "DOA," he said sharply. "Get away! Move away!"

Roeder ran from the classroom and headed left, and his partner, Fanslow, broke across the hall to the right, looking for the rest of the wounded. Fanslow found Peter Munro and carried him back to the classroom, then retrieved Robert Trossman from Classroom 11. All the wounded were laid out on the floor near Nicky Corwin.

•

Chief Timm arrived and entered the school, where the hallways were becoming increasingly chaotic as confusion spread. He first went into what appeared to be a deserted room. As he was turning to leave he heard a rustling under a table and a child's head popped out. "Can we come out now?" asked a boy. "Are we going to get shot?"

"You'll be okay," Timm said. "Just stay there. You're not going to be shot."

Timm found Classroom 7 and saw the bloodstained floor, the wounded children, the riot of papers and the kicked-over desks. Officer Rich Carlson was helping Patty McConnell, Bob Kerner and other arriving paramedics clear the area and sort the victims by the severity of their wounds.

"My tummy hurts so bad," Robert Trossman groaned. "I can't breathe. Am I going to die, mister?"

"No, no," Timm said. "You're going to be fine."

A fire department paramedic pressed on the gaping wound in Robert's chest as his mother looked on in horror. "I bet this is more attention than you've gotten in a long time," he said to the boy.

Robert smiled.

Dick Streedain, the principal, returned to the classroom and the paramedics told him Nicky, who was then covered by a sheet, was dead.

•

Joel Corwin received a telephone call at his law office in Chicago from a woman at the school. She told him in a voice ragged with emotion there had been "an emergency" and that he and his wife should get there as soon as possible. Nothing else. Just "an emergency."

He remembered that Linda was at the golf clinic at the nearby public course and he called the clubhouse. She was in a group practicing sand-trap shots when a man ran out to get her, saying her husband was on the phone and it was very important.

Linda's mind turned back several months to the time she was called off the tennis courts when Michael had chipped a couple of teeth and she had to take him to the dentist. But as soon as she heard the panic in Joel's voice she knew something much more serious had happened—maybe one of the school's boilers had blown. The school board had just been talking about replacing one of the boilers.

She ran to her car and Joel headed for the street to hail a taxi for the half-hour trip home—there was no time to catch the train.

•

A second paramedic panicked badly. He was a Vietnam veteran who had once been assigned to cleaning out a schoolhouse that had been bombed, and he appeared to suffer a flashback as he looked over the carnage. He rushed over to Nicky's body, tore the sheet off him and began trying to administer cardiopulmonary resuscitation. Then he picked up the body, which ought to have been left where it had fallen for purposes of the police investigation, and carried it to a stretcher for transportation to a hospital.

Meanwhile, Dick Streedain realized he had two children still missing—one from Classroom 7 and one from Mary Lind's class—and no real idea if the gunwoman was still hiding in the school or if she was headed to another classroom in another school.

Don Monroe began calling other districts and telling them to lock the doors to their schools, protect their children.

•

Rich Carlson took Amy Moses over to Sergeant McConnell, Winnetka's chief of detectives. "Patty," he said, "this is the teacher. She was in the room."

"Who did this?" McConnell said, assuming that the attacker would be someone known to the school community.

"I don't know," Moses said. "It's a woman. She's about thirty years old..."

McConnell interrupted: "Would you know her if you saw her again?"

"I'll never forget her," Moses said. "I'll never forget her face. She had red hair, cut kind of short, and—"

"We're going to try to go up and down the streets to find her," McConnell interrupted. "Can you come with us?"

"Absolutely," Moses said.

McConnell and Moses would not leave each other's sides all day. She, like Floyd Mohr, wasn't your usual cop. She had been a literature major at the University of Illinois at Chicago and had quit school twelve hours short of her degree to become a police officer. But where Mohr was serious and low-key, McConnell was engaging and high-spirited, a salt-of-the-earth type. When popular Chicago deejay Jonathon

Brandmeier needed one-day replacements for his vacationing news announcer, McConnell took her handcuffs down to the radio station and went on the air with him as "Patty, the Love Cop."

McConnell and her partner, Bob Kerner, took Moses out to the squad car. A teacher yelled at them that the gunwoman had headed west on foot, so they headed up to Tower Road and proceeded in that direction, looking down every side yard and behind each tree. Because of the funeral traffic, they drove along the left side of the road.

In the car, Moses repeated over and over, "My God, I wish she had shot me and not my children. I wish she had shot me."

•

"You're my hostages," Laurie said to Ruth Andrew and her son Phil, her voice steady, her eyes calm. She moved to the center of the kitchen. "Get over to the other side of the room. I have a gun."

They didn't take her seriously. "What's going on?" Phil asked.

"Come on, get over on the other side of the room," Laurie said.

"Who are you? Where are you coming from? What's going on?" both Andrews asked.

"I'm running from the police," Laurie said, once again assuming the role of the victim. "I was raped in my car and I shot at the guy who did it. I ran here."

"Did you hit him?" Phil wanted to know. "Is he hurt?"

"I don't know," Laurie said. "I just ran because I was scared."

"Where did you get those guns?"

"My car," Laurie said. "They were in the glove compartment."

Phil tried to get a closer look at the guns to see if they were real. Suddenly he caught a glimpse of the slugs in the chamber of the .32. "So where's your car?" he asked, hoping to keep her distracted.

"Forest Glen," said Laurie, recalling the name of the street where the Rushes lived. "I left it there."

Phil asked Laurie where she was from; she said Glencoe. He asked her where she'd gone to school; she said the University of Wisconsin.

"Yeah?" said Phil. "I go to U. of I." He paused, aware of how awkward his attempt at chitchat sounded. "Why don't you give me the guns?" he said.

"No," said Laurie. She recoiled slightly. "I'm afraid."

"Do you think we should call the police?"

"I'm afraid of the police," she said.

Phil could see her point. If she had, in fact, shot her attacker, he could be telling the police anything—that she was simply a crazy person who had gone after him for no reason. Who knew what the cops might do under such circumstances? On the other hand, Phil thought, the story was pretty incredible. Women just don't get raped in their cars in the middle of the day in Winnetka, and women getting raped don't just grab a pair of pistols out of the glove compartment and open fire.

Phil was standing close to Laurie, who was not brandishing her guns but holding them by the handles, down at her side. He was a full foot taller than Laurie and could have grabbed and subdued her at that moment, but he worried that doing so might just further traumatize her.

"Do you want a glass of water?" he asked.

"Okay," she said.

As he was filling the glass at the sink he said, "Do you want my mom to go get you a pair of pants?"

"No," she said. "I don't want you leaving the room. You'll call the police."

"You should get on the phone, then," Phil said. "Isn't there someone you could call?"

"I could call my mother," Laurie said. "She lives in Glencoe."

"Go ahead," Phil said. "Then you'll be on the phone so my mom can go upstairs and get something for you to wear. Okay?"

"Okay," she said. She took the phone from its cradle on the wall and dialed. Phil saw that the number had an 835 prefix—Glencoe, just like she'd said. Ruth Ann Andrew left the room. She had every chance to use the second line, a children's telephone, but didn't. The girl with the guns seemed frightened, not dangerous. Phil had everything under control and her husband was expected home any minute.

Edith answered the telephone when it rang at the Wasserman house at 10:57. "Hello," she said.

"Mom," Laurie said. "I've done something terrible. People won't understand. I'm going to have to kill myself."

26

The
Suspect

Amy Moses remembered everything about the woman—the skeletal design on her medical school T-shirt, the yellow shorts with the drawstring waist, the way her reddish shoulder-length hair appeared to have been permed. From the back seat of the police sedan she leaned forward between the seats so her head was between Sergeant McConnell and Detective Kerner. "She's a little taller than I am," she said. "Kind of heavy."

"If we see her," McConnell cautioned, "I want you to get down in the back seat."

McConnell was playing calm and steady, but she too was frightened. The scene at the school had been awful almost beyond comprehension—blood, death, chaos among the innocents. And the woman they were looking for was probably not going to go quietly. She had nothing to lose.

Moses more easily gave vent to her anguish. Every so often she would break the mood in the car by crying out, "Oh, my God, she shot Nicky!" or, "Oh, my God, she shot Lindsay!"

When they reached what McConnell decided was the western boundary of their search—Hibbard Road, one quarter mile from the school—she called for the area to be sealed off.

•

Floyd Mohr heard the description of the attacker broadcast on the police radio and he, too, began driving around the school area, looking.

Suddenly he saw a car drive past with a red-haired woman in the passenger seat. Showtime. He put out on his radio that he was following a suspicious vehicle southbound on Locust Street and might need backup. He also called for the witness, Amy Moses, to be brought to the scene. Mohr, Winnetka lieutenant Joe Sumner and two other officers pulled the car over at the intersection of Locust and Vine streets, three blocks from the school. Mohr drew his gun, took cover behind his car and screamed at the women to throw the keys out of the car. Don't move. Don't even move.

The women were petrified. Just as Mohr and Sumner were preparing to approach the car to question them, McConnell, Kerner and Amy Moses drove by.

"Does this look like her?" McConnell asked.

"It's definitely not her," Moses said.

"It ain't her!" McConnell called out. The trio continued their cruise of the neighborhood.

•

At Hubbard Woods, the classmates of the children who had been shot were locked inside the principal's office, shaking, crying, asking for their mothers and fathers.

Streedain opened the door and looked in on them several times, and each time they jumped up and said, "We're going to be shot! We're going to be shot!"

He was doing his best to intercept shocked and grieving parents who were starting to arrive at the school, and he had the sad duty of being the first to talk to Linda Corwin. She had parked beyond the fire engines and run to the front entrance of the school. She'd noticed as she passed inside that people were turning their heads away from her, avoiding eye contact.

"What happened?" she cried. "What happened?"

No one said anything. Streedain hurried over to her, his shirt stained brightly with Lindsay Fisher's blood. "It's the worst possible thing that could ever happen," he said. "This crazy person came in the school and started shooting kids." He paused only half a second. "And I hate to tell you this, but she shot Nicky."

"Is he dead?"

Streedain said yes, he was.

Linda cried, "Oh, Nicky! Nicky! No!" Streedain embraced her, then she walked away and Chief Timm came and took her by the arm and led her to a bench to sit down.

"I'm very, very sorry," he said.

The irony was that Nicky normally wouldn't have been in Classroom 7 at 10:40 A.M.—that was his period for advanced math with third-graders. It was only because of Bike Day that he'd been in the line of fire at all, and only because Linda had decided not to let Nicky skip a grade when his first-grade teacher suggested it, and only because the Corwins had decided to leave Minneapolis to come to Chicago, and only because they had chosen Winnetka...Such was the bitter arithmetic of tragedy.

Timm turned away. The pain of his own loss eight years ago—their baby, five days old, born prematurely, hardly had a chance—returned sharply. One of his officers came up beside him. "Do you want someone to go talk to the reporters?" he asked.

Timm snapped to. He went to a window and looked out. Scores of journalists were waiting outside beyond the yellow police barriers. The news had raced literally around the world—calls were even then coming in from Australia, Germany and England. Could this horrible story possibly be true?

•

Floyd Mohr drove back to the school, where he walked in for a look at the mess inside Classroom 7, then wandered back outside to see how the investigation was proceeding. Chief Timm and Winnetka fire chief Ron Colpaert were discussing the awful coincidence of the fire at the Rushe house, and how it still appeared possible that the baby-sitter was trapped inside. Her name was Laurie something, that was all they knew, and they couldn't find her.

The words "baby-sitter" and "Laurie" clicked immediately in Mohr's mind. He excused himself and broke for his car, jumped in and drove quickly back to the Rushes', cutting over curbs and sidewalks and clipping bushes, dodging the streams of pedestrians and cars headed the other way toward the school.

"Who's the homeowner here?" he asked as he approached a group gathered around the back of a paramedic van.

"I am," said Marian Rushe. Her hand and arms were bandaged. After she had run away from the house and looked back, she realized that Laurie was probably not still inside—her car was gone. She was beginning to confront the terrible possibility that her baby-sitter had tried to kill her.

Mohr had the same theory. He identified himself to Marian and asked her if they could go to her house to talk.

"My house is on fire," she pointed out.

"Oh, yeah," Mohr said. He led her to a house next door and began grilling her wildly. "Now, what's your baby-sitter's name?"

"Laurie Porter."

Mohr was relieved for a moment, but pressed ahead. "Do you know her phone number?" he asked.

"She lives in Glencoe, I think," Marian said. She was very calm, especially compared to Mohr.

"Is it 835-1263?" Mohr said. He had a professional fascination with numbers—telephones, license plates, addresses.

"Yes. How did you know?"

"What kind of car does this lady drive?"

"It was blue," Marian said. "A Japanese car."

"Was it a Honda?"

"Yes," Rushe said. "But wait. She didn't have her Honda, she was driving a white—"

"Toyota?"

"Yes. How did you know?"

Mohr felt as though his beating heart was going to pop through his bulletproof vest. "Was the license number NW 000?"

"Yes, how did you know?"

At 11:04, an agonized Floyd Mohr broke into the police radio traffic. "The suspect's name is Laurie Porter, P-o-r-t-e-r.

Her real identity I believe to be Laurie Dann, D-a-n-n. She lives at 346 Sheridan. She's gained a lot of weight. The same description as the baby-sitter. She's driving a white, Japanese car..." He paused to breathe hard, then continued to ramble. "It has a registered plate of NW 000. I'm sure it's her. [Marian Rushe] gave me a phone number which I called, that's her phone number. [Rushe] calls there all the time and asks for Laurie Porter and that's who she gets. Her father has an office off Skokie Boulevard. It's right across from the Edens Theater."

Mohr called for someone at the Glencoe station to pull a copy of Laurie's Highland Park mug shot out of his files and rush it to Hubbard Woods.

Five minutes later, Officer Rich Carlson found the getaway car hung up on the rock in the driveway at 1200 Hamptondale, its engine still running. The initial suspicion was that she was inside that particular house, but a phone call there reached a trio of domestic servants, one of whom came out to tell police that she had seen and heard nothing and she didn't know who the car belonged to.

•

The Evanston Hospital emergency room had been placed on full alert when the call came that critically wounded shooting victims from a Winnetka school were on their way.

"Oh, geez," thought Dr. Jeffrey Vender, director of medical-surgical intensive care. "Why are they bothering us with another simulation on a Friday?"

The hospital had just gone through a disaster drill a month earlier, and it seemed awfully soon to be dragging everybody through another one.

But word passed quickly that this was no exercise. And almost as soon as the true gravity of the situation became known, children started to arrive.

Lindsay Fisher, the most seriously wounded of the survivors, was all but dead. The bullet had punctured her right lung, her liver and her stomach. Her heart was empty but still beating, and she registered no appreciable blood pressure. Nurses tried to insert intravenous lines but could find no blood vessels that hadn't collapsed.

A team of surgeons lead by Dr. John Alexander and Dr. Stephen Sener put an adult-sized, 16-gauge intravenous tube straight into her left atrium and transfused blood directly into her heart, a common procedure during normal surgery but an extraordinary step for treating a patient in shock.

Dr. David Winchester, the hospital's chief of surgery, and Dr. Richard Larson took Kathryn Miller, Drs. Charles Drueck and John Golan tended to Mark Teborek, and Dr. Willard Fry began operating on Robert Trossman.

The chaos was less pronounced six miles away at Highland Park Hospital. Peter Munro had come severely wounded in the abdomen but conscious, and Dr. Mart Jalakas, the same physician who had treated Russell Dann's ice-pick wound, was on hand to oversee X-rays, blood-typing and the starting of intravenous lines.

Paramedics trying to treat Nicky Corwin in the ambulance had put a tube into his lung to try to get him breathing and started heart massage, but he showed no signs of life when he arrived in the emergency room. Jalakas put in a second tube to drain blood from the boy's chest and continued heart massage.

•

As the story spread, it grew. When the news reached the Skokie office of Cook County felony prosecutor Nancy Sidote, the official who had met with Laurie, Norm and Edith to explain why no charges would be filed in the alleged knife rape, the number of children killed was eleven. She rounded up two assistants and headed for the school.

One of the civilians who heard the confused reports and raced to the school was James McManus, the father of a third-grader inside and an author whose 1984 first novel, *Out of the Blue,* involved a five-year-old girl who is kidnapped from the playground at Hubbard Woods by people who mistake her for the daughter of wealthy parents.

The jacket of the book boasted with eerie prescience that McManus' story showed how "random violence can reach out to touch the lives of the innocent."

•

Alice Horevitz was told to move her first-graders down

the hall to the school library because evidence technicians were taking over the west corridor. When she made the announcement, the children rushed at her and began tugging at her clothes imploringly. "Please, please!" they said. "We don't want to go!"

"We're only going down to the resource center," she said.

"We don't want to go out there, please don't make us go. It's dangerous. Please Mrs. Horevitz, don't make us go."

She faltered. She didn't want to go either. When she opened the door, she felt like it was leading into a gas chamber.

The students stood in line clutching one another and shuffled down the hall as though playing choo-choo train. When they got to the library they closed the doors behind them and cuddled with their teacher in the corner.

"What happened?" they wanted to know.

"I don't know," their teacher replied. "Something terrible."

"We're scared," they said.

"I'm scared, too," she said.

•

After several more unsuccessful passes through the neighborhood, Sergeant McConnell and Amy Moses dropped off Bob Kerner at the intersection of Kent and Hibbard roads so that he could make his way back east toward the school through the overgrown back yards.

The two women then returned to the school, where there was still no sign of the missing students. Were they hostages? Were they wounded and lying in the underbrush somewhere near the school after trying to run for help?

Then, just to add to the general distress, a car or TV van outside backfired and everyone crouched down.

As that first hour wore on, Streedain and Monroe became overwhelmed by the number of would-be decision-makers who had descended on the school—at least fifteen mental health care workers, ten clergymen, most of the school board members and innumerable law enforcement and court officials.

Everyone had a different opinion about what to do with the children, when to let them go.

"Time out!" Monroe said. "There are too many people here. I have to make the decisions."

•

A mug shot of Laurie Dann was rushed to the school from the Glencoe police department, and Amy Moses identified her immediately as the woman who had been in her classroom.

At 11:30 A.M., dog teams began arriving on the scene at the end of Hamptondale Court, where Lieutenant Sumner was preparing to search the house at 1200 in case Laurie had slipped in without the domestics noticing. He had other teams of officers combing the backyards to the west of the house, pushing through the underbrush and hopping fences. Mohr, who had hurried back to the school after making the identification on Laurie, was part of the hunt, and was side by side with Deputy Chief Clauser from Wilmette and Lieutenant George Carpenter and Patrolman Malcolm Caskey from Winnetka. They hopped a backyard fence and found themselves behind the Clements' house, where Laurie had broken the window. They felt almost like they were standing in the middle of a forest preserve.

It was 11:46. Suddenly an excited voice broke into the radio traffic—forget the house at 1200 Hamptondale Court; a nearby resident was reporting a hostage situation at 2 Kent Road. A woman had walked into the kitchen and was holding the family prisoner.

The officers began heading through the yard toward 2 Kent when the air rocked with the shattering report of a gunshot. There was nothing to do but run toward it.

Within thirty seconds, Mohr and Kerner were in the front yard of 2 Kent. They saw Vincent Wolf and his nurse sitting out taking the sun next to the gate, so Clauser and Carpenter provided cover while Mohr and Kerner hurried to the old man's side—he was shaking badly and couldn't speak.

"He's sick!" the nurse cried. "He can't move."

They dragged the old man in his chair along the asphalt.

Mohr crashed into the garage door with his back and the door swung open. They hid him away behind a car and took up positions in the bushes by the gate that led to the backyard, their guns drawn.

27

I've Done Something Terrible

The shot had come from Laurie's .32, a sudden, unexpected explosion. Phil Andrew could not believe she had done it. It made no sense. After all he had tried to do for her...

She had been distraught and suicidal when she first reached her mother on the phone, and Phil edged over next to her and touched her lightly on the arm. "Oh no," he said. "No one's going to have to do that."

She jumped back. "I want you away from me," she warned him.

"Mom, I've done something terrible," she said again. "These are nice people here, I don't want to hurt them."

After several minutes of listening to Laurie's bewildered babble, Phil could tell she wasn't getting anywhere with her mother. He asked for the phone and she handed it to him.

"My name is Phil Andrew," he said, trying to strike a coherent contrast to Laurie. "Your daughter is here. She came in with two guns and told us we're her hostages. She said she was attacked, she shot her assailant and now she's afraid of the police."

"Really," she said.

Phil was stunned that she seemed so detached.

"Has she ever done anything like this before?" Phil asked. "Does she have a history of this?"

"No," Edith said. Then she paused. "Would you please see that my daughter gets home safely?"

It was the kind of situation Norm would usually handle, but he was even at that moment driving Edith's car up to Madison to clear out Laurie's room in the Towers.

"I'll do what I can," Phil said.

He hung up and looked at Laurie, who was, in turn, looking hard at him. When he would relax, she would relax. When he would begin looking around nervously, she would become agitated, too.

His mother returned to the kitchen carrying a pair of yellow, cut-off sweatpants for Laurie. She accepted them and set both guns on the kitchen counter in order to unwrap herself from the plastic, discard it in the trash can under the phone and put the shorts on. Although she was naked under the bag, she made no effort to hide herself or to turn while changing, and the thought passed through Phil's mind that she probably had been raped; only a woman who had just been violated would be so casual about her own nakedness.

He also saw his opportunity to take the guns away, and he reached out quickly and got his hand on the .22 Beretta. As he grabbed it, Laurie snatched up the .32 and brandished it. "Give me that back," she said.

"No, I'm going to keep it," Phil said. He made an obvious show of removing the cartridge and putting it in one pocket of his shorts while putting the gun itself into the opposite pocket. He knew the rudimentary workings of the revolver because he had once trained for a modern pentathlon, in which one of the events is target shooting with a .22.

Phil then heard his father, Raymond, fifty-one, come in the house, returning from a brief errand that delayed him after the conclusion of the funeral. He was a former senior vice president for Bell and Howell Corporation who had gone out on his own in the early 1980's as an executive for hire, and was at the time acting president of Stocker Corporation— he was virtually the archetype of the successful North Shore businessman. Phil met him in the door of the kitchen. "We have a situation here," he said tightly. "This woman has a gun. She says she's been attacked and she shot her assailant. Why don't you sit down."

Raymond took a seat at the counter. "That certainly explains the police cars," he said. "They're all over the place. I almost thought they weren't going to let me come down the road."

Heightened panic showed in Laurie's eyes.

"We've talked to her mother," Phil said. "She's in Glencoe."

"Is she coming over?" Raymond asked.

"No," Phil said. He turned to Laurie. "Maybe we should get her on the phone again?"

At 11:07, Laurie called Edith back and resumed apologizing and lamenting. "No one will understand," she told her mother. "It's terrible." She was pacing, wielding her gun, her finger on the trigger. Phil beckoned again and again for her to hand him the receiver. Finally she gave it to him.

"Can't you come over?" he pleaded.

"I don't have a car," Edith said. "My husband has the car."

"Can't you take a cab? Borrow a neighbor's car?" Phil said. "You've got to come here and help us."

"No, I just can't," Edith said. "I can't."

Phil passed the phone across the kitchen to his father, who spoke sharply to Edith. "Tell your daughter to give up her gun," he said. "We're all in danger here. I just came in and the police are down on the corner setting up. You've got to tell her to give up the gun."

Laurie clamped down on the switch-hook, cutting off the call.

"We're not through," Raymond said, taking the same stern tone with Laurie he had taken with Edith. "Call her back."

Laurie complied so quickly that the number rang busy because Edith hadn't hung up on the other end yet. On her second try the line was clear, and Raymond continued his harangue. "I don't know what's happened here, but she's got to give up the gun," he said.

Finally, exasperated at Edith's bland and noncommittal responses, he handed the phone back to Laurie. She commenced again with her miserable yet unspecific apologies. "I'm sorry to both of you, Mom and Dad," she said.

Their conversation went on and on, and Phil and his father conferred quietly in the background. Should they jump her? Seize the other gun? End this ridiculous standoff before it turned tragic? They decided against it. She seemed haunted, insecure, afraid—very unlikely to harm anyone except maybe herself. Grabbing her would mean running the risk that the gun would go off, hitting either her or one of them. They decided to wait.

"Goodbye," Laurie said at last. "Goodbye, goodbye. I'm sorry. This is it, goodbye."

Right after she hung up, Ruth Ann threw up her hands. "Listen," she said, almost scolding Laurie. "My daughters are coming home from school soon and we don't need any more people involved in this. Anyway, the police will follow them in."

"Oh, that's no good," Laurie said. "We need to keep them out."

"We'll send my mother outside," Phil said. "She'll be there so the girls won't come in."

"Okay," Laurie said. "Fine."

Ruth Ann hurried out the front door and into the yard. To her left down the block, a policeman was guarding the entrance to Kent Road and directing traffic away as the manhunt through the neighborhood continued. She ran up and told him what was happening in her house.

•

Back in the kitchen, Phil was still working at calming Laurie down. "My summer job is in the State's Attorney's office," he told her. "I know how the system works. Nobody's going to hurt you—really. I'll stay with you. If you give me the gun, I'll go to the police with you and be sure they don't hurt you. I won't leave your side."

His sincerity was improvised and Laurie wasn't buying it. She knew Phil had no idea of the enormity of what she had done and how impossible it was going to be to save her. She had run out of options, exhausted all of her plans.

"You've got to give up the gun," Raymond, the father, said, this time pleading even harder. His main worry at that point was not that Laurie would discharge her gun, but that the police would storm the house and they would get caught in the crossfire. All the police had to go on, after all, was what they had been told by the man Laurie said tried to rape her.

"Look, this is no good," Phil said, standing. "We're just going to leave now. You're endangering us so we're going to leave." He and Raymond headed for the door.

"No!" Laurie cried, pointing the gun at them. "Stop! Don't leave!"

•

The officer at first thought Ruth Ann was just some nutty lady trying to get in on the action, but when her description of the woman in her house matched the description of the suspect, he put out the call that Floyd Mohr and the other officers heard at the other end of Kent Road:

"I have a woman with me. We're at Hibbard and Kent. She says she has a woman in her kitchen. One girl in her kitchen holding her son and her father hostage. The address is number 2 Kent Road. Number 2. There's a woman with a gun."

•

Phil and Raymond Andrew stopped at Laurie's command.

"How about if just I stay?" Phil said. "Let my dad go. I'll stay and make sure nothing happens to you. Okay?"

She nodded. "Okay," she said.

Raymond left and Phil remained standing, leaning against a wall near the microwave oven. "You've got to give me the gun," he said again. "It's going to be all right. Nothing is going to happen to you, I promise."

She was five feet away from him, looking around the kitchen and out the windows distractedly. She seemed worried but somehow calm, with the gun pointed toward the floor, her finger still on the trigger.

Phil could not take his eyes off its black barrel. "How fast am I?" he thought. "Can I get that gun from her? Can I get the jump?" They were the same sorts of thoughts that used to go through his mind when he perched on the starting blocks before swimming races. "Can I do it? Can I do it?"

He hesitated. He still had time. His parents were safe. Laurie could be manipulated.

She quickly looked out the window and straight back at her hostage. Without saying a word or changing expression she raised the .32 and fired it into his chest.

Phil spun with the force of impact and saw Laurie move away from him. As he staggered and fell, he dove around a corner into the pantry.

"She knows she didn't kill me," he thought as he pushed the pantry door closed with his foot and squirmed deep into a corner. "She's going to try to shoot me again."

Phil had yet to feel the pain of the bullet, which had ripped through his lung and lodged a fraction of an inch from his heart, but he quickly found himself having trouble breathing. Concentrating hard, he took the gun and cartridge out of his pockets and assembled them, then pulled himself to his feet. He stood by the entryway of the pantry, the gun raised in his shooting hand, and listened. No sound. She could be hiding. She could be right on the other side of the wall.

He opened the door carefully inward, peered out, then led the way into the kitchen with the Beretta. He was prepared just to shoot it out with her—he was quicker, younger and, unlike her, knew what to do with a pistol. But she had vanished—not concealed behind the counter, not hiding in another doorway. He backed out of the kitchen cautiously, turning, waiting for the ambush that never came.

Laurie was on the stairs to the second floor. As soon as she'd shot Phil she scurried from the kitchen. She was trapped, no way out, no way to finish the rampage as she'd planned. She found the central staircase and started up. It was a nice house, familiar in its sturdy, North Shore opulence and bigger by a fair margin than her parents' home in Glencoe. At the landing she turned to the right at the head of the stairs, walked through a sewing room and wandered down a hall, past one closed door.

Phil, meanwhile, had backed all the way out of the kitchen and through the door leading into the yard. As soon as he was clear he made a break for the gate that led out through the side wall to the driveway. His run turned into a stagger as he burst through.

"I've been hit!" he yelled, waving the gun in his left hand and trying to keep moving. "I can't believe it! I can't believe she shot me."

Mohr and Kerner, still in position near the gate, were startled by the sudden, bloody apparition. "Police officers!" they screamed, training their guns on Phil as he threw down the gun and collapsed in front of them. "Don't move!"

Phil's senses were alive. He could hear the hip radios crackling, someone reporting shots fired, a man down, and his own father in the background crying, "My son! Get help for my son!"

Kerner advanced on Phil and kicked the gun into the bushes, just to be sure. The kid was sucking for air, so he and Mohr grabbed him and dragged him off behind a tree. A paramedic stanched the flow of blood with a four- by five-inch bandage.

The life was draining out of him. "Am I going to make it?" he asked.

"Yeah, you're going to be fine," said Mohr, trying to sound as though he meant it.

The day was still beautiful—particularly so in the Andrews' yard, with flowers everywhere and buds on the trees. Mohr could smell freshly cut grass in the air, he could smell the soap on Phil Andrew's body and the tangy odor of the blood flowing out of the awful wound. Time for him was creeping along, virtually suspended at this peculiar and horrifying moment. Laurie Dann, he thought. Jesus. All the times he had talked to her, listened to her, *believed* her, and now this. "Why?" he said to himself over and over. "Why, Laurie? Why?"

It was 11:49. An ambulance was on the way.

•

Upstairs, Laurie reached the end of the hallway and turned left. Ahead of her was an open door leading into a bedroom shared by two teenaged girls—Kathy and Trish Andrew, starters on the New Trier High School basketball team, one of the best in the state. A college admissions guidebook, *Newsweek* magazine, a Dr. Martin Luther King, Jr., biography and an opened copy of the weekly *Winnetka Talk* were scattered on the floor between the twin beds, and the themeless bric-a-brac all about included a plastic Cubs batting helmet, an Alf doll on the floor next to the window, class photos, Cabbage Patch kids, several teddy bears and a trash-can-sized popcorn container with the cartoon character Baby Bopper on the side.

Laurie walked past the boom box on the floor by the door and the curling iron and the answering machine out on the dresser, and picked her way past a few scattered clothes on the gold, green and yellow shag carpet. It was a bedroom where girlhood and young womanhood collided exuberantly, and Laurie stood there at the foot of one of the beds and listened to sirens close in around her.

•

Edith called the Towers at 11:54. Norm hadn't arrived yet.

•

An ambulance from Northbrook pulled up at the road block at the corner of Kent and Hibbard roads at 11:55, but could not go in after Phil. Both the paramedics and Winnetka lieutenant Sumner, who had arrived to take charge, worried that the ambulance would be an easy target as it passed the Andrews'. They wanted to wait until a large contingent of officers could cover the front of the house.

Phil Andrew remained conscious on the ground, aware of everything around him, feeling the sun beat on his exposed chest. "It's too beautiful a day to die," he thought.

The paramedics wanted Mohr and the other police officers to bring the victim down the road themselves, but his injuries were clearly too severe to move him. Mohr couldn't wait. He ran past the front of the house as fast as he could and headed for the ambulance.

"Go down there," he said. "The guy's dying!"

"You're fucking crazy," the driver answered. "Get the fuck out of here."

The paramedic in the passenger seat climbed out and went to the rear of the ambulance and Mohr got in. "Just drive," he said.

"No fucking way. I'm not going to get killed."

"Get down then," Mohr said. "You run the gas and the brake. I'll steer. We're going in."

The driver crouched on the floor and worked the accelerator pedal with his hand. Mohr guided the ambulance with his left hand and held his gun out the window with his right, training it on the windows of the big white house.

They passed the windows without incident and parked where they were safely shielded by the garage.

"Give me the fucking stretcher," Mohr said. "We'll bring him to you. You just stay fucking here."

The officers quickly hoisted Phil onto the stretcher and ran him to the back entrance of the ambulance. Once he was inside they pounded on the side and yelled, "Go! Go!"

Phil was on his way to Highland Park Hospital. It was 12:09 P.M., more than twenty minutes after he'd been shot.

•

One minute later, Edith called the Highland Park police department.

28

Did They Catch the Lady Yet?

Emergency room doctors at Highland Park Hospital continued without success for the better part of an hour to stimulate Nicky Corwin's heart and make it beat again, but the effort proved futile. Just past noon, Dr. Jalakas decided there was nothing more to do. The boy was dead.

He went to the private grieving area off the emergency room and told Joel and Linda Corwin that resuscitation efforts had been stopped. For the second time that day Nicky had been pronounced dead. Jalakas briefly described the wounds and said it looked as though the bullet went right through the boy's heart.

It had to be a short conversation because Jalakas was needed again in the emergency room to treat yet another shooting victim who had just been wheeled in, a college-age male with a slug from a .32 in his chest.

•

Law enforcement officials swarmed Kent Road. The perimeter of the Andrew house was surrounded by the Emergency Services Team of the Northern Illinois Police Alarm System (NIPAS)—a crack unit of twenty-nine officers from twelve local police departments that had only been activated three weeks earlier—along with approximately eighty backup officers. They sealed off the residence from all angles, and sharpshooters done up in camouflage and eye-black moved into place in surrounding homes.

It looked like a perfect web had been thrown up around the killer, but there was still a nagging doubt. The police calculated that a full ten seconds had elapsed between the time Laurie fired the shot that hit Phil Andrew and the time the backyard of the Andrew house had been covered. Not a long time, but enough.

Lieutenant Sumner oversaw the establishment of a command post in the Berghorst home at 12 Kent Road, two doors east of the Andrew home. The family was traveling in England and the house-sitter volunteered the use of the home for the private interior headquarters to complement the more public center near where the reporters and photographers were clustering at the corner of Kent and Hibbard roads.

Just as everything was nearly in place, a huge shotgun blast split the air.

"Holy shit!" said Floyd Mohr, spinning around in the position he had taken behind a tree. "Holy fuck!"

It was a misfire. An accident. The tragedy of errors just went on and on.

•

Laurie's ex-husband, Russell, had come through his root canal that morning and was having lunch at the Green Acres Country Club with his brother, his father and an insurance client when the Highland Park police tracked him down by phone through his office. They told him about the shooting in Winnetka and that they thought Laurie was probably responsible. She seemed to be holed up in a house, the officer said, and he should probably get down to Winnetka as fast as he could in case they needed him to talk her into surrendering.

He had to collect his thoughts, which were alternating between shock and a certain cool feeling of vindication. Now maybe they would believe him—Laurie was out of her mind, a lunatic. They had let it come to this, the goddamned cops. And now they needed his help. Well. He went back to the table and finished his soup. Then he left for the offices of Dann Brothers where he found his sister crying hysterically.

She had been watching TV at 11:30 that morning when a special bulletin broke into regular programming to announce the incident at Hubbard Woods School. Details were sketchy, and Susie called Jeff on his car phone. "Doesn't that sound like something Laurie would do?" she said.

Jeff didn't laugh. It did.

She got in her car and headed out for a golf lesson. She kept the radio tuned to the all-news station to see if they had any breaking information. The teletype sound effect clattered in the background. The announcer had another bulletin. "Authorities in Winnetka have just announced a tentative identification of the suspect," he said portentously. "She is Laurie Dann, also known as Laurie Porter, a thirty-year-old—"

Susie immediately did a U-turn in the middle of the road and headed for Russell's office nearby. She was shaking so bad she could hardly drive.

"I know," were Russell's first words when he saw her. "I'm on my way there."

Susie then reached her friend, Jan Sider, who had herself received a mysterious packet of juice in her mailbox that morning, to ask if she could come pick her up. Russell left and drove his Saab toward Winnetka at speeds of more than 110 miles per hour, just daring the police to stop him this time.

"Laurie's taken a bunch of people hostage," he told his attorney, Rick Kessler, when he reached him on the car phone. "She's shot some kids at a school, too. I'm on my way. What should I do?"

•

Even though Laurie was thought to be safely pinned inside the Andrew house, police departments up and down the North Shore stationed officers outside of schools, where shades were being pulled down and large windows barricaded with cafeteria tables. In Glencoe School District 35, the superintendent ordered all 925 students bussed home, even though half of them normally walked. All elementary schools in Wilmette went on immediate lock-down, posting custodians to intercept strangers at all doors and canceling recess. The police rounded up New Trier High School students who had strayed to a convenience store down the block and returned them to school. In fear and confusion, four students ran to a car, got in and peeled away.

The police told residents in the Hubbard Woods School area to get inside with their children and lock their doors. For some reason, though, no one ever told the day laborers mowing the lawn across the street from the Rushes'. They just kept working.

In Evanston, several elementary school students sat at their desks and secretly wrote out their wills.

•

"The woman is a thirty-year-old baby-sitter whose first name is Laurie," said the radio announcer. "She lives in Glencoe and goes by the last names Porter, Dann and—"

Dr. Barry Gallup, who was in his van running an errand on his day off, turned to his wife. "Wasserman," he said in unison with the announcer.

"No way!" Diane said. "There's no possible way."

"No question in my mind," Barry said. It was the same girl he had dated for two years in high school. "She called for me twice, remember? She was depressed. Now she's degenerated. It's got to be her."

"Authorities don't know at this time if the woman is still in the house at Kent Road," the announcer said.

"They don't know!" Barry cried. He turned to head for home and picked up the car phone to call the woman who was watching over their daughter that morning. "Get her in the house," he said. "Turn on the alarm."

When they pulled in their driveway, a woman from across the street ran over. "There's a killer on the loose!" she yelled. "Get your kids indoors."

•

Beth Rosen was out and arrived home a little past noon. Her housekeeper was very distressed. "There's this woman and she shot a classroom filled with children," she said.

Beth knew instantly that it had to be Laurie—it was the same feeling private eye Frank Bullock had when he heard the news on the radio in his office. He didn't even wait for confirmation on the name of the suspect, but got in his car and headed for Winnetka.

•

The two children who were missing after the attack eventually turned up. One had run right under Laurie's shooting arm, out the door and all the way home; the other was hiding in another teacher's classroom, cowering amid the confusion.

But despite this momentary relief, officials inside Hubbard Woods School were facing a huge, unprecedented problem of crisis management. Parents were demanding to be let inside to see their children, some so vehemently that they had to be physically restrained at the door. Reporters and cameramen were at every corner of the building shouting for the latest news, and evidence technicians were sifting through the crime scene, shooting videotape, gathering up whatever they might need in the event of a trial.

After consulting with police, social workers and Cook County felony prosecutor Nancy Sidote, school officials decided it would be best to keep all the children inside until the end of the normal school day at 3:15—the only exceptions would be the children from Classroom 7, who would be reunited with their parents as soon as possible after they had been interviewed by investigators. They wanted to keep the students in the safest possible location and away from the hysterical ministrations of their parents to reinforce the idea that school was still a safe place and to be sure that their testimony as witnesses was not corrupted. District employees and counselors met parents at the door with stout resolve and directed them to cordoned off areas where they could talk to one another and to social workers.

Principal Dick Streedain, superintendent Don Monroe and other district officials congratulated themselves for this decision in the aftermath of May 20, but it was far from popular that afternoon. Shouting, weeping parents insisted that the mental health of their children—their need for family comfort—ought to come first, and that they should have the right to take their children home if they wanted to. "Don't you know they need support?" some shouted at Chief Timm when he emerged.

Several of the parents of the children from Classroom 7, who were admitted to the building but kept separated from their children until the appropriate interviews could take place, were very worried about their children being "interrogated" as they put it. A couple of the parents said they absolutely would not allow their children to be interviewed unless Sidote or a member of her staff could give them a written guarantee signed by a child psychologist that such questioning would not have a detrimental impact.

Sidote didn't have time for that kind of paperwork, but she promised that a psychologist would say it would be best to ask a few questions and encourage the kids to talk about it.

•

Pizza Hut, McDonald's and Long John Silver's donated lunch for those held down in the school. Most of the students were still in their classrooms talking with the parade of professionals there to help them. As soothing as the adults tried to be, they had no answers to the blunt, obvious questions: What happened? Why? Did they catch the lady yet?

One of the first-grade girls in Alice Horevitz's class sobbed convulsively. "She's in my house!" the girl said. "I know she's in my house!"

Dick Streedain took it upon himself to go from room to room along with Dr. Mary Giffen, a psychiatrist from a Northbrook clinic and an expert on death and loss, and explain what had happened as best he knew.

He began with the children from Classroom 7, who had been moved out of Streedain's office into a fourth-grade classroom temporarily vacated during the field trip. They were seated together on a carpet remnant where students usually gathered when their teacher read to them. At the perimeter of the room stood several teachers and crisis team workers.

Streedain started by telling them the story of *Alexander and the Terrible, Horrible, No Good, Very Bad Day*, a book by Judith Viorst about coping with misfortune. "Well, we have had a terrible, horrible day here," Streedain said. "A woman came into our school, went to the bathroom, shot Robert

Trossman, and then came to your room and she shot at some of you. Everyone who was hurt is getting the best possible care at the hospital. But Nick has died. Nick was shot and he died. He was a friend to everyone."

After Streedain left to take his grim tidings to the next group, Amy Moses helped Patty McConnell interview the children of Classroom 7.

"This is Patty McConnell and she's a policewoman," Amy began, the introduction being necessary because McConnell was still in street clothes. "I want you to tell her what happened in our classroom, to describe the lady. Because we want to catch her."

The women both sat on the floor with the second-graders and just let them talk. "We know Nicky died," several of them volunteered right away.

McConnell was both relieved and surprised by how calm the children were. They seemed to be handling the situation with considerably more composure than many of the adults frantically milling around inside and outside the school.

"Can we tell you about Nicky, about what he was to us?" one of the children said. "He was the smartest boy in class and he was such a good athlete," another said. "And he was real nice," said a third. "He was the teacher's helper a lot," added yet another.

"Now we're not going to be able to play fairly on the playground," one said.

"Why?" Amy Moses asked.

"Because Nicky knew all the rules," the student said. "And he always reminded us."

"What happened in there?" McConnell began gently.

Among them, the children were able to fashion together an account similar to the account Amy Moses had already given. They didn't seem to remember that Laurie had been in the room twice and their memory of her exit route was different, but the essentials were the same. They said she had come in, that she had walked up to the front of the room and she had a gun. "Then," they said, "we saw Nicky get shot."

•

At Highland Park Hospital, Joel and Linda Corwin were

taken into the emergency room to see Nicky one last time and say goodbye. Linda touched him—he was still warm. It was so confusing. She just wanted to pick him up and carry him home and tell him everything was okay.

"What a beautiful child," she said through her tears.

•

Susie's friend Jan Sider came by Dann Brothers and took her to the Ravinia School to pick up Brian. They took him over to the Young Men's Jewish Council to get his little sister, Lisa, and when Susie heard Lisa wasn't there and that Laurie had been by the school that morning with a can of gasoline, she went nearly wild with fright. Then Brian tugged on his mother's sleeve and said a strange lady had been to Ravinia, too, and had started a fire.

Lisa was safe. She was just on a school trip over at Highland Park High, where her class was seeing a play. A police officer took over for Jan Sider and drove Susie first to the high school to get Lisa and then to Red Oak Junior High to get Adam. From there they went directly to the police station.

Jean Leivick, director of the Young Men's Jewish Council, reached Jeff by calling him on the car phone. "You have to be strong," she told him. "Susie is hysterical."

When Jeff arrived home, his house was surrounded by police officers and squad cars.

•

In the yard at Hubbard Woods School, much of the initial fear had subsided, replaced with a wrenching grief, confusion and anger—some of which was directed at the media. A neighborhood resident tried to charge a reporter a parking fee for a space in front of his house and other residents shouted at cameramen to stay off their property.

Many of the parents turned away from photographers and declined interviews. Several asked the school officials to ban the media from school property. Winnetka was not the kind of town to wear its emotions on its sleeve or to embrace publicity. To many, the attention was grotesque and the fascination with their pain sickening and ghoulish. What, after all, was there to say? The unthinkable had happened. A killer had violated the sanctuary of an elementary school classroom. Children had been shot in the least likely of places. The world was mad. If you'd pretended to yourself before that it wasn't, you now knew you were wrong.

29

No
Answer

A small army of police officers bunkered in around the Andrew house and awaited further orders. Lieutenant Sumner, who was in charge of the standoff while Chief Timm worked at Hubbard Woods, chose a cautious plan of attack. Laurie was totally alone and—unless she had slipped out during the ten-second gap in police coverage of the house—totally surrounded. She had one gun left. She could do no more harm unless they gave her the opportunity, and she had already demonstrated that she wasn't the least bit afraid to shoot people.

If he sent members of the Emergency Services Team to storm the house, they would undoubtedly capture or kill Laurie. But at what cost? Perhaps one life. Perhaps two or more if she were lying in wait. And maybe she had some kind of bomb on her and would set fire to the house as well. Under the circumstances, as long as things were calm, Sumner decided it was better to wait. They could coax her out, make her surrender, get some answers.

So the standoff continued: everyone against Laurie Dann. The police called to her through bullhorns—"Laurie, let's get it over with," said their tinny voices. "You need help"—and placed numerous calls to the Andrew residence, hoping she would answer.

The phone rang and rang and rang.

•

When Russell Dann arrived at the mob scene developing on Kent Road, he was taken to the interior command center at the Berghorst home and put in the den. He told the commanders that they might be in for a very long day if they simply intended to wait, because Laurie could easily crawl off and hide in a closet and not say a word for days.

For a time, then, everything was quiet. No sound came from the house and police were still waiting to see if and when Norm and Edith Wasserman would arrive to help with their daughter.

Russell paced nervously, then stepped out onto the back patio where he caught sight of Detective Floyd Mohr, also pacing.

The lull in activity had forced Mohr to feel for the first time the full force of his combined shock, fear, anger, sorrow and guilt. He had talked to Laurie dozens of times, counseled her, taken her to the prosecutor's office and, at a certain level, trusted her. Then not only had she betrayed him, but also her case had dogged and haunted him in a way that nearly defied coincidence, as though she were placed in his way over and over to teach him some kind of lesson. But what lesson?

Mohr's commanding officers had briefly discussed removing him from the scene. He was obviously distraught, and the situation called for calmness. They chose to let him stay because of his connection to the suspect, but were keeping him out of the way in the backyard until he was needed.

When he saw Russell, he felt a surge of compassion and self-pity. "I'm sorry," he said, his voice breaking. "You were right. I was wrong."

"She fooled a lot of people," Russell said, trying to be magnanimous.

"My own kids, they mean more to me than anything," Mohr said. "I don't know what I'd do if anything happened to them." He could barely bring himself to look at Russell. "How can you ever forgive me? I was wrong. I feel terrible."

"It's okay, it's okay," Russell said. "If you can learn from your mistakes and prevent this from happening again, you'll become a better man."

"I've learned a lot from all this," Mohr said. "I'm a better person." He gave Russell a clumsy bear hug. "I owe you big time," he said. "I owe you one."

Mohr walked away, still agitated. Several minutes later, Lieutenant George Carpenter of Winnetka took him by the elbow. "Come with me, Floyd," he said. "We're going to talk."

Carpenter led Mohr to an upstairs bedroom, got him a box of Kleenex and sat him down. "You've got to control yourself," he said. "You've got a lot more work to do today. I know you've been through a lot already and it's not over yet, but we need you here. And you're no good if you're not in control."

Mohr snapped to as if slapped in the face. He promised he would be okay.

•

Marc Boney, the building manager for the Kellogg Living/ Learning Center in Evanston, was on his lunch hour when he heard that a woman had gone berserk and shot up a schoolhouse in Winnetka. Awful. He returned to work and was sitting at his desk when Andrew Burke, his student director, leaned his head into the office.

"Marc, what was the name of that woman we had all the problems with last summer?"

"Laurie Dann," said Boney with a sigh. How could anyone forget?

"She's the one who did those shootings," Burke said.

"No way!" Boney hurried to a television to turn on the special reports. Because there was still a slim chance that Laurie remained on the loose, he called the Northwestern Department of Public Safety and alerted the staff at the Kellogg Living/Learning Center to be on the lookout.

•

Pearl Gelb, who hadn't seen or spoken to Laurie since the previous November, was at work at a business consulting firm in Northbrook when one of her younger sisters called. "It's her!" she screamed.

"What's her?" Pearl said.

"Oh, my God!"

"What's going on?" Pearl demanded. At her sister's direction she turned on the radio. When she heard what had happened in Winnetka and who was responsible, she sat back in a daze. She had never even heard Laurie raise her voice in anger. The girl had hardly seemed to have a temper.

She called her mother, Betty, who had just heard the news herself and was preparing to drive down to Kent Road to see if she could be of help.

"She could be on her way up to get you," Pearl said. "Go find the gun, load it."

"What are you talking about?" said Betty. "If I opened the door and she was there, I'd just hug her."

"Over your dead body you'd hug her," Pearl said. "Get the gun."

•

As more and more information came out about Laurie's life and her associates, north suburban police departments rushed to defend the homes of those who knew her and might be her next targets.

When Cassandra Pappas arrived home from a visit to her daughter in Glenview, officers met her in the driveway and escorted her inside the house. They knew that her son Dean had been friends with Laurie, and they wondered if Cassandra could locate him and have him go to Kent Road and negotiate.

She excused herself and went off where she could call him in privacy.

"I'm going to go get her out?" Dean said incredulously. "Let her family do it. With my luck, she'll blow me away. I'm not going to go. I'm not James Bond. No. Let them. If the police want to know where I am, tell them I'm in China."

•

An FBI agent found Dr. Steve Witt making his hospital rounds. "Laurie Dann is holed up in a house in Illinois," he said. "We need your help to coax her out."

"After all the harassment?" he said, offended by the request. "Why should I do that?"

The agent did not mention that it appeared that Laurie had shot seven people, something that his wife, Barbara, was just learning from her father. Friends from Chicago had called him.

Steve got away as quickly as he could and together they watched the Cable News Network reports and hoped that Laurie would stick a gun down her throat and end it all.

•

The police had determined that Russell's relationship with Laurie was so poisoned that he was unlikely to be of much use, so they left him to his devices.

Russell borrowed one of the telephones that had been hastily installed by terrified Illinois Bell linemen in the kitchen of the command center at the Berghorst home and called his date for that night. She wasn't in, so he left a message on her answering device—he wasn't going to be able to make the White Sox game.

He entertained himself watching the earnest affectations of the suburban commando cops all done up like Vietnam, as though they were fighting a nest of guerrillas instead of one frightened crazy woman. The whole thing reminded him of kids playing G.I. Joe.

When he saw a reporter was watching him as he stood outside, he took off his shoe and, just for laughs, held it up to his ear as though it were a telephone.

He talked to Mohr again after the young detective had settled down. Mohr began on an apologetic note. "Maybe I understand now," he said. "Maybe I understand what you were going through."

"So you see?" Russell said. "You see what she's like?"

Mohr nodded. "I didn't know, and now I know."

"When did you figure it out? That it wasn't me?"

"Maybe a week ago," Mohr said, thinking of the FBI reports.

"A week, you've gotta be kidding," Russell said. "Are her parents supposed to come over?"

"I hear they'll be here any time."

"I don't want to see them," Russell said. "I don't want to deal with them."

"That's fair," Mohr said. He arranged for Russell to have the den to himself, and the two of them then turned on the television to watch the news reports. The information already assembled on Laurie's life and hard times was impressive—yearbook shots, neighbor interviews, law enforcement records from three states—but the reporters kept calling Russell "Rusty." He really hated that.

•

Norm Wasserman was driving toward Madison when he heard the radio bulletins about what his daughter had done. He returned to Glencoe to pick up Edith, and they arrived together at Kent Road shortly after two o'clock. Both parents were crying. Norm was wearing a white golf shirt and jeans, and walking with both hands jammed into his front pockets. Edith, in slacks and sweater, had looped her left arm through her husband's right. The police led them to the living room of the Berghorst home where they were separated from Russell in the den by a set of sliding doors.

"She's my little girl," Norm said, highly agitated as he looked out the window. "And they're treating her like a wild animal. Look at these people with army outfits and guns. All they want to do is kill her."

He said he felt faint, and Mohr, who by then had calmed down considerably, insisted he be checked over by paramedics to see if he were having a heart attack. "If this is true," Norm said, "if this is Laurie and she did these things, my life is over."

•

Mohr interviewed Norm briefly and found out Laurie had been seeing Dr. Greist in Madison. He then tracked down Greist to ask him the now familiar question he had asked of Dr. Greendale and Dr. Epstein: "Do you think Laurie could be homicidal or suicidal?"

"She never showed any signs of violence," Greist answered. "I never could have visualized her committing this large an act of violence. She was a very quiet little girl I'd been treating. She had some problems with rituals and not being able to touch certain things."

"Is it possible she could have many personalities?" said Mohr, who was desperately trying to explain to himself how he too could have been so fooled.

"Well," said Griest in his usual, even, cautious manner, "now that I think about it, it's possible."

•

Jeff and Susie Taylor and their three children remained under police guard at the Highland Park police station while bomb squads swept their home for explosives and officers waited inside by the phone in case Laurie called.

Susie went from being frightened to being angry. "I told them so," she said loudly. "I told them this was going to happen. I knew this was going to happen. Why didn't they listen to us? Why couldn't they listen to us?"

Jeff told her to hush.

•

As information started to come together about Laurie Dann, her rampage appeared to have some parallels to the 49th Street Elementary School playground shootings in Los Angeles on February 24, 1984. In that attack, a twenty-eight-year-old mentally disturbed man sprayed rifle fire at more than a hundred children as he crouched in the window of his second-story apartment across the street from the school.

The gunman, Tyrone Mitchell, had a long history of threatening and irrational behavior before his attack; he killed one child; and the police surrounded the house he was occupying for hours afterward.

The Winnetka tragedy was also reminiscent, in some respects, of the McDonald's Massacre in San Ysidro, California, on July 18, 1984. Twenty-one people were slaughtered and another fifteen were wounded in that attack.

These killings galvanized Los Angeles County authorities to establish a special Mental Evaluation Unit, a multiagency team of law enforcement, court and mental health care workers to coordinate information and keep track of potentially dangerous people as they cross jurisdictional lines.

Unfortunately, no such unit existed in Illinois.

•

Steven Davis, an acquaintance of Russell's from high school and from college days in Ithaca, came to Kent Road. He wasn't allowed behind the barricades, but he entertained reporters by giving them just the sort of quotes they were all dying for. "I can't say that I'm surprised," he said. "When you grow up in this area that I grew up in on the North Shore, there's a lot of parental and family pressure that can cause the children of the family some unusual pressures. You have to be more than everybody else because you grow up in one of the wealthiest areas in America."

•

At Carmela and Company, the Northbrook beauty salon where Edith always had her hair done, the employees were shocked. All those years, and they didn't even know she had a daughter.

•

Norm was frustrated by the standoff and responded eagerly when Mohr relayed a request from Gary Stryker, commander of the Northern Illinois Police Alarm System, that Norm help get Laurie out of the house.

"I'll go in there," Norm said. "I want to go in there. I'm going in there."

"No, you're not," Mohr said. "We'd just have another hostage situation. And if you try to go in, I'm going to have to do whatever I can do to restrain you."

"I'm not the kind of person that fights," Norm said, suddenly mild-mannered.

But just to be sure, Mohr found the only suitable tether handy—the cocker spaniel's leash in the hall closet at the command center—and looped it around Norm's waist before they left the house. And so the cameras recorded the pathetic spectacle of Norm Wasserman on a leash, walking with his head down toward the front of the Andrew house.

He began shouting. "Laurie," he cried, his ragged and distorted voice echoing through the trees. "Get on the phone, please pick up the phone. Talk to me at least. Let me know you're all right. Can you hear me? Come on out."

No response. He tried again. "Please, Laurie, come on out of there. Everything's going to be okay."

Back in the command center, though, Edith was not so sure. After her husband had left with Mohr, she turned to county prosecutor Nancy Sidote, who had taken responsibility for tending to the Wassermans because of her earlier dealings with them.

"I feel so sorry," Edith said. "I feel very sorry for all the mothers of the other children and the families of all the other children. I had no idea Laurie was like this. How could she ever hurt kids? She told me on the phone when I talked to her, 'I'm sorry, Mom. I'm sorry for everything. None of this is your fault. I'm really sorry.' Last night she was so excited about being with those children. She made Rice Krispies treats and she brought them special drinks and she was practically dancing around the kitchen. She was so excited about preparing these little lunches for the kids and going to this fair, she was really happy to be doing that."

"I'm a mother, too," Sidote said. "I have a son in grade school. Do you have any other children?"

"Yes, I have a son in Texas," Edith said. "He's doing very well. We have grandchildren and we're really happy about them. I just...we just don't know what happened with Laurie." Edith paused. "What would happen if they do arrest her? I know she'll have to be punished, but what would happen to her?"

"That's something we shouldn't worry about now," Sidote said. "If Laurie needs help, Laurie will get help. But obviously these charges will be real serious."

"This sounds terrible for a mother to say," Edith said. "But, you know, she's in so much trouble I think it would be better if she didn't come out of this alive."

•

Scott Freidheim's golden retriever, Boots, was vomiting blood. He'd eaten the entire plate of Rice Krispies treats left on the family's front porch that morning and was the first creature—man or beast—to suffer noticeable ill effects from Laurie's early morning drop-offs.

Boots was to survive. Scott, who hadn't made the connection between the dog's distress and the treats, figured that the curious note "from your little sisters" might have something to do with a sorority pledge class having to bake goodies for Psi U alumni.

•

Armand Dann arrived at the police barricade at Hibbard and Kent and could not get through. "My name is Armand Dann and she was my daughter-in-law," he explained.

The sentry narrowed his gaze impassively. "I don't care who you are," he said. "You're not coming in."

•

At the end of the regularly scheduled school day at Hubbard Woods, parents were called into the school classroom by classroom to be reunited with their children. Administrators encouraged them to take a back exit in order to avoid the crush of cameramen still out front. They also announced a crisis counseling session for parents and children to be held at seven o'clock that night on the second floor of the Winnetka Community House.

•

At 3:40, when the school was calm and all the children had gone home, Chief Timm left to join Lieutenant Sumner, NIPAS team leader Sergeant Gary Stryker, Nancy Sidote and FBI agent James Bogner at Kent Road. The NIPAS team had the interior perimeter secure, and Winnetka and other local police forces were holding the outside perimeter.

They took their small group to another house on the street for a living room conference to figure out their next move. As time went on they were more and more sure that Laurie was still alone inside the Andrews'—two Kenilworth policemen said they pretty well had the backyard covered during that worrisome ten-second gap in which Laurie might have escaped; and no sightings had been reported anywhere all afternoon.

One way to roust her was to launch tear gas into the house, but after some discussion they ruled it out because tear gas sometimes has no effect on people with mental illness, and to use enough gas to saturate such a large home might start a fire or an explosion. Timm reflected that the Andrew house alone—which looked to him like a small hotel—had to be worth a million easy. It was not a bad guess.

And given that Laurie had set a fire in one school, taken gasoline into another, torched the Rushe house and left a can of gasoline in her getaway car, it seemed possible she had a bomb with her inside the house. Ruth Ann Andrew said Laurie was carrying only her guns, but anything now seemed possible. She might have stashed flammable liquids outside the back door before coming in. She might have planted devices inside the Andrew house earlier in the morning. It seemed unwise at that point to underestimate her or hurry her along if she didn't want to be hurried.

Two police dogs from Northbrook were on the scene, and the FBI said sensitive listening devices and motion detectors were on the way but were held up in traffic. Sidote said that, to be safe, they ought to try to secure a judicial order before using listening devices on the house. This was one case they didn't want to screw up.

Some of the officials returned to the Berghorst kitchen, but kept their conversation low so as not to further distress the Wassermans in the next room, who had refused a television set and were agonizing in silence. Edith was nesting on the couch and Norm moved from the couch to the chair facing her when he wasn't pacing. They both had stress headaches; Edith refused aspirin but accepted Sidote's offer of a cup of tea during one of the prosecutor's visits to the room to check up.

Because Kent Road was a dead end and the Red Cross service truck could not get to the command post without driving through the theoretical line of fire, those bunkered in had no outside source of food or drink all afternoon. After a while, they decided to set aside good manners and began raiding the cabinets and the fridge, eating crackers, brewing coffee and making themselves at home for the long haul.

Every so often, homeowner Ted Berghorst would call in from England to find out what was new and to be sure someone was minding the dog.

•

The FBI in Madison thought to take control of Laurie's room in the Towers and to check with the U.S. Attorney's office in advance of a search that started at 3:45. The move was significant not only for what the search turned up, but also for the way it stands in contrast to what happened later that evening in Glencoe at the Wassermans' house.

•

At 4:30, Timm held a news conference at the corner of Kent and Hibbard roads. As he approached the media from his side of the police tape, a fistfight broke out between a sound technician from one station and a camera operator from another. Everyone was antsy—including the Chicago-area residents who were continuing to watch the drama unfold live—because nothing seemed to be happening and the small-town police were starting to look ineffectual. One woman with a handgun had been holding the entire North Shore at bay going on five hours now.

Timm said he had nothing new to report and said no action was planned because there had been enough violence already. He refused to be more specific because electricity was still going into the Andrew house and, as far as he knew, Laurie was watching him speak at that very moment.

•

Many Winnetka residents had gathered with the reporters outside the yellow tape sealing the end of Kent Road, waiting for word. Author James McManus, after learning his child was safe, turned his attentions to his next fear—that Laurie would be carrying a copy of his book, *Out of the Blue*, just like Mark David Chapman had been carrying J.D. Salinger's *Catcher in the Rye* when he killed John Lennon.

•

The Corwins went with Nicky's body to the funeral home in Wilmette, where they were overwhelmed not only with their grief but also with the necessity of planning for the services and burial. Linda was worried that the rabbi who would deliver the eulogy would not really know Nicky, and so she wrote up a few short paragraphs for someone to read at the funeral.

Once she had finished, she and Joel realized that her statement might better serve as a statement to the reporters who were desperate for information and family comments from the Corwins:

A gifted athlete, a gifted artist, a gifted student; a child full of love and humor; a child who made his parents weep with joy at his talent

and his attractiveness. He loved people; he loved organizing games; he
played basketball, hockey, baseball, soccer; he drew pictures that
showed a keen eye for detail and a vivid imagination; a sweet and loving
child who had concern for others. Nick enjoyed a role of helping
others and lending support whenever he could. He was a very tough
competitor in his athletic games, but a sensitive and kind child off
the field or court. He brightened our lives with such a brilliant light that
we cannot believe he's gone.

When they came back home, several dozen friends and
relatives visited to sit with them. In the backyard, Johnny and
Michael played ball with a friend.

•

By 5:15, Timm had started to worry. Night was beginning
to fall over Winnetka and the Andrew house was shrouded in
shadows. Darkness was Laurie's one chance in a thousand of
slipping out of the house undetected and into the dense woods
all around. They couldn't wait forever.

Sergeant Stryker suggested getting portable flood lights
and illuminating the entire house, but Timm argued that the
area was like a jungle at night and to wait much past dusk
would be taking an unnecessary chance.

•

Highland Park police officers took Jeff and Susie Taylor
and their kids to the Deerbrook Hyatt Regency in Deerfield
where it was thought they would be safe. They checked in at
about 5:30 under the name "Cole," which Jeff chose because
he worked for the Cole Taylor bank.

Two officers stayed with the Taylors inside the hotel,
where the children watched comedy programs on TV in an
effort to take their minds off the events of the day. When room
service brought hamburgers to the door for dinner, the family
was told to hide in the bathroom until the waiter had left and
the coast was clear.

Now, Jeff thought bitterly, now they're concerned with our
safety. Now they believe there's a danger.

•

A little before seven o'clock, Sergeant Stryker asked Norm
to go to the front of the house again to try to talk to Laurie, as

he had been begging to do all afternoon. Mohr again tied him to the leash, walked him to the front of the house and this time gave him the bullhorn.

He began pleading. "Please, come out of there," he said. His voice broke with sorrow. "If you can hear me, please. Laurie. Please come out. Laurie. Pick up the phone. Laurie. Pick up the phone. Please. Please."

He didn't know it, but he was simply a diversion, meant to hold his daughter's attention while an assault and canine team could enter from the rear of the house.

•

A twelve-man assault team accompanied by a police dog and two handlers from Northbrook entered the Andrew house through basement windows at 7:10. The team, dressed in black, was led by Deerfield patrolman Eric Lundahl, who had been a year behind Laurie at Highland Park High School in 1973 but had no recollection of her.

It took the officers ten minutes to check and secure the basement and first floor. Norm Wasserman's wretched appeals were still sounding out front.

The dog went ahead first to reconnoiter, and when it returned almost immediately from the second floor, Lundahl turned with alarm to one of the handlers. "Is that bad?"

"That's good," the handler said. "It probably means there's a dead body up there."

At 7:23, four members of the entry team came into the bedroom of Trish and Kathy Andrew and found Laurie lying facedown in a small pool of her own blood, the .32 at her feet, her head turned to the left and resting on her right arm where she fell on it, her left arm extended. A single bullet had gone through the back of her mouth and through her brain stem. Her eyes were open, her face was slightly swollen and the tip of her tongue was clenched between her teeth. Blood had splashed down onto her legs as she spun and fell.

Chief Timm was summoned quickly. He looked at the body. "Is this it?" he thought. "All this mayhem and she takes the easy way out? And that's all?"

Patty McConnell, who was back at the station nervously chain-smoking with Amy Moses, felt relief when she heard that the crisis was over, but also anger that she would never get the chance to talk to Laurie and find out why she did what she did.

•

Police escorted Norm Wasserman back to the command center from where he had been calling through the bullhorn. He was standing several feet away from his wife when Nancy Sidote came into the room and put her arms around Edith. Just then, Floyd Mohr began to talk to him.

"I'm very sorry," Nancy said quietly. "I'm sorry, she's gone. She took her own life."

Simultaneously, Mohr told Norm, "She's dead. She killed herself. Shot herself."

Edith seemed relieved, Sidote thought. Norm, however, buried his face in his hands, then cried out, "Why? Why? Why? Why? Why didn't she wait for me? Why didn't she wait? Why didn't she talk?"

Edith turned to Mohr. "Did she suffer?"

"No," he said. "It was quick."

•

"I want to go home," said Russell in the other room when he heard that his ex-wife was dead. He tried to imagine the pain she must have been feeling inside to have done what she did—the hurt, the hate, the alienation. He felt an unexpected sorrow. "I just want to go home," he said again.

•

Laurie's parents wept and embraced each other. After a tactful minute had passed, Mohr approached them to offer his condolences. He said he didn't think they should drive themselves home given how they were feeling. Norm balked at first but finally agreed.

Sidote said it might be best if they were to go to a friend's house, as reporters were bound to be crawling all over their residence and they probably shouldn't be alone.

"We're so ashamed right now, there's no one we can be with," Edith said. "Who would understand this? We can't talk to anyone. We just have to go and be in our own home together."

They remained firm on this point, so Mohr put them in

the back seat of his Fairmont sedan and they escaped unnoticed by the media.

"I'm sorry, I'm sorry," Norm repeated over and over on the ride back, speaking to no one in particular. "Just look at my daughter, God, they treated her like an animal."

"Why would she do that?" Edith said. "How could this happen?"

It was eight o'clock when they arrived at the house on Sheridan Road. Mohr walked Norm and Edith to the door and, at the last minute, asked if he could come in. "I need to look in her room," he said. "I think it's real important to see if there's any evidence for the case."

"What case? The case is over," said Norm, suddenly angry. "She's dead. What the hell do you guys want? Leave us alone."

Mohr pressed him. "There could be a danger to you, a bomb or whatever, or maybe evidence of a danger for someone else."

"I'll give you five minutes, and five minutes only," Norm said.

"You don't have to come in if you don't want to," Mohr said. "I'll do it by myself."

"I'm not leaving you alone in her room," Norm said.

They turned right inside the front door and walked down the hallway to her room. The yellow shag carpeting and the single bed against the wall were familiar to Mohr, who had visited Laurie's room several times before in the course of other investigations. Usually, though, the room was a shambles. That night, however, it was very tidy.

"Please don't disrupt things," Edith told him. "The maid was just here today. Be as neat as you can be."

Inside Laurie's closet were a dozen *Penthouse* magazines on the top shelf. On her dresser were bottles of pills, toiletries, an appointment book, a used bus ticket from Madison to Northbrook and a bag from the Marksman gun shop. Inside the bag was the box for the .357 Magnum. Mohr picked up the bag and Norm began to remonstrate: "I want you out!" he said.

"I need more time," Mohr said. He and Norm were very

much on edge, both feeling a surreal sense of loss, anguish and guilt. Mohr was also worried he might uncover a booby trap and be blown sky high.

In a drawer he found the syringe that, he would learn later, Laurie had used to shoot poison into the fruit juice packets. He put the syringe into the Marksman bag, then lifted up the mattress. There he found another *Penthouse* magazine, which seemed to enrage Norm.

"What are you doing?" he cried. "You have to get out of my house. Now. Take whatever you have and get out of my house." Mohr had never seen him so forceful.

The doorbell rang and Edith went to let in those who were arriving to comfort them, including Norm's sister, Idele, and her husband, Harry, and Peter Weinberg, who owned a chain of clothing stores where Norm did the books. Mohr moved over to the dresser to grab the calendar and the bus ticket, but Norm stopped him. "No!" he said. "That was Laurie's and you can't have it."

Mohr stepped back and Norm continued. "You need to leave now, please, leave my house," he said. "This is a tragedy and our lives are destroyed." He began to weep. "And my daughter, my baby..."

One of the guests came over to Mohr. "Mr. Wasserman wants you to leave," he said firmly.

And so Mohr left. Later he would come under much quiet criticism for not making any effort to freeze Laurie's room as part of the crime scene. If he were less emotionally involved in the case, other policemen said, less trusting, he would have considered more strongly the possibility that there was important evidence hidden somewhere in the room or in the house that Norm and Edith might later have reason to destroy or dispose of.

Mohr did not have a neat excuse. Pressed on the point later during an emotional recounting of his actions that day, he shifted in and out of the present tense while describing his state of mind at the doorway. "First of all, it's not my case and I'm not the supervisor involved, and I'm personally in no mental shape to think about really what I'm doing right now. I hate to say this, but I think about it. I wasn't the supervisor there. What happened is, right now I'm totally drained right now. I'm not thinking clearly again. All I want to do is stop my body for a little while."

•

Around the corner on Montgomery Avenue, the Pappas family was having dinner. Both Dean and Cassandra had tears in their eyes.

"What are you thinking?" Cassandra asked her son.

"I'm thinking that this is a tragedy all around," Dean said. "Not only for the boy who was killed and his parents, but all around. Laurie was a good person inside. What happened to her, God only knows. I don't."

•

At 9:22, Norm and Edith called their son, Mark, in Austin and spoke to him for fifteen minutes.

•

Jennifer Nehls, the massage therapist, walked into the living room of her house in Madison, saw Laurie's face on TV, and simply began swearing.

Haley Bareck, Laurie's old dining companion from the Towers, had been at work all day at the Chas A. Stevens clothing store and had overheard bits and pieces of news about a shocking tragedy in Winnetka. She arrived at her parents' house just in time for the ten o'clock newscast.

"Did you hear what happened?" her mother said.

"Of course," she said. "Do they know who did it yet?"

"Let's watch and see," her mother said.

Haley stood behind the couch. And suddenly, there was Laurie's mug shot, staring impassively from the TV screen.

For the first time in her life, Haley fainted away and crashed to the floor. She woke up several minutes later screaming and made her sister sleep upstairs with her that night.

•

Lindsay Fisher survived two hours of surgery and a total blood transfusion, but remained in critical and unstable condition Friday night in Evanston Hospital. She was conscious but on a respirator.

Kathryn Miller was in critical but stable condition at Evanston Hospital, as were Mark Teborek and Robert Trossman.

Peter Munro was at Highland Park in serious but stable condition.

•

Floyd Mohr put his gun and badge away, went to Bennigan's and put back eight bottles of Miller Lite in half an hour. He was not usually a drinker.

His partner drove him home. All Mohr remembered was that he couldn't feel his lips and his wife had to undress him and put him to bed.

•

Russell Dann was home alone, screening his telephone calls with his answering machine. His mind was racing a million miles a minute. He wanted to tell everyone, "Fuck you," as in, "Fuck you, I told you so."

30

The
Aftermath

The morning after the shooting spree, a call came to the Winnetka police department for Lieutenant Sumner.

"I am an attorney representing Norman Wasserman," said the man on the other end, "and we are demanding that you return the Toyota today."

"We're done with it," said Sumner. "Come and get it." He was puzzled by the demand. The entire nation had been rocked by Friday's juxtaposition of school, suburbia and murder. The *New York Post*'s Saturday front page was screaming "Berserk!" and other, less excitable newspapers coast to coast were splashing the story prominently on the front page—the classroom, the last sanctuary, had been violated. A certain innocence was gone, murdered by a wealthy young baby-sitter inexplicably gone mad. No parent would ever feel quite the same way again about seeing children off to school or leaving them in the care of strangers.

And, Sumner thought, Norm Wasserman was worried about his car.

Shortly thereafter, Norm appeared at the Winnetka police department. Patty McConnell thought he looked much older than his fifty-eight years, raw and whipped, as though he hadn't slept.

"I'm very sorry about your daughter," she said. "If there's anything I can do, please call."

Norm shook her hand. "Thank you," he said, his voice dripping with misery.

Sumner approached Norm. "We're going to Wisconsin and I'd like you to sign a waiver so we can look at your daughter's psychiatric records up there," he said.

"Well, you know, I talked to a friend who's a lawyer, and there is really no reason for me to sign anything," Norm said. "It wouldn't hold water. She was an adult."

"Okay," Sumner said. "But I also want to set up a time to talk to you and your wife. I want to interview you."

"We're really distraught right now," Norm said. "We're very embarrassed and hurt about what happened. We also lost a daughter."

"Fine," Sumner said. "Why don't you take a few days? Maybe you ought to get away, leave the area. But as soon as you feel strong enough, I'd like to sit down and talk."

"Okay," Norm said.

•

Lindsay Fisher underwent two more operations Saturday, one to stop ongoing bleeding in her diaphragm and the other to clear fluid out of her lungs. She remained in critical and unstable condition in Evanston Hospital.

Robert Trossman and Mark Teborek started the day in critical condition but seemed to be mending quickly and were upgraded to serious and moved out of intensive care to pediatric wards. Peter Munro, Kathryn Miller and Phil Andrew were also reported in serious but stable condition.

•

A sobbing Linda Corwin talked to a *Chicago Sun-Times* reporter about her slain son: "I told one of my friends that the only thing wrong with him was that he was perfect," she said.

•

School district superintendent Don Monroe held a special gathering for parents and students at Hubbard Woods Saturday. His purpose was to get the children back across the threshold of the schoolhouse as soon as possible and to reestablish the classroom as a safe place in their minds.

Some 250 of the school's 300 children came to school nearly all with at least one parent. The program opened with a general assembly during which Dick Streedain gave condition reports on all the injured and assured the children that the events of the previous day were freakish and unusual—such a thing had never happened before and, God willing, would never happen again.

Amy Moses was there. Media accounts—including a story being prepared by the *National Enquirer*—were hailing her as a hero who saved untold numbers of lives by fighting with Laurie and refusing to gather the children in the corner when Laurie ordered her to do so. Yet a quieter sentiment said that Nicky Corwin was dead and five other children were in the hospital because Moses hadn't recognized Laurie for a dangerous outsider and challenged her immediately; because she hadn't been as strong as the regular teacher, Amy Deuble, a tall, fit blonde woman who had once been a middle-school gym teacher. Moses could read the heartless second-guessing in the contemptuous eyes of some of the parents. Her fault.

Then the rumor started: Amy Moses had been dating Russell Dann. If she hadn't been in Classroom 7, the tragedy never would have happened.

It was all her fault.

•

When the large assembly broke up, the students went with their parents back to their homerooms where they were met by teachers and counselors who encouraged them to talk about what they were feeling.

The discussion in Classroom 7 was led by social worker Walter Rest, the director of a local community counseling center. The children sat in their regular seats and their parents sat next to them, either scrunched side by side onto the tiny chairs or on the floor. The first theme Rest tried to develop was that the kids should keep their faith in humanity. "Most people are still to be trusted," he said.

He explained a little about mental illness, and said that because Laurie Dann's thinking was faulty, her behavior was faulty, too.

"Did we do anything to make her sick?" one of the children asked.

"No," Rest said. "Many people tried to make her better, but they were unable to do so."

Others asked why Laurie had shot at some children and not at others, indirectly expressing guilt that they had been spared. Some felt guilty because they were glad they weren't hit.

Throughout the school, a few of the students demanded that the school post policemen in every room, but most were adamant that life continue normally and that the building not be locked up like a cage.

A fifth-grade girl asked why people were praying for Laurie. The Reverend Michael Weston, a Catholic priest at Sacred Heart Church in Winnetka, later answered her question in a homily. "What she did she could not have done if she were in her right mind," he said. "She certainly was not humanly responsible for what she did. Jesus said, 'Pray for your persecutors,' and we pray for Laurie Dann."

A mother reported that her daughter had play-acted putting on a bulletproof vest and shooting Laurie. Many other children had looked in their closets and under their beds the night before to see if Laurie had come back to life and was after them again.

•

And, in a sense, Laurie did come back to life on Saturday.

After the assembly at the school concluded, Sergeant McConnell and Lieutenant Sumner waited on the curb in front of the school while Chief Timm crossed the street to tell the gathered media what had been said.

A Glencoe police officer drove his squad car right up in front of McConnell and Sumner and jumped out. "Patty, I have to tell you," he said. "We had a little girl poisoned in Glencoe today. It was a juice package left on her door, it was stamped 'Sample' and it's all connected to Laurie Dann."

McConnell listened with growing alarm as the officer explained how this and other reports of tainted juice in Glencoe appeared related to Laurie's baby-sitting. "Oh, my

God," she said. She hurried to Timm's side and began tugging on his sport coat.

"Can this wait until after the interview?" Timm said.

"Herb, this is real important," McConnell said. "I don't think it can wait."

Within hours, the true scope of Laurie's attack on the North Shore was starting to become clear, and word went out that people should not eat or drink any food samples found in their mailboxes and that the schools Laurie had visited should throw away all their snack foods.

The warnings were only partially successful—well over a dozen people ultimately ate or drank the poisoned treats. Fortunately, Laurie had not taken into account that the arsenic solution she had stolen was highly diluted at one thousand parts per million. Her most seriously affected victim outside of Boots the dog was Northwestern University sophomore Greg McCullough, a member of Alpha Tau Omega who had eaten a Rice Krispies treat. He was called away from a Big Ten track meet in Ann Arbor, Michigan, hospitalized for emergency tests and released in good condition.

Laurie's enormous ineptitude had dogged her to the end. If she had been successful in all she wanted to do on May 20, she would have fatally poisoned at least fifty people, shot to death at least a dozen schoolchildren, incinerated three members of the Rushe family in their home and burned down two schools with 440 children inside.

•

The Rushe family, whose house was uninhabitable for the rest of their time in Winnetka because of smoke and fire damage, moved in with David and Rosemarie Hawkins, friends to whom they had recommended Laurie as a baby-sitter.

Young Patrick and Carl were upset that Laurie was dead. They couldn't comprehend what she had done, only that they had loved her.

The Rushes, too, were the subject of dark rumors and mutterings from those who sought to find a coherent motive for Laurie's rampage and thereby understand her incomprehensible final madness. The Rushes had been stupid enough to hire Laurie Dann, and then Marian's announcement that the family was leaving town lit the fuse. That must have been it.

Sunday, May 22

The churches were packed Sunday morning in Winnetka as residents looked for solace and meaning through God.

"We gather as a community whose heart has been ripped out," said the Reverend David Goodman, preaching at the Winnetka Bible Church.

After services, many people simply wandered the streets of Winnetka with their families, as though Nicky Corwin's death had reminded them of something they had forgotten.

•

Shooting victim Lindsay Fisher's condition stabilized after she'd undergone three nearly total blood transfusions. She was still on the respirator, but wrote a note to her father asking if she had missed a soccer game. She also asked him to bring her favorite shorts to the hospital and said she wanted to go home.

Robert Trossman, Kathryn Miller and Mark Teborek remained in serious but stable condition; Pete Munro was upgraded to fair. Phil Andrew, also upgraded to fair, was able to walk eighty feet between hospital rooms.

Greg McCullough, the Northwestern track team member, was even well enough Sunday to run a leg of the 400 meter relay at the Big Ten Outdoor Track and Field Championships in Ann Arbor. His team finished sixth.

•

The Evanston Hospital Crisis Intervention Unit held a session on post-traumatic stress in the basement of the Winnetka fire station that afternoon, but it was poorly attended. The policemen said they'd rather play softball.

"How could somebody who doesn't know me talk to me about something I lived through and they didn't?" Mohr said later, explaining the defensive reaction that he and many of his colleagues first had to these and similar sessions.

But when he looked at the chart of symptoms of post-traumatic stress, he saw he was virtually a textbook case—anxiety, obsession, anger, inability to sleep, vomiting, diarrhea.

•

Dean Pappas was in his front yard Sunday when he saw Norm Wasserman jogging toward him. "Hi," Dean said.

"Hi," Norm said. He seemed to jog a little faster as he passed.

•

Johnny and Michael Corwin wanted to see their brother, Nicky, one more time. Linda had promised, but couldn't bring herself to take them to the funeral home, so Joel took them.

The boys each slipped a note into the coffin. Michael, the older boy, wrote, "Nick was the greatest brother anyone could ever have. He was always so nice to everyone and was always helping them. He was a great athlete and a great student. He didn't ever deserve any of this. We'll never fully get over the grief and he'll always be with us. We love you Nick."

Johnny, who was just learning his letters, drew a picture of a baseball player and wrote "I love Nick" all over it.

Monday, May 23

A steady drizzle started at dawn Monday on the North Shore and turned into a downpour shortly before ten A.M., when funeral services for Nicky Corwin began at Temple Jeremiah in nearby Northfield. Some 1,500 mourners filled every seat in the huge, modern sanctuary and stood two and three deep along the outer walls.

A small, closed coffin rested at the head of the central aisle.

"We're here this morning with hearts heavy, confused and troubled," said Rabbi Robert Schreibman in his eulogy. "We ask ourselves, 'Why?' We wonder what we could possibly say to relieve such inconsolable grief. We search for words of explanation, but we find none. Nicky is gone long before his time."

To the Corwins he said, "The answer we look for—to find comfort for ourselves, and to comfort you—eludes us."

The rabbi praised Nicky as "a wonderful and promising

child with so much to give," and noted that "the pain is great because the joy was immense."

Referring to the torrents of rain falling outside, he said, "So deep is our sorrow, so great is this loss, that we know that God, too, is weeping."

He concluded, "Nicky lives on in the timelessness of time, in all of our hearts and memories. We ask for God's help to rise from our grief, and turn to each other and to love one another, share love with those who need it. Amen."

The funeral cortege led by a silver hearse wound wearily for seven miles through Northfield, Winnetka, Wilmette and Evanston to the gravesite at Memorial Park Cemetery in Skokie.

Several hundred of the mourners reconvened at the maroon awning over the grave, pressing close to hear the final prayers.

"God gave, and God has taken away," Rabbi Schreibman intoned. "The dust returns to earth as it was, the spirit returns to God who made us.... The spirit itself cannot die."

Linda Corwin remained doubled over in grief and Joel held her in his arms.

The rabbi then said the Kaddish, a traditional Jewish prayer for the dead, and the family left the burial site. Several of Nicky's friends stood at the gravesite before the coffin was lowered into the ground. One of them, a little blond boy in a black windbreaker, touched the side of the coffin and mouthed a single word: "Goodbye."

•

Laurie Dann was also supposed to be buried Monday in Skokie, but to avoid controversy or the appearance of insensitivity, her burial was moved to Shalom Memorial Park in northwest suburban Palatine. It was a private ceremony attended by perhaps a dozen family friends. Her body was lowered into an unmarked grave, and workers at the graveyard were given strict instructions not to reveal the location to anyone.

•

Floyd Mohr returned to the Wassermans' home Monday. Edith was home but Norm wasn't, and she let Mohr search Laurie's Honda. She would not allow him back into Laurie's room.

"We totally cleaned it out, anyway," she said.

The appointment book Mohr had seen Friday night was gone forever.

•

Thirteen bicycles were still locked in the racks at Hubbard Woods School as they had been all weekend, left behind and temporarily forgotten.

The doors opened at one P.M. for an abbreviated school day. Most parents walked their children to the front doors.

At 2:30 P.M., children, teachers and administrators held another memorial service for Nicky. His class had put together a book in which they recorded their memories of their fallen friend. "The name Nicholas means 'giver of gifts,'" said Don Monroe. "So they put together a book called *The Gifts That Nicholas Gave Us*." The words from the children are not as eloquent as Linda Corwin's, but they are just as revealing:

The gift Nick gave to me was helping me spell things.

Nick taught me how to play kickball.

Me and Nick had a fight about a marker and after the fight Nick gave me the black marker.

The gift Nick gave to me was the first friend from Hubbard Woods.

The rumor in the school community about Amy Moses dating Russell Dann was gaining strength. Moses had given one quick news conference during which the subject never came up, and Russell had refused to make any statement whatsoever. Officials at the school finally felt obliged to pass the rumor on to Winnetka sergeant Patty McConnell, who then had the unpleasant task of calling Moses in to ask her about it.

McConnell had earlier in the day been put in charge of a twenty-six-member, multijurisdictional task force to investigate the tragedy. One of the first things the task force did was to establish a hot-line number for people to call with any relevant information about Laurie, her family, her friends and her associates to find out if she had acted alone and, if so, what er motivation might have been. McConnell needed all the leads she could get, and wanted to talk to anyone who had anything to say.

The Amy Moses–Russell Dann story, though, turned out to be rank fiction. The two had never even met. Also false was the other report that the Rushes' impending move to New York had somehow triggered Laurie's rampage—her planning for a day of rage appeared to have gone back at least two months.

A titillating angle to the story—that Russell and Laurie had invested in pornographic films when they were married—was also much less exciting when the whole truth came out later. It was a small investment in their portfolio and the movie company produced soft-core, R-rated features, and it only came to the public's attention because Laurie's divorce attorneys had tried to use the information to cast Russell in a bad light.

•

Illinois governor James Thompson called Monday for legislation to prevent people who have "exhibited bizarre behavior and [who] have consistent run-ins with authorities" from obtaining guns. But, he added, "the general public at large is never going to be protected against the person who goes berserk..."

•

Dr. Greist received a tainted packet of vegetable juice in the mail Monday. Jane Sterling, the woman whose children Laurie tried to lure to Hubbard Woods School, got a packet of Ocean Spray cran-raspberry juice laced with arsenic.

Lindsay Fisher, the most seriously wounded of the shooting victims, remained in critical condition at Evanston Hospital. She had been weaned from the respirator, and her doctors reported with some amazement that her injured right lung, liver and stomach showed signs that they would heal completely.

Kathryn Miller, Robert Trossman, Mark Teborek and Peter Munro were upgraded to fair condition and moved out of intensive care. Phil Andrew was also upgraded to fair, but he remained in intensive care at Highland Park Hospital.

•

Later in the afternoon, Joel Corwin brought his sons back to the cemetery. Together they walked the damp grounds around where Nicky was buried, looking at other graves and reading the names and dates.

One of the people had died at age eighty-eight. "That's how long a person should live," Joel told his sons. "Eighty-eight, not eight."

•

Russell Dann would only talk on the record to *Nightline*. While reporters from all over the country were frustrated by his persistent silence, he was volunteering to appear on ABC-TV's late-night news forum to talk about the breakdown in law enforcement that led to Laurie's rampage. He said his purpose was to outline how the system had failed and, by doing so, help prevent another such tragedy from occurring.

Host Ted Koppel circled Russell carefully in their live interview that night, starting with the ice-pick incident, moving on to the harassing telephone calls, then returning to the ice pick with an unexpectedly hard question: "At some point, you were asked to take a lie detector test, right?"

Russell faltered. He admitted to failing the test, said it was the worst day of his life, then—mistakenly—admitted that Laurie had passed a lie detector test on the same incident.

"That either says something about lie detector tests," Koppel offered, "or it says something very bizarre about the two of you."

Russell answered that lie detectors don't work, and he went on to ramble about the grief of the Corwin family and the need for gun control, but the damage was irreversible. He'd looked awful—shifty, defensive, untrustworthy.

After a commercial break, Glencoe chief Robert Bonneville followed Russell on the hot seat and looked magnificent in comparison.

"Given the same set of circumstances," he told Koppel, "without changes in law or our freedoms we cherish so much, I can't sit here and honestly tell you, Ted, that anything would be different."

Tuesday, May 24

Phil Andrew was moved out of intensive care in the very early hours Tuesday morning and upgraded to fair condition. Lindsay Fisher was upgraded from critical to serious.

Once the wounded victims seemed to be safely on the mend, the headlines turned inevitably to the issue of gun control. Supporters of stringent gun control seized the opportunity presented by Laurie's rampage to attempt to revive a bill prohibiting the sale or manufacture of handguns that had died in committee in the Illinois House of Representatives the previous year.

"I am hopeful that the tragedies of last Friday will get through the thick heads of the members of this General Assembly that we have a responsibility for the life, the health and the safety of our citizens," argued State Representative Barbara Flynn Currie during an acrimonious debate with her colleagues.

"Look at this issue for what it is," answered Representative Robert Piel. "I think you should be ashamed, Representative Currie, because you are pulling a sham and a farce to the media at the expense of these children in Winnetka. All it is is a grandstand."

The motion to revive the bill failed by an overwhelming margin, but the routed antigun forces, bolstered by the support of Chief Timm, announced that they would continue their fight on the local level.

•

The normal school schedule resumed at Hubbard Woods, but two police officers stood guard at the entryways. Additional officers were assigned to other schools in the district for the rest of the week.

Dick Streedain announced that he and the guidance counselors would be spending most of every day simply walking from class to class to calm and reassure the children. Unfamiliar adults, even parents, would not be allowed into the building.

Regular Classroom 7 teacher Amy Deuble was given a full-time aide and the assistance of a teacher from the National

College of Education to help her tend to the special needs of the second-graders who had watched their classmates gunned down. They planned to devote a large part of every day to writing, acting and talking about the incident and corresponding with those in the hospital.

•

Nicky Corwin's youth league baseball team, the Cubs, got together to compose a letter to Joel and Linda:

It is sunny and breezy. It is Tuesday and we have a game tomorrow. We need to practice today because we just can't go right into a game without Nicky. The team drifts in one by one and starts throwing the ball around. Then we sit on the outfield grass and begin to talk. Our game is in Winnetka tomorrow and Nicky won't be there. We're all very sorry. When we think of Nicky we feel sad. He could pitch. He could hit. He could field. He listened. He was determined. He got along with everyone. We will play tomorrow and try our best as Nicky always did.

Late Tuesday, Joe Sumner and Robert Kerner of the Winnetka police department and Detective Martin Paulson of the Wilmette police department left for Madison as part of the task-force investigation.

Wednesday, May 25

Laurie's father released his first and only public statement five days after the shooting. "Mrs. Wasserman and I reach out to all the families in their suffering," it said. "We suffer with you. Our prayer is that time will help alleviate the pain."

Norm Wasserman's "reaching out" did not include signing a release as executor of Laurie's estate that would have allowed Dr. Greist and his assistant Yoram Shwager to discuss her psychiatric treatment with Sumner, Kerner, Paulson and FBI agent Miller.

They met with Greist Wednesday afternoon after searching Laurie's room at the Towers, and played a four-and-a-half-hour game of cat and mouse. Sumner, with a malfunctioning tape recorder hidden in his briefcase, questioned Greist specifically and hypothetically, directly and obliquely, trying to pry out information. Greist, who was accompanied by a hospital lawyer keeping him on a tight rein, didn't say anything particularly enlightening.

Sumner was finally able to compel Greist to hand over his written records by threatening him with a grand jury subpoena. The ostensible legal reasons for the subpoena were that Greist's files might show that Laurie was part of a larger conspiracy or that she had other intended victims who might not yet have discovered their poison. It was a stretch, really, and Sumner knew it. The plain truth was that he just wanted to find out why Laurie did it—the great mystery.

But when Sumner finally got the files, he saw that Greist was as much in the dark as everyone else. Laurie had moved to Madison to be treated by him, and he'd seen her only a few times. The graduate student had done most of the work.

•

At four o'clock, postal authorities found a leaking brown envelope in Russell Dann's post office box in Highland Park. The reason he even had a post office box in the first place was to protect himself from Laurie.

The Highland Park police called in a bomb squad from a nearby military base as a precautionary measure. There was no return address on the envelope. X-rays followed by a further examination revealed the package was not a bomb, but a foil package of Hawaiian Punch.

At Hubbard Woods School, the first of a series of weekly discussion and counseling sessions began at 7:15 in the evening.

Thursday, May 26

By the time the task-force investigators arrived at the apartment Laurie had leased for the summer in Madison, the building manager had in hand an overnight-mail letter from Norm Wasserman that included a copy of the lease Laurie had signed for the upcoming year.

It began, "Dear sirs: As you are probably aware, Laurie Dann is deceased as of May 20, 1988." It went on to direct the management to release his daughter's possessions to Robert Kann, Norm's cousin, and added, "I would appreciate your returning her $300 security deposit."

Kann had just called, the rental agent said. He said he was on his way over.

The investigators found a shopping cart full of belongings in the new apartment, including a bottle of clomipramine, Laurie's gun-owner's permit and more than a hundred birth control pill containers.

When Kann arrived, Sumner pulled him aside for an interview. Kann, a gaunt, nervous man in his forties with a facial resemblance to Norm, didn't want any trouble. "Keep whatever you want," he told Sumner. "Take it."

•

Telephone records from the office of Dr. Phillip Epstein show two calls Thursday afternoon to the Lud Bock Pharmacy in Montreal, the drugstore through which Epstein had prescribed the experimental clomipramine for Laurie. The records show only one other call from Epstein's office to the pharmacy in the previous six months.

•

Mark Teborek was quietly discharged from Evanston Hospital early Thursday afternoon and became the first of the shooting victims to go home. Robert Trossman and Kathryn Miller were upgraded from fair to good condition, Lindsay Fisher was moved out of intensive care and listed in fair condition, while Peter Munro and Phil Andrew remained in fair condition.

The names of the victims were becoming numbingly familiar to Chicago-area residents, but with the exceptions of the all-American boy Phil Andrew and the murdered Nicky Corwin, information about the other children was hard to come by. Lindsay and Kathryn liked soccer. Peter liked hockey. They wanted to come home from the hospital and that was more or less it. Their parents had all met and agreed to keep the publicity and the interviews to a minimum, and Lindsay's father, George Fisher, asked the media to honor their "God-given right to privacy."

The children were to remain names and hospital charts, smiling faces in a class picture. As George Fisher later said, he wanted Lindsay to become famous someday for something *she* did, not for something that was done to her.

Friday, May 27

Exactly one week after Laurie Dann had pulled him into the bathroom and shot him in the chest, Robert Trossman was released from Evanston Hospital. He was two days shy of seven years old.

Lindsay Fisher's remarkable recovery continued and she was upgraded to good condition.

Summer 1988

The shootings came up in class discussion every day at Hubbard Woods for the rest of the school year. The kids seemed to need to talk about it, and the teachers would sometimes just say, "I have a bad memory. Can you tell me again what happened?"

The kids from Classroom 7 reenacted the shooting in the form of a play over and over. Children who hadn't witnessed the shooting turned it into a playground game, taking turns assuming the role of Laurie Dann and her victims. The fears and sleepless nights persisted. One girl suggested that her father quit his job and become a policeman in order to better protect the family; a boy lined up G.I. Joe dolls outside his bedroom door for protection each night.

Brian Taylor, Susie and Jeff's middle child, had nightmares of being chased by people with guns or having his family slaughtered. In one dream, he was having a birthday party and someone popped out of a huge cake and sprayed the room with gunfire.

•

Patty McConnell's task force, which included investigators from her own department as well as from Glencoe, Northfield, Wilmette, Glenview, Niles, Deerfield, Northbrook, Highland Park and the Cook County sheriff's office, kept scratching for clues in case No. 88-3443. Their files were filling up with minutia—citizens reporting that they thought they'd seen Laurie once shopping at the White Hen Pantry and so on—but it was slow to add up and the people who might have been able to help the most weren't talking. Russell wanted little to do with the North Shore police and remained virtually in seclusion after the *Nightline* debacle. He gave interviews to the *Chicago Tribune* and *People* magazine, but only on the condition that he not be quoted or identified as the source of any information.

Norm and Edith made several appointments to speak to Lieutenant Sumner in Winnetka but always backed out at the last minute, saying they were too distraught to be interviewed. Their friends would add very little; the man who painted their house said he had been instructed to keep his mouth shut.

Everyone had a lawyer. It got to be almost a joke with the task force—someone would call the hot line and say he had seen Laurie somewhere or knew her at one time, then he would balk at answering any further questions and say he had to consult with his attorney before saying anything else.

•

When Floyd Mohr reached Mark Wasserman by telephone in Texas as part of the investigation, Mark said that he hadn't seen Laurie in two years and that she was always friendly, quiet, shy and timid.

"I can't believe she did this," Mark said. "My feeling is that my parents didn't tell me about all of her troubles—just the OCD."

The results of Laurie's autopsy, released June 2, weren't particularly revealing either. The report showed therapeutic levels of both clomipramine and lithium carbonate in her blood as well as caffeine, but no alcohol or illegal drugs. The Canadian connection through which Laurie got the clomipramine piqued the interest of the Illinois Department of Professional Regulation, which said that it was investigating Dr. Epstein's conduct.

That night, shooting victim Peter Munro was released from Highland Park Hospital. Only Lindsay Fisher and Phil Andrew were still hospitalized, both now in good condition. Mark Teborek was already riding his bicycle to and from school.

•

Linda Corwin published a statement of thanks to the community in the June 2 edition of the weekly *Winnetka Talk*:

It is because of the love that we have received from all corners that we can find something positive in the loss of our dearest Nick. We see that Nicky has left in his wake all the best that humanity can offer—the reaching out of parents to their children, the reaching out of people to one another to comfort the bereaved and the injured, the reaching out of children in a show of caring and love that we would never have imagined.

We have said often over the past week that Nick always wanted us to do the noble thing; he would strive always for grace under pressure. His life stands as a shining example to us of what we should strive for in dealing with his loss.

Hubbard Woods School had returned all of Nicky's classroom projects, including several storybooks he had written and drawn pictures for. Two creations seemed chillingly prescient—the first was a lengthy talking-animal story he titled "Randolph's Adventure," in which the villain, a dog named Dirty Dan, shoots his victims while at play, killing a character named Mickey. The second was a drawing of his mother, standing alone, with a balloon caption coming from her mouth reading, "Where is my son?"

•

Floyd Mohr went through the contents of the Wassermans' garbage at ten o'clock in the morning two weeks after the crime. He found powdered boric acid, lithium carbonate, clomipramine tablets and one empty box that once contained a Daisy 2 over-the-counter pregnancy test kit.

Later that afternoon, someone in Dr. Phillip Epstein's office placed another call from his phone to the Lud Bock Pharmacy, the first of two such calls in June.

Phil Andrew was released from Highland Park Hospital

on June 5. Two days later, during the height of public specula-
tion about the role of prescription drugs in Laurie's mad
rampage, the U.S. Food and Drug Administration removed
some of the shadow from clomipramine by approving it for
wider use—a prelude to the agency's general approval of the
drug issued in January 1990. An FDA spokesman said the
agency action was unrelated to Laurie's case.

That Friday, on the last day of school at Hubbard Woods,
Lindsay Fisher was allowed to take a special excursion to
Hubbard Woods to spend a half hour at Book Club Breakfast.
She was discharged from Evanston Hospital the next afternoon,
three weeks and one day after she'd been wheeled in without
blood pressure or vital signs.

•

After examining the information gathered by the Winnetka
police department task force for its report on Laurie Dann,
Chief Timm was prepared to harshly criticize Norm and Edith
Wasserman for what he saw as their failure to recognize the
threat that Laurie's condition posed to the community, and to
cooperate in Greist's effort to institutionalize her. But when he
ran a sharply worded draft by the village lawyers, he said, he
was advised to tone it down.

The final draft, released June 15, forced the public to
read between the lines:

We are...convinced that opportunities existed prior to May 20th for Ms.
Dann's condition to have been successfully addressed. Unfortunately, it
is apparent these opportunities were missed because critical information was
not sufficiently provided to police authorities or mental health practitioners
to adequately address the deteriorating mental state which Dann exhibited.
It was also apparent that many opportunities for prosecution were lost
either through withdrawal of criminal complaints, insufficient evidence or lack
of cooperation from Ms. Dann or other interested parties.

The report did not include any hint of the obsession the
investigators had with trying to figure out what exactly was in
Laurie's mind that day and the hours they spent with one
another playing the "what if?" game.

What if Dr. John Greist in Madison had contacted Norm

five days before May 20 and told him that he had learned the FBI was looking into allegations that Laurie was threatening the life of an Arizona doctor? Would Norm have taken his daughter's guns away? Would he have agreed to take immediate steps to have her hospitalized?

What if Officer Carlson had not happened to be directing traffic on the corner of Tower Road and Gordon Terrace? Or what if Laurie had successfully turned around at the end of Hamptondale Road and found her way out of the neighborhood? She would have been long gone by the time the police arrived at Hubbard Woods—where would she have gone? The office of Dann Brothers? It was right off the highway headed north. Washburne Junior High? Thirteen-year-old Jennifer Rushe attended school there and the building held unpleasant memories for Laurie from her own youth. Home? She had no money and no extra clothes in the car. She might have returned to Glencoe and tried to pretend to her mother that nothing had happened, or she might have gathered supplies, dumped her guns and attempted to flee the state. To Arizona? To Madison? She had the ability to live like a bag lady and could have disappeared into dozens of American cities.

And what if Phil Andrew had wrestled both guns away from her and she had been arrested and brought to justice? Would there have even been a trial? And what would it have revealed?

•

Investigators were also left with a number of possibly relevant loose ends. One is that a bus driver in Evanston swore he saw Laurie wandering the streets after midnight on the morning of the killings, and that several buildings on the Northwestern campus were spray painted with graffiti letters reading "NWU." Most students refer to the school as "NU"; "NWU" was always Laurie's little idiosyncrasy.

Another woman, a senior citizen, came forward and said she had given a woman who looked like Laurie Dann a ride from a Winnetka church to a house in Wilmette one Sunday in April. The hitchhiker said her name was Laurie and she was contemplating suicide.

A husband and wife in Highland Park swore they saw Laurie standing forlornly in their backyard late on the Saturday afternoon before Friday, May 20. She said she was looking for a shortcut she used to take when she lived in the area and went to an elementary school that's now closed. The sighting was close to the Wassermans' first house in Highland Park, but it occurred on the wrong side of the school to have been a shortcut Laurie used in her youth; further, this sighting occurred within hours of when she was reported in the company of Jesse Roeper in the Towers.

•

Floyd Mohr was crossing the street in front of the Glencoe firehouse on the day of the final task-force debriefing when he saw Norm Wasserman coming up the street in Edith's Toyota. Mohr stopped and Norm pulled over to say hello. Mohr asked how things were going and Norm said, "Well, okay. Edith is feeling really anxious and afraid," he added. "She's ashamed to come out of the house. She's feeling really bad."

"I'd still like to talk to you someday about this," Mohr said. "About everything."

"Maybe someday," Norm said. "But I can't talk to you now. I've got to go."

•

Principal Dick Streedain wrote a poem for the Corwins that he gave them on June 17. He called it "Nicky":

A child whose life was symbolic
 of the best of childhood.
A child known equally well
 for being a teacher as well as a student.
A child whose hunger for learning
 and expression was without peer.
A child whose friendships
 had no boundaries.
A child whose wisdom
 far exceeded his years.
A child who deeply experienced
 in his brief life
 the fullness and wholeness of life
 which God only chooses
 for a select few.

Shooting victim Peter Munro returned to the Highland Park Hospital for ulcer surgery on June 20.

On June 26, two hundred North Shore residents met in Temple Jeremiah for a meeting to discuss how to go about banning handguns in their communities. Phil Andrew spoke to the assembly.

"I am here as a victim, not as a representative of an organization," he said. "I am here because I was shot in my kitchen, and the necessity of gun control hit home to me."

George Fisher, Lindsay's father, became co-founder of Winnetka Citizens for Handgun Control.

•

Over the summer, the Towers apartments in Madison implemented a new, strict admissions policy. Each new resident had to submit a copy of his university acceptance letter before being eligible to sign a lease. No longer would anyone be allowed in on just their say-so.

•

On August 1, Norm sold Laurie's 1982 Honda to a Northbrook woman who worked at his bank. The car was in near mint condition, as Laurie had only put 21,000 miles on it in six years.

Norm and Edith also held a sale of their household goods as part of their ongoing effort to sell their home and retire to Florida. Pam Berman, one of Laurie's former baby-sitting clients, saw an ad for the sale and decided to go before she realized whose house it was. Once she was there she was intrigued by several paintings of the English countryside, but decided not to buy them because of the memories they would hold.

She also took the opportunity to look into several closets to see if she could find the shoes Laurie had stolen from her. Friends who were with her also looked in vain for scratches on the insides of closet doors or any other evidence that Laurie had been kept locked in the house like some kind of wild beast.

•

More than three thousand letters of sympathy from around the world were mailed to Joel and Linda Corwin, and they accumulated in stacks in Nicky's bedroom. At first Linda was going to try to answer each one of them personally, but after a while the pain became too great and the letters just sat.

She felt embraced and supported by the community for the most part, but there were times when she saw people turn away from her and avert their eyes, as they had that terrible morning at school.

"Winnetka was a town that liked to think of itself as perfect," she reflected later. "This incident was the stain on the white linen tablecloth that you try to cover up."

The great symbol of this internal civic struggle was the debate in late August over the idea of renaming Edgewood Park, eight blocks from the school, after Nicky Corwin. Proponents of the idea, including Joel and Linda and the commissioner of the local youth soccer league, said it would be a fitting memorial gesture and wholly appropriate because Nicky used to play there all the time. Cathy Kinsella, whose daughter, Meg, was in Classroom 7, led the drive that gathered more than one thousand signatures in favor. She said she saw renaming the park as a healing step for the community and a way to conclude a period of mourning.

Those who opposed the idea were less vocal, but they felt that renaming the park would simply serve to prolong the memories and needlessly remind future generations of a terrible incident. Nicky was not a hero, he was just a victim, they said. To honor him would be unfair to families who had also lost sons and daughters to other tragedies or to war.

In the end, the Winnetka Park District bowed to the loud faction of those who wanted the park renamed. Those who felt it necessary to remember won a victory over those who wanted to forget.

31

New
Beginnings

Hubbard Woods sponsored three group-counseling meetings for parents and teachers over the summer and had a social worker on duty for private counseling. Before the school year started again in the fall, teachers, children and parents met at dawn on a Saturday morning in a lakefront park. They sang songs, talked and watched the sunrise. Everyone in attendance wore a bright yellow button that said, "Hubbard Woods School—new beginnings."

School opened on September 6, a day every bit as sunny and warm as May 20 had been. All exterior doors were locked except for the main entrance, where a monitor checked every visitor and issued them visitor tags—some schools had taken to calling them Laurie Labels.

It was an ordinary back-to-school scene, with hugs and smiles all around. The oddest aspect of the morning was the hall-of-mirrors media game across the street from the entrance, in which one TV station camera operator spent most of his time attempting to videotape other TV station camera operators in action to try to show that there was an intrusive excess of TV station camera operators on the scene, which there wasn't.

Former substitute teacher Amy Moses was not back in the classroom. She had expected to land the full-time position that had opened up at Hubbard Woods, and was discouraged not to have been given an offer. The reason, she heard, was that a small group of parents who blamed her for allowing the tragedy to happen had lobbied quietly with the district against hiring her on the grounds that her presence would be an unpleasant everyday reminder of Laurie Dann for the children. Disgusted with the politics of the situation, she gave up on teaching altogether and began looking for work in publishing and writing.

•

Lisa Taylor's teacher contacted Susie and Jeff early in the school year. She was worried because all of Lisa's art projects concerned guns and people getting killed, and whenever her turn would come to tell part of a progressive story, she would kill off the main character.

•

Russell saw Norm in September at a Shell station on the border of Highland Park and Northbrook. Russell walked right by with his head down, pretending not to see his former father-in-law.

Later in the month, Patty McConnell won the Illinois Female Police Officer of the Year award from Illinois Women in Law Enforcement for her actions on May 20 and for her role in heading up the task force.

•

Just as it looked as though the wounds had started to close and the nation could write off Laurie Dann's attack as the result of a unique and unrepeatable chain of circumstances, nineteen-year-old former mental patient James William Wilson opened fire inside Oakland Elementary School in Greenwood, South Carolina.

His September 26 shooting spree in a cafeteria and third-grade classroom killed two children and wounded seven children and two adults. After he was arrested he said that in the months before his rampage he had read the *People* magazine cover story on Laurie Dann every day.

"I could understand where she was coming from," he said. "I think I may have copied her in a way."

Wilson, who had been hospitalized for depression three

times, told a newspaper reporter that his thoughts while firing were of his own unhappy experiences as a child.

•

Norm and Edith sold their home on Sheridan Road in Glencoe for $475,000 in early November and retired permanently to their vacation condominium on South Ocean Boulevard in Boca Raton. Their five-story, forty-unit building was constructed in 1975 with a vaguely Spanish theme, and it included a heated pool, covered parking and rights to use the beach across the road.

The first family that bought their Glencoe house was scared away before even moving in by a note they found on the door reading, "This is the home of a deranged killer." They quickly sold the house to another family, which attempted to exorcise the house by securing permission from the village to legally change its address.

•

Chief Timm had trouble for months sleeping through the night. One of his recurring nightmares was that he would be walking down a street, turn a corner and come face-to-face with Laurie Dann. One night, his wife told him, he cried out, "Get her!"

In Floyd Mohr's nightmares, his own car had the vanity license plate bearing the question that continued to haunt him: Y LORI Y?

•

On January 17, 1989, crazed drifter Patrick Purdy, twenty-six, opened fire with an AK-47 automatic rifle on an elementary school playground in Stockton, California. He killed five and wounded twenty-eight before taking his own life. It was a far more brutal crime than Laurie Dann's, but, in a sad way, it was not as shocking.

The children at Hubbard Woods School found voice for some of their feelings in writing letters to the children in Stockton; Principal Dick Streedain and Classroom 7 teacher Amy Deuble were summoned to California to help the Stockton administrators handle their crisis.

•

Joel Corwin filed a wrongful-death lawsuit against Norm

and Edith Wasserman on February 28. His complaint charged specifically that Norm and Edith helped buy Laurie's guns with their credit cards, that they promised the police they would keep the guns away from her and didn't, that they deliberately withheld crucial information from Dr. Greist and that they and Epstein undertook to provide her with an experimental drug that can cause violent behavior in psychotic individuals. Because Laurie's parents managed her finances, arranged for her treatments and acted on her behalf in almost all ways, the complaint went on to say, they should be held responsible for the death of Nicky Corwin.

The families of five of the six other shooting victims also filed suit against Norm and Edith Wasserman; they settled out of court with the Wassermans' insurance company in late 1989 and received undisclosed sums. In the Corwin suit, the Wassermans' attorneys initially tried and failed to have it dismissed on the grounds that Laurie was an adult and they could not be held responsible for her actions. The Corwins' attorneys considered this ruling a significant victory and settled the case for a reported $1 million in early 1991.

The resolution, Corwin's lawyer, Al Hofeld, believes, will set an important precedent concerning the responsibilities of parents for the actions of their adult children.

•

The Winnetka Presbyterian Church held an interfaith forum on "Suffering and the Search for Meaning" in early April of 1989, shortly after voters passed an advisory referendum calling for a ban on the ownership and sale of handguns in Winnetka.

That result was offered as a positive aspect of the tragedy. It also brought parents and children, neighbors and friends closer together, some said. It made for better relations between community members and the members of their police and fire departments because the events of May 20 reminded everyone that these civic employees are not simply an extension of their household help but vital guardians of public safety and order.

But it was left to Rabbi Schreibman, the Corwins' clergyıan, to issue what may ultimately stand as the last word on ıch events:

"Suffering is not there to test us or to help us or give us ıumility or correct us," he said, "but it may do all those hings. We have no choice but to live through suffering vithout answers."

•

The ceremony to rename Edgewood Park after Nicky Corwin was held on April 22, eleven months after his death. 'he granite marker placed on the site reads:

Nick Corwin's years were full of life and enthusiasm. His kindness, illingness to help others and sense of humor made him a cherished ıember of our community. Winnetka places great value on its children and ıe loss of any one of them is a loss to us all. Nick Corwin Park is ıedicated to all the children in the community, past, present and future.

As for Laurie Dann, her legacy was gun control.

Prior to her attack on the children of Hubbard Woods chool, three Chicago suburbs had outlawed the sale and ossession of handguns. In the year after, Deerfield trustees ınned the local manufacture and sale of handguns; trustees ı Wilmette, Highland Park and Winnetka banned their sale ıd possession. Later in 1989, the Illinois General Assembly ımended state firearms laws to prohibit "violent, suicidal, ıreatening or assaultive" individuals from obtaining or hold- ıg Firearm Owner's Identification Cards.

Laurie Dann should not have had guns—that much is lear. The rest of her life remains a patchwork of didn'ts, ouldn'ts, and might-have-beens. Her problems, given the ıstory of depression in her family, may well have had their ıots in genetics. Her capacity for distortion and lies, and ıe unreliability of all her statements, made it impossible for ıose close to her, such as Russell Dann, and even her ıoctors to discover what exactly had created this tortured ıind.

She was a lonely child who grew into an unhappy young ıoman, starved for affection she evidently felt she never got rom her family or other women, unable to forge friendships

and close relationships, and deeply resentful of the succes
of others. She both found and lost herself in romantic lov
and ended up a helpless, overmedicated emotional wrec
who controlled her own life through bizarre rituals, and th
lives of others through intimidation.

Behind her mask of evil is a pathetic face.

•

"They got Laurie Dann," snarled a man who phone
Winkelman School in Glenview early in the year, "but the
didn't get me."

Several months later, a woman called Hubbard Wooc
School and told the secretary that a bomb was set to go of
Principal Streedain herded the children outside for "ur
scheduled recess" while the police searched the building fc
nearly an hour.

Both calls were cranks, but as the anniversary dat
approached, a security guard was posted inside the fror
doors at Hubbard Woods and the other elementary schoo
in Winnetka, and round-the-clock building protection wa
added.

Absenteeism on Friday, May 19—the day set aside t
remember the tragedy and commemorate how far the stu
dents and staff had come—was twice as high as usual. At a
all-school assembly in the afternoon, each grade sang a son
and presented a memory of Nicky Corwin.

Amy Moses came back for the assembly and the recep
tion that followed in the company of Sergeant Patty McConne
(both women had started smoking again on the day of th
tragedy and were still unable to quit). McConnell and Mose
were uncomfortable with what they thought was the sel
congratulatory air of the assembly, and Moses was disturbe
that Amy Deuble, whose class she had been substitute teach
ing on May 20, did not talk to her or even look at her.

McConnell and Moses left after fifteen minutes.

•

Some one hundred community members attended
memorial service for Nicky Corwin held in Temple Jeremia
on May 1, 1989. The service was to mark the conclusion c

e yearlong period of mourning, and it included messages
om six different area clergymen.

"Children live in a small world," said the Reverend Andrew
ietsche of Winnetka's Christ Church. "Their homes and fami-
es, their schools, playgrounds and athletic fields; this is their
orld. And it was precisely that world that was invaded and
pped apart on May 20. And all that can be assumed, all that
n be taken for granted, all that can be counted on, all that is
e right of every child—life, peace, security, spontaneity, innocence—
as taken away that day by firearms. And in the weeks after
at event we could not be comforted, for our children were
ot."

He went on, "Now we put our mourning behind us.
nd we do so in order that our lives may now give meaning
 the tragedy. What was done cannot be undone. Evil had
s day, but if we are never able to live again, then evil will
ave had a greater victory. Evil will have triumphed and we
ill be dead."

•

Norm and Edith Wasserman bought a new condo in a
ricier part of Boca Raton.

The Corwins stayed in their house on Locust Street,
urrounded by memories of Nicky—pictures of him and by
im now dominate the house more than ever before, the
elves, the end tables, the credenzas. A mounted, framed
ewspaper feature story about his life hangs above his par-
nts' bed, the same bed he used to crawl into in the morning
 be with his mother after his father was awake.

"It's been hard for the boys," said Linda of her two
urviving sons. Her voice was uncommonly thin, her eyes sad
nd heavy. "They don't like to see their mom cry every day.
ut they're getting used to it, I guess. I do have a great faith
 the afterlife now. Sometimes Michael consoles me by
aying, 'We'll all be together again.'"

•

Late on a sunny weekend morning in Winnetka almost a
ear and a half after Laurie's rampage, a stranger stood at a
istance from Hubbard Woods School taking it in: the outer
oor to Classroom 7; the entryway made famous in hun-

dreds of TV news reports and photographs; the sidewa
Laurie ran down as she made her desperate bid to escape.

A small group of children hung on the jungle gym an
ran across the yard under the vigilant eyes of their paren
A mother left the playground area holding the hand of h
daughter, a girl of perhaps three or four with wispy blon
hair and a clown's face on her sweatshirt. As they cross
twenty yards in front of the stranger, the mother gave him
quick, hard look—a new look. It said:

Who are you? What do you want? Go away.

Index